RECONCEPTUALIZING TEACHER EDUCATION

RECONCEPTUALIZING TEACHER EDUCATION: A CANADIAN CONTRIBUTION TO A GLOBAL CHALLENGE

Edited by Anne M. Phelan, William F. Pinar,
Nicholas Ng-A-Fook, and Ruth Kane

University of Ottawa Press
2020

University of Ottawa **Press**
Les **Presses** de l'Université d'Ottawa

The University of Ottawa Press (UOP) is proud to be the oldest of the francophone university presses in Canada as well as the oldest bilingual university publisher in North America. Since 1936, UOP has been enriching intellectual and cultural discourse by producing peer-reviewed and award-winning books in the humanities and social sciences, in French and in English.
www.press.uottawa.ca

Library and Archives Canada Cataloguing in Publication

Title: Reconceptualizing teacher education : a Canadian contribution to a global challenge / edited by Anne M. Phelan, William F. Pinar, Nicholas Ng-A-Fook and Ruth Kane.
Names: Phelan, Anne M., editor. | Pinar, William F., editor. | Ng-A-Fook, Nicholas, editor. | Kane, Ruth, 1957– editor.
Description: Includes bibliographical references.
Identifiers: Canadiana (print) 20190226919 | Canadiana (ebook) 20190230487 | ISBN 9780776631127 (softcover) | ISBN 9780776628844 (hardcover) | ISBN 9780776631134 (PDF) | ISBN 9780776631141 (EPUB) | ISBN 9780776628851 (Kindle)
Subjects: LCSH: Teachers—Training of. | LCSH: Multicultural education. | LCSH: Culturally relevant pedagogy—Study and teaching.
Classification: LCC LB1707 .R43 2020 | DDC 370.71/1—dc23

Legal Deposit: First Quarter 2020
Library and Archives Canada

Production Team
Copy editing   Michael Waldin
Proofreading   Barbara Ibronyi
Layout   Counterpunch Inc./
               Linda Gustafson
Cover design   Steve Kress

Cover image   Gorman, Richard, *Miniatures Series No. 4*, painting, canvas, oil, 115.8 cm x 128.5 cm (45.6 in x 50.6 in). Courtesy of The Robert McLaughlin Gallery.

© University of Ottawa Press 2020
All rights reserved. No part of this publication may be reproduced or transmitted in any form or by any means, or stored in a database and retrieval system, without the prior permission.

In the case of photocopying or any other reprographic copying, please secure licenses from:

Access Copyright www.accesscopyright.ca
1-800-893-5777

For foreign rights and permissions:
www.iprlicense.com

This book was published with the help of a grant from the Canadian Federation for the Humanities and Social Sciences, through the Awards to Scholarly Publications Program, using funds provided by the Social Sciences and Humanities Research Council of Canada.

The University of Ottawa Press gratefully acknowledges the support extended to its publishing list by the Government of Canada, the Canada Council for the Arts, the Ontario Arts Council, the Social Sciences and Humanities Research Council and the Canadian Federation for the Humanities and Social Sciences through the Awards to Scholarly Publications Program, and by the University of Ottawa.

Table of Contents

Introduction
Anne M. Phelan, William F. Pinar, Nicholas Ng-A-Fook, and Ruth Kane 1

1. Reconciliation in Teacher Education: Hope or Hype?
   Jan Hare 19

2. Reconceptualizing Teacher Education in Ontario: Civic Particularity, Ethical Engagement, and Reconciliation
   Kiera Brant-Birioukov, Nicholas Ng-A-Fook, and Ruth Kane 39

3. Accounting for the Self: Teacher Education in a Post–Truth and Reconciliation Context
   Avril Aitken 67

4. Using Methods of Juxtaposition to Jolt Teacher Understanding: Exploring Ethical Forms of Pedagogical Practice
   Teresa Strong-Wilson 91

5. "Tenants of Time and Place": Teacher Education as Translational Practice
   Anne M. Phelan 115

6. From Africa to Teacher Education in Ontario
   Phyllis Dalley 141

7. Unknowing the Child: Towards Ethical Relations with the Precarious Other
   Melanie D. Janzen 169

8. Teaching as a Learned Profession: The Evolution
   of Inquiry in a Teacher Education Program
   Anthony Clarke 191

9. A Renewed Understanding of Learning to Teach:
   Aristotle, Confucius, and My Mother's Stories
   Ying Ma 215

10. Knowing, Thinking, Living: Teacher Education
    in the Most Enlightened Age
    Theodore Christou 237

11. George Grant's Critique of Education: Civic Particularity,
    Academic Erudition, Ethical Engagement
    William. F. Pinar 257

INTRODUCTION

Reconceptualizing Teacher Education: A Canadian Contribution to a Global Challenge

In October 2017, the editors of this collection hosted a national symposium of Canadian curriculum and teacher education scholars to articulate a response to our collective concerns about the impact of global policy on teacher education. The title of the invitational symposium was Reconceptualizing Teacher Education: A Canadian Contribution to a Global Challenge; *it was funded by the Social Sciences and Humanities Research Council of Canada, and it took place at the University of British Columbia, Vancouver. This collection of essays is the result of that symposium, and it is aimed at provoking an international dialogue about teacher education in and for our times.*

Global Policy and Teacher Education

The first two decades of the new millennium have witnessed unprecedented appraisal, analysis, and educational policy formulations related to teaching (K–12) across the western world. In turn, teacher education has been immensely impacted, as "governments around the world intent on systemic reform of education to improve their country's global competitiveness ... see the reform and progressive management of teacher education as a key component" in the restructuring process.[1] The goal of current education reforms is to elevate the importance of capital—human, financial, and corporate—as the value governing all entities big and small. The deluge of reform has involved a standardization of the social and operational meanings of professional practice and teacher identity. It has meant, among other things, the emergence of what can be called "bureaucratic professionalism,"[2] an attempt by some governments to regulate the very idea of what it means to be professional by declaring improved standardized national (for example, SATS in England; NAPLAN in Australia) and international (TIMMS, PISA) test results as the sole determinant of teacher success.

An excessive focus on standardization and accountability distorts the educational aims of professional practice.[3] This is detrimental to professional pride and integrity, and leaves teachers less time and enthusiasm for teaching as a moral endeavour.[4] The scope of teacher decision-making is restricted because of government-mandated, outcome-based curricula.[5] Questions of worthwhile knowledge and experience are viewed as procedurally resolvable rather than normative questions, embedded in a moral evaluative framework, and requiring teachers' thoughtful deliberation. The orthodoxy that "quality" teaching assures "quality" learning for all students leads to the push to identify effective and efficient interventions that can be generalized across a range of contexts, in order to bring about pre-determined outcomes.[6] The World Bank's emphasis on technical solutions uninformed of contextual and historical analysis is a case in point (for example, in the establishment of national testing centres in Tajikistan and Angola).[7] The neglect of national and cultural circumstances means that education becomes less of a social and cultural relationship and more of an economic and commodity relationship[8] based on notions of "best returns on investment."[9]

The role of teachers as interpreters of national cultures, protectors of forms of particularity within civic communities, and mediators between tradition (past) and innovation (future) is ignored. The neglect of academic study and an emphasis on teachers' behaviours, performances, and outcomes means that teacher education becomes, at best, a problem-solving activity and, at worst, a training exercise whereby teachers learn to choose those technical means best suited to externally mandated objectives.[10] The upshot is the teacher deprofessionalization underway in countries such as the United States, Australia, and the United Kingdom but also endorsed by *World Bank 2020*.[11] An impoverishing instrumentalism and a comforting consensualism haunt teacher education,[12] representing a retreat into the unequivocal, systematic, and amnesic world of modernity.[13]

It is vital to the future of teacher education, and concomitantly public education, that we imagine alternatives to the homogenization of educational experience that globalizing policies install. What is needed, in part, are vocabularies that enable educators to discern and articulate educational purposes *beyond capital* and which focus on the kinds of educational experience that might prepare the young to lead good and worthwhile lives, in the company of others, in each particular society.[14] Education so understood raises important questions for the profession and the public, including: What characterizes good and worthwhile lives? What knowledge is of most worth, to what purposes, and in whose interest? What intellectual, moral, and civic virtues should be promoted? Who decides and on what basis? These questions are focused on the *legitimacy* of what we do in the name of education in particular places and communities. Education so understood foregrounds "the cultivation of classrooms, curriculums and student orientation toward exploring meaning, the nature of knowledge, the condition of the world, human relations or the human spirit, or coordinates of existence different from those of the status quo."[15] Education so understood invites a complicated conversation[16] between the entanglements of the past in the present and our hopes for an uncertain and ill-defined future.

A Canadian Reframing: "Cultivating Responsiveness"

Asserting a distinctively Canadian alternative is not to say that teacher education in Canada has been immune to standardization. In Ontario, for example, the Ontario College of Teachers[17] has created the *Accreditation Resource Guide* as well as an accreditation template, which each faculty of education must use to assess whether or not it meets the government's predetermined criteria. The broader impulse of Canadian faculties of education, however, is to honour teachers as intelligent, inquiring, and perceptive.[18] The Association of Canadian Deans of Education recognizes, for example, that "effective initial teacher education … encourages teachers to assume a social and political leadership role" in a "continuing dialogue with local, national, and global communities."[19] Moreover, the particular historical and political circumstances of Canada as a multi-state, multi-cultural, peace-keeping experiment attempting to address its own history of colonialism and cultural genocide are increasingly acknowledged in teacher education policy and practice.[20] There is growing recognition, for example, of the ways in which the uniqueness of local cultures and histories animate the curriculum as it is lived by teachers and students.[21] Most significant in this regard, and providing the backdrop of many chapters in this volume, is the effort to address the challenges identified in the Truth and Reconciliation Commission *Calls to Action*,[22] to redress the legacy of residential schools "created for the purpose of separating Aboriginal children from their families, in order to minimize and weaken family ties and cultural linkages, and to indoctrinate children into a new culture—the culture of the legally dominant Euro-Christian Canadian society."[23] As a result of the Truth and Reconciliation Commission (TRC), there are increasing attempts to emphasize (teacher) education's role in "cultivating responsiveness"—acknowledging our responsibility for, experiencing our implication in the suffering of Indigenous peoples, and taking action—among settler Canadians.[24] In this regard and in this volume, Pinar succinctly identifies the three-fold professional responsibilities of Canadian educators today: remembrance, reparation, and reconciliation.

Cultivating responsiveness involves "coming to grips with our ontological conditions of plurality, contingency, and freedom"[25]—denied by excessive standardization and cultural homogenization. Plurality refers to our sharing a fragile world with others—who are equal to us but distinct in biography and perspective from us—and depending on one another to render our action meaningful by mutual acknowledgement.[26] Contingency reminds us that while it might be tempting to invoke standardization and accountability as historical constants or educational obviousnesses, it isn't as a matter of course or necessity that things have turned out the way they have. Curriculum and teacher education, as we now know them, have come about through a play of forces, strategies, encounters, and blockages—a pluralization of causes.[27] Finally, the idea of freedom signifies the human capacity for action. By focusing on our complicity we not only acknowledge our respective vulnerabilities and the role of contingency in history, we defend against an everyday kind of thoughtlessness.[28] The path to responsiveness is not without its challenges, however, and remembrance, reparation, and reconciliation place enormous demands on our cognitive and affective resources. This is perhaps why we flee these experiences, decide not to think too much about them, and "disavow our responsibility."[29] In *Burdens of Political Responsibility: Narrative and the Cultivation of Responsiveness*, Canadian political theorist Jade Schiff invites us to consider how we retreat into thoughtlessness, bad faith, and misrecognition, three dispositions that inhibit responsiveness.

> When we are thoughtless our conscience fails us, or we abandon ourselves to the seductions of ideology, or we are simply overwhelmed by how much there is to think about. When we are in bad faith, we take ourselves to be passive objects rather than active subjects, helpless in a world for which we deny any responsibility. When we are subject to misrecognition, we take our socially constituted, historical, contingent world to be a natural one, and so do not see how to transform it; or, indeed, that transformation is even possible.[30]

How do we become attuned to the distortions—thoughtlessness, bad faith, and misrecognition—that mark educational and, as Schiff would have it, political conversations? How do we face and navigate global policy conditions, and their seductive ideologies, without submitting to them and becoming "a cog in their machineries"?[31] As teacher educators and teachers are we willing to expose our educational lives to critical reflection when the moment calls for it?

Central Themes: Academic Erudition, Civic Particularity, and Ethical Engagement

The central themes presented in this book offer a counterpoint to the tendencies toward the homogenization of educational experience that globalizing policies implement. And in an effort to cultivate in teachers a deep capacity for responsiveness, the authors in this collection variously assert—as crucial themes of teacher education—the importance of initial and continuing professional education that foster teachers' intellectual freedom and study; that advances an informed and critical appreciation of civic particularity and historical circumstance; and that cultivates ethical (pedagogical) engagement with ideas and histories—their own and their students—animated by analysis, critique, interpretation, and resymbolization.

Academic Erudition

At the turn of the twentieth century, Canadian historian Frank Underhill condemned the rationality of educational administration in the United States that prevented teachers from exercising the academic—intellectual—freedom assumed by university-based scholars.[32] Without ongoing academic study—animated by the canonical curriculum question: what knowledge is of most worth?—teachers cannot participate in the complicated conversation government-issued curriculum guidelines require of them. They are unable to address questions about the school subjects they are contractually compelled to teach, but also the human subjects they are ethically obligated to engage, each, as circumstances allow, in their own way.[33] The effort to understand one's own and one's students' situations requires historical knowledge—knowing where one is, what time it is, what has been done, what might have been done, what needs to be done still—in this place. Without knowledge of history teachers cannot take up their mediating, even reconstructionist, role between the old and the new, the past and future.[34] Canadian curriculum scholars recognize that remembrance requires respect, an attitude but also the knowledge obtained through ongoing study, witnessing to what is learned through and by teaching.[35] It is here that the singularity of the teacher as thinker and as a member of a profession that understands its collective responsibility for remembrance, reparation, and reconciliation—albeit in another historical context—is evident. Animated by remembrance, teaching structured by study stitches the how, why, and what of teaching tightly together, woven and rewoven by educators working separately together, in time, place, and circumstance. The role of teacher education in cultivating careful study of what teachers are called upon to teach while pursuing their own studies of what they as intellectuals are committed to understanding and communicating cannot be overstated.[36]

Drawing also on the theme of academic erudition, in chapter 8 or this volume, Anthony Clarke argues that "if teaching is a *learned profession* then the ability to be curious about, to study, and to inquire into one's practice is a defining feature of that practice" (191). He tracks the evolution of inquiry within the context of one North American teacher education program, considering how inquiry is taken up variously during five historical periods since the program's inception.

Also asserting teaching as an intellectual endeavor, William Pinar while sympathetic to the integration of thought and action via inquiry—understanding curriculum and creating it must co-evolve, he writes in Chapter 11—insists on the importance of "a certain immersion in the subject, both academic and human" (265). Pinar extends the stakes of teachers' intellectual work when he claims that without academic erudition, teachers cannot know the past or what they as educators can do now to rebuild it via ethical engagement with our students—in all their particularity—in the present. Echoing Canadian scholar, George Grant, Pinar writes "the task of thought is to humble oneself before the mystery of the world, seeking understanding" (Pinar, 2014, 9).

In Chapter 9, Ying Ma illustrates such a pursuit of understanding with due humility, not deference, to the authority of the past. Finding herself at the intersection of Eastern and Western traditions of thought, she initiates a conversation between Aristotle, Confucius, and the largely forgotten voices of teachers in China during the Cultural Revolution. Ying Ma, a Chinese scholar in Canada, signifies the importance of finding one's own words within the dominant discourses of any historical era or geographical place—the essence of thought.[37] Juxtaposing two major ethical vocabularies and using them to read her mother's stories of learning to teach, Ying Ma illustrates how teachers might live datively, confronted by and addressed, questioned, challenged, and formed by the world and their study of it.[38]

Theodore Christou, in Chapter 10, seems to agree with Ying Ma, arguing for study as a way of life for teachers; study, not only of one's practice but also one's discipline, becomes the premise and possibility of teachers' thought and action. Christou wants teachers, and they in turn their students, to couple thought with reality and experience, enabling them to engage in the world via judging and acting.

What of teaching as a learned profession at a time of reconciliation? What knowledge ought to pre-occupy teachers? Jan Hare speaks to current efforts to include "Indigenous perspectives, histories, and pedagogies" in teacher education programs across Canada, given impetus by the work of Canada's Truth and Reconciliation Commission (TRC). "Reconciliation," she writes in Chapter 1, "is fast becoming a vehicle for expression, concern, attention, and action in educational spheres." While Hare sees some promise in reconciliation as a framework for teacher education, she raises significant questions about the conceptual confusion surrounding the idea of reconciliation and specific curriculum content—teacher candidates need opportunities to study Indigenous-settler history, including residential schools if reconciliation is to be a transformative framework—and the role of non-Indigenous teacher educators. For the profound shifts in settler-Indigenous relations, reconciliation, she concludes, may give us pause, enable reflection, and reawaken consciousness so that "we may engage in action, change, and transformation" (32).

Civic Particularity

The particular remains primary, if within globalization and its lowest common denominator: homogenization through standardized assessment and omnipresent technology. Despite these circumstances, the distinctiveness of national histories and local cultures continues to animate the curriculum as it is enacted every day by educators in specific classrooms in specific schools, in specific nations, regions, and locales. Nowhere is this more resonant than in the Canadian context where particular regions and cultures have given rise to unique political traditions and complex social realities.[39] Teachers are obligated to honor the civic particularity of this multicultural, linguistically plural, occupied place where they encounter the entire world in one classroom.[40] Particularity is thus political and cultural and personal. Subjectively situated, teachers are attuned socially to those children and colleagues in their midst but also to those who dwell distant from the immediacy of their everyday lives. The classroom is "a civic square and a room of one's own."[41] Teachers teach what needs to be taught, that knowledge of most worth, as circumstances—personal, local, regional, national, worldwide—call upon them, students themselves of what they are committed to understand and communicate. If curriculum is conceived as complicated conversation, Canadian scholars argue,[42] collective acknowledgement of particularity can promise not parochialism, but cosmopolitanism: self-conscious, self-critical, dialogical encounters with texts—understood to include ideas and experiences, articulated by those present and absent.[43]

In Chapter 4, Teresa Strong-Wilson heeds Pinar's call "to restore temporality—a sharp sense of the past, enabling discernment of the present and foreshadowings of the future—to the complicated conversation that is the school curriculum." Drawing on Pinar and Grumet's *currere*, Rothberg's multidirectional memory and implicated subject, and Sebald's idea of coincidence, this author theorizes and illustrates a pedagogy whereby practicing teachers can engage with and negotiate the multiple and often fraught histories of their students in relation to their own histories and understandings as teachers. It seems, the author concludes, that one cannot teach to the subject until one feels it oneself as a subject, an implicated subject.

It is such a subjective journey of implication Anne M. Phelan undertakes in Chapter 5. Inspired by Jane Urquhart's allegorical novel *Away*, she explores two historical events: Ireland's Great Famine

(1845–1847) and the assassination of the Canada's first Minister of Agriculture and Immigration, Darcy McGee, in 1868. The author examines their intersections with her own history as an Irish teacher educator in Canada by focusing on three meanings of "away"—as transformation, exile, and betrayal—revealing the persistent entanglements of colonialism across societies and histories. Phelan argues that if teacher educators are to resist unwarranted standardization and cultural homogenization that global educational policies attempt to install—if we are to cultivate responsiveness in prospective teachers—we will have to unfurl the knot of our own civic particularity in this place.

Resonating with Strong-Wilson and Phelan and echoing the idea that the first ethical obligation of an educator is to know thyself, Avril Aitken proposes that "thinking with and about subjectivity—what it is, its repercussions, one's own subjectivity and that of others—must be viewed as fundamental to teacher practice and professionalism and, therefore, central to the work of teacher educators" (67). Taking a psychoanalytic perspective, she argues that we each bring our distinctive subjectivities into new "relationship[s] fraught with unconscious desires and shadows from the past" when we enter the classroom. As such, she advocates closer attention to the psychic life of the teacher—the root of particular conflicts as experienced (transference) and the ways that our states of being are "imagined as being experienced by another" (projection). Interestingly, she tests her own hypothesis by considering the language used by settler and non-Indigenous teachers, working in a remote First Nation, in relation to reconciliation. Aitken identifies the experience of loss as significant in opening up questions about individual and collective responsibility for reconciliation—"the loss of the image of Canada the good, the loss of the fantasy of becoming the good citizen teacher, and the loss of certainty that through planning and reason the problems of teaching and learning can be solved (79)."

Ethical Engagement

The ethics of teaching today means not only memorizing rules of professional conduct but remembering those who have summoned us—our own teachers and parents perhaps, policymakers, and other officials—and those who summon us still, to this our calling to educate the public.[44] The first ethical obligation of the educator is to "know thyself"—as both member of a "colony (first politically of France and

Great Britain, later economically of the United States) and colonizer (of Indigenous people, and later the French, within its own borders)."[45] Teacher education can offer opportunities for teachers to deconstruct education, curriculum, and pedagogy as explicit tools of colonialism and European imperialism through which Western notions of race, language, and nation were formed, disseminated, and continue to be reproduced in classrooms throughout the world.[46] It can use today's classroom, where students from those colonies and beyond gather, to deconstruct mythologies about particular forms of knowledge and identity. Canadian faculties of education are struggling to take up the challenges identified in the Truth and Reconciliation Commission *Calls to Action*[47]: How do we teach our students to take collective responsibility for a history not of their making but which must be of their remaking? Several authors in this volume examine the role of teacher educators in cultivating responsibility in the face of challenges posed by such challenging inheritances.

In Chapter 2, Kiera Brant-Birioukov, Nicholas Ng-A-Fook, and Ruth Kane describe and interrogate efforts to build "a reconciliatory-minded" teacher education program in Ontario and to prepare ethical teachers, mindful and responsive to their obligations at this time of reconciliation. Drawing upon Cree scholar Willie Ermine, the authors argue that ethical engagement "requires co-constructing a curricular and pedagogical space *in-between* Indigenous and Settler epistemologies and their respective material, social, and metaphysical realities. Within this curricular and pedagogical space, educators must seek to create and engage a 'theatre for cross-cultural conversation.'"[48] Such conversation entails "an honest engagement with the historical particulars," such as the history of residential schooling and the appropriation of lands. That said, when dialogue about reconciliation, partnership, and treaties are curricular priorities in teacher education, the challenges are great: student teachers may take recourse to bad faith narratives wherein they disavow any responsibility for a historically contingent world, which they deem as natural. To promote an agenda that destabilizes settler-dominant narratives, these authors write, teacher educators must continuously re-centre "ethical engagement and the nurturing of historical consciousness" at the forefront of teacher education curricula (56).

In Chapter 8, Melanie Janzen suggests that settler-dominant narratives and their proclivity for mastery of the Other are reflective of the prevailing paradigm of schooling itself—technical rationality.

She enlists the work of Judith Butler to illustrate how schools frame teachers and students as recognizable within particular relations of power—subject-object/master-slave. Such framing is evident within current discourses of evaluation and assessment but is at its most dangerous in regard to those most precarious students—children from marginalized communities, many of whom experience extreme poverty. Rather than welcome and serve those children, Janzen argues, we render them unrecognizable and undesirable. She concludes, on a hopeful note, that teaching as an ethical relation is possible in our schools—if not without risk for both teachers and students—and that this must be underscored in teacher education.

In Chapter 6, Phyllis Dalley is also concerned about the lack of hospitality extended to marginalized others. She draws our attention to the challenges posed when university teacher education programs are a place of transition for professionals emigrating from "French Africa" to "French Canada." Racialized adult immigrants and new Canadians enrolled in teacher education in Quebec meet with difficult challenges during practica and have been the object of exclusion both in schools and within the university. Inclusion, she writes, is a process dependent upon the willingness of us all "to modify the status quo and co-construct a common space." Inclusion requires that we move in a dialectical fashion between an ethic of care and an ethic of justice. Our appreciation and enactment of inclusion, we might add, are also dependent on the types of vocabularies—counter narratives, even—we have at our disposal.

In Closing

The fundamental question shaping the Canadian dialogue, and we believe relevant to a global conversation about the integrity of teacher education in particular places serving particular communities, is: *What curricular conditions would need to prevail for teacher education to foster teachers' intellectual leadership, an appreciation of civic particularity and historical circumstance, and a capacity to engage ethically (pedagogically) with students' histories and ideas?* Put simply, what conditions would need to exist for teacher education to cultivate responsiveness? The lessons learned from the Canadian context relate to the significance of history, difference, and scale of aims.

The centrality of history in any reconceptualization of teacher education reverberates throughout this volume. How can we challenge the historical foundations of our past, if teacher education and teacher candidates do not know that past? Here we are thinking of how teacher education historically worked hand in hand to help support the state formation of Canada. Such a formation was in negation of Upper and Lower Canada, as well as several different First Nations communities who agreed to sign treaties that were never fully respected by what would later become John A. MacDonald's government. However, such agreements were signed in place between different nations (French of what is now Quebec, English, First Nations). Up until 2015, for the most part, only the two solitudes of French and English Canada were recognized across the provincial curriculum. Prior to 2015, certain provinces and territories had been more proactive toward addressing First Nations, Inuit, and Métis civic particularities within the school curriculum and in teacher education (Nunavut, Saskatchewan, Manitoba). However, other provinces, such as Ontario and Quebec, have moved much more slowly.

As well as knowing our national, provincial, and local histories, openness towards reading our histories differently (as juxtapositions) is crucial. Teacher educators need to write different kinds of interpretations of the past for teacher candidates to study. Or, at the very least, provide pedagogical opportunities for teacher candidates to reread the formation of their subjectivities in relation to different historical narratives that edge their way beyond the curricular periphery. In the chapters put forth in the collection, we see scholars rereading our own and others' experiences while attempting to reconceptualize how we might juxtapose them with prior readings inside and outside the provincial and territorial contexts of teacher education.

There is an increasing openness in Canada, we believe, among members of our various research communities (Canadian Society for the Study of Education as well as others in Canada), faculty of education administrators, and school communities, depending on where they are located, to addressing civic particularity. That is not to say there are not elements of nationalism (alt-right) here in Canada. While certain countries in the world seem to be closing their borders, trade, and conceptions of teacher education and teachers—witness Brexit in the United Kingdom—others are trying to acknowledge how such historical policies toward nationalism have created certain historical harms. Whether teacher education can ever, at least here in Canada, refrain from being a settler colonial educational endeavour is a key question, of course. We recognize that teacher education is replete with efforts at restructuring, but attempts to reconceptualise teacher education in ways that both acknowledge and challenge the past that formed it are another matter entirely. This requires what Christou[49] calls historical mindedness in the field of teacher education itself. In Canada this entails an appreciation of specific historical policies that were put in place to ensure the formation of Canada and its respective provincial educational systems (including teacher education).

Curricular responsiveness to difference is intrinsic to the very concept of Canada, however great the dissonance between concept and event, a dissonance to which public reasoning—especially public-school teaching—aspires to be responsive. Given differences among the first English-speaking settlers—the English, the Irish, and the Scots—it became obvious that reason alone could provide the only non-violent means to solve problems of irreconcilable difference. Leslie Armour and Elizabeth Trott suggest that this earliest responsiveness to difference among English-speaking Canadians led to a "concern with public education which the need for public reasoning was bound to feed."[50] That educational concern coupled with the federal system of government designed in part to protect regional interests led to systems of thought with "distinctive national characteristics,"[51] evident in the essays collected herein. Armour and Trott add that given the great diversity of early Canada—a diversity only multiplied many times since the early colonial period—there developed a sense that "society must be held together by aims of great generality and of fundamental importance."[52] It is these scales of aims, they suggest, that hold Canadians together. We are suggesting this scale of aim—responsiveness to the demands of truth and shared aspirations for reconciliation—characterizes the Canadian contribution to teacher education worldwide.

Anne M. Phelan
William F. Pinar
Nicholas Ng-A-Fook
Ruth Kane

Notes

1. Furlong, "Globalization," 46.
2. Green, *Understanding and Researching Professional Practice*, 4.
3. Clark and Phelan, *Teacher Education and the Political*.
4. O'Neill, "Called to Account."
5. Ball, *Education Policy and Social Class*.
6. OECD, *Teachers Matter*.
7. Vally and Spreen, "Human Rights."
8. Smyth, "Teachers' Work and the Politics of Reflection."
9. Carnegie Corporation of New York, *Teachers for a New Era*, 9.
10. Grumet, "Generations."
11. Pinar and Zhang, *Autobiography*.
12. Clark and Phelan, *Teacher Education and the Political*.
13. Hartley, "Shoring Up the Pillars of Modernity."
14. Coulter and Wiens, *Why Do We Educate?*
15. Brown, "Vocation," 74.
16. Pinar, *What Is Curriculum Theory?*
17. Ontario College of Teachers, *Accreditation Resource Guide*.
18. Kane, "Teacher Education Landscape"; Clarke and Erickson, *Teacher Inquiry*; Phelan, "'Strange Pilgrims'."
19. Association of Canadian Deans of Education, *Accord on Initial Teacher Education*, 3.
20. Butler, Ng-A-Fook, Vaudrin-Charette, and McFadden. "Living between Truth and Reconciliation."
21. Ng-A-Fook and Rottmann, *Reconsidering Canadian Curriculum Studies*; Phelan, "Power and Place"; Pinar, "Curriculum as Social Psychoanalysis."
22. Truth and Reconciliation Commission of Canada, *Calls to Action*.
23. Truth and Reconciliation Commission of Canada, vi.
24. Schiff, *Burdens*, 14.
25. Schiff, 16.
26. Arendt, *The Human Condition*.
27. Foucault, "Questions of Method."
28. Clark and Phelan, *Teacher Education and the Political*.
29. Schiff, *Burdens*, 8.
30. Schiff, 10.
31. Brown, "Vocation," 63–64.
32. Tomkins, *A Common Countenance*, 264.
33. Pinar, 'The Synoptic Text Today' and Other Essays.
34. Tomkins, *A Common Countenance*.
35. Ng-A-Fook, *Indigenous Curriculum of Place*.

36 Ruitenberg, *Reconceptualizing*.
37 Phelan, *Teacher Education and Curriculum Theorizing*.
38 Griffiths, *Intellectual Appetite*, 20.
39 Chambers, "As Canadian as Possible."
40 Hasebe-Ludt, "Teaching across Traditions."
41 Pinar, *What Is Curriculum Theory?*, 47.
42 Smith, Ng-A-Fook, Berry, and Spence, "Deconstructing a Curriculum of Dominance."
43 Pinar, *Worldliness*.
44 Janzen, "Aporia of Undecideability"; Forghani-Arani and Phelan, "Heterogeneous Classrooms"; Pinar, *Worldliness*.
45 Chambers, "As Canadian as Possible," 228.
46 Willinsky, *Learning to Divide the World*.
47 Truth and Reconciliation Commission of Canada, *Calls to Action*.
48 Ermine, "Ethical Space," 202.
49 Christou, *Curriculum History*.
50 Armour and Trott, *Faces of Reason*, 4.
51 Armour and Trott, 15.
52 Armour and Trott, 21.

Bibliography

Arendt, Hannah. *The Human Condition*. Chicago, IL: The University of Chicago Press, 1998 (original work published 1958).

Armour, Leslie, and Elizabeth Trott. *The Faces of Reason: An Essay on Philosophy and Culture in English Canada 1850–1950*. Waterloo, ON: Wilfred Laurier University Press, 1981.

Association of Canadian Deans of Education. *Accord on Initial Teacher Education*. Accessed on April 14, 2017, http://www.csse-scee.ca/docs/acde/ACDE_Accord_on_Initial_Teacher_Education.pdf.

Ball, Stephen. J. *Education Policy and Social Class: The Collected Works of Stephen J. Ball*. London, UK: Routledge, 1990.

Brown, Wendy. "The Vocation of the Public University." In *What Is Education? An Anthology on Education*, edited by Anton Bech Jorgensen, Jakob Jule Justesen, Nana Bech, Niels Nykrog, and Rasmus Bro Clemmensen, 55–90. Copenhagen, DK: Dansk Ungdoms faellesrad, 2015.

Butler, Jesse K., Nicholas Ng-A-Fook, Julie Vaudrin-Charette, and Ferne McFadden. "Living between Truth and Reconciliation: Responsibilities, Colonial Institutions, and Settler Scholars." *Transnational Curriculum Inquiry* 12, no. 2 (2015): 44–64.

Carnegie Corporation of New York. *Teachers for a New Era: Transforming Teacher Education*. New York, NY: Carnegie, 2006.

Chambers, Cynthia. "'As Canadian as Possible under the Circumstances': A View of Contemporary Curriculum Discourses in Canada." In *International Handbook of Curriculum Research*, edited by William F. Pinar, 221–252. New York, NY: Lawrence Erlbaum, 2003.

Clark, Matthew, and Anne M. Phelan. *Teacher Education and the Political: The Power of Negative Thinking*. London, UK: Routledge, 2017.

Clarke, Anthony, and Gaalen Erickson. *Teacher Inquiry: Living the Research in Everyday Practice*. London, UK: RoutledgeFalmer, 2003.

Christou, Theodore. *The Curriculum History of Canadian Teacher Education, 1900–2000*. New York, NY: Routledge, 2018.

Coulter, David L., John R. Wiens, and Gary D. Fenstermacher. "Why Do We Educate? Renewing the Conversation." *The 107th Yearbook of the National Society for the Study of Education* Vol. 1. New York, NY: Wiley-Blackwell, 2008.

Ermine, Willie. "The Ethical Space of Engagement." *Indigenous Law Journal* 6, no. 1 (2007): 193–203.

Forghani-Arani, Neda, and Anne M. Phelan. "Teaching in Heterogeneous Classrooms: The Play of Reason and Unreason." In *Transnational Spaces and Regional Localization*, edited by Angela Pilch-Ortega and Barbara Schröttner, 191–204. Münster, New York, München, Berlin: Waxmann, 2012.

Foucault, Michel. "Questions of Method." In *The Foucault Effect: Studies in Governmentality*, edited by G. Burchell, C. Gordon, and P. Miller, 73–86. Chicago, IL: University of Chicago Press, 1991.

Furlong, John. "Globalization, Neoliberalism and the Reform of Teacher Education in England." *The Educational Forum* 77, no. 1 (2013): 28–50.

Green, Bill, ed. *Understanding and Researching Professional Practice*. Rotterdam, NL: Sense Publishers, 2009.

Griffiths, Paul J. *Intellectual Appetite: A Theological Grammar*. Washington, DC: The Catholic University of America Press, 2009.

Grumet, Madeline R. "Generations: Reconceptualist Curriculum Theory and Teacher Education." *Journal of Teacher Education* 40, no. 1 (1989): 13–17.

Hartley, David. "Shoring Up the Pillars of Modernity: Teacher Education and the Quest for Certainty." *International Studies in Sociology of Education* 10, no. 2 (2000): 113–131.

Hasebe-Ludt, Elizabeth. "The Whole World in One Classroom: Teaching across Traditions in a Cosmopolitan Environment." *Interchange* 30, no. 1 (1999): 39–55.

Janzen, Melanie. D. "The Aporia of Undecideability and the Responsibility of the Teacher." *Teaching Education* 24, no. 4 (2013): 381–394.

Kane, Ruth. "The Teacher Education Landscape of My Imagining." In *Engaging in Conversation about Ideas in Teacher Education*, edited by Caroline Riches and Fiona J. Benson, 39–47. New York, NY: Peter Lang, 2009.

Ng-A-Fook, Nicholas. *An Indigenous Curriculum of Place: The United Houma Nation's Contentious Relationship with Louisiana's Educational Institutions.* New York, NY: Peter Lang, 2007.

Ng-A-Fook, Nicholas, Awad Ibrahim, and Giuliano Ries, eds. *Provoking Curriculum Studies: Strong Poetry and Arts of the Possible in Education.* New York, NY: Routledge, 2015.

Ng-A-Fook, Nicholas, and Jennifer Rottmann. *Reconsidering Canadian Curriculum Studies: Provoking Historical, Present and Future Perspectives.* New York, NY: Palgrave Macmillan, 2012.

OECD. *Teachers Matter: Attracting, Developing and Retaining Effective Teachers.* Paris, FR: Organisation for Economic Co-operation and Development, 2005.

O'Neill, Onora. "Called to Account." Lecture 3, BBC Reith Lectures. http://www.bbc.co.uk/radio4/reith2002/lectures.html.

Ontario College of Teachers. *Accreditation Resource Guide.* Toronto, ON: Ontario College of Teachers, 2015.

Phelan, Anne M. "Power and Place in Teaching and Teacher Education." *Journal of Teaching and Teacher Education: An International Journal of Research and Studies* 17, no. 5 (2001): 583–597.

———. "'Strange Pilgrims': Disillusionment and Nostalgia in Teacher Education Reform." *Interchange* 27, no. 3–4 (1996): 331–348.

———. *Curriculum Theorizing and Teacher Education: Complicating Conjunctions.* London, UK: Routledge, 2015.

Pinar, William F. *On the teachings of George W. Grant. Critical studies in Education.* 55, 1 (2014), 8–17.

———. "Curriculum as Social Psychoanalysis: The Significance of Place." In *Curriculum as Social Psychoanalysis of Place*, edited by J. L. Kincheloe and W. F. Pinar, (167–186). New York, NY: SUNY Press, 1991.

———. *'The Synoptic Text Today' and Other Essays.* New York, NY: Peter Lang, 2006.

———. *What Is Curriculum Theory?* 2nd ed. New York, NY: Routledge, 2012.

———. *The Worldliness of a Cosmopolitan Education: Passionate Lives in Public Service.* New York, NY: Routledge, 2009.

Pinar, William F., and Zhang Hua, eds. *Autobiography and Teacher Development in China: Subjectivity and Culture in Curriculum Reform.* New York: Palgrave Macmillan, 2015.

Ruitenberg, Claudia., ed. *Reconceptualizing Study in Educational Discourse and Practice.* New York, NY: Routledge, 2017.

Schiff, Jade L. *Burdens of Political Responsibility: Narrative and Cultivation of Responsiveness.* Cambridge, UK: Cambridge University Press, 2014.

Smith, Bryan, Nicholas Ng-A-Fook, Sara Berry, and Kevin Spence. "Deconstructing a Curriculum of Dominance: Teacher Education, Colonial Frontier Logics and Residential Schooling." *Transnational Curriculum Inquiry* 8, no. 2 (2011): 53–70.

Smyth, John. "Teachers' Work and the Politics of Reflection." *American Educational Research Journal* 29, no. 2 (1992): 267–300.

Tomkins, George S. *A Common Countenance: Stability and Change in the Canadian Curriculum.* Vancouver, BC: University of British Columbia Press, 2008/1986.

Truth and Reconciliation Commission of Canada. *Truth and Reconciliation Commission of Canada: Calls to Action.* Retrieved from: http://www.trc.ca/websites/trcinstitution/File/2015/Findings/Calls_to_Action_English2.pdf.

Vally, Salim, and Carol Anne Spreen. "Human Rights in the World Bank 2020 Education Strategy." In *The World Bank and Education: Critiques and Alternatives,* edited by Steven J. Klees, Joel Samoff, and Nelly P. Stromquist, 173–187. Rotterdam, NL: Sense Publishers, 2012.

Willinsky, John. *Learning to Divide the World: Education at Empire's End.* Minneapolis, MN: University of Minnesota Press, 1998.

CHAPTER 1

Reconciliation in Teacher Education: Hope or Hype?

Jan Hare

Policy directives have motivated the changing curriculum of Canadian teacher education programs to be inclusive of Indigenous content, perspectives, and learning approaches. The Association of Canadian Deans of Education established priorities for Indigenous education as early as 2010, with goals that emphasize improving teacher candidates' knowledge of and experiences with Indigenous knowledge systems.[1] More recently, teacher regulation bodies are developing new standards for the teaching profession concerned with implications for Indigenous education. For example, starting in 2019, the province of Alberta expects the following competency in order to maintain an Alberta teaching certificate: "A teacher develops and applies foundational knowledge about First Nations, Métis, and Inuit for the benefit of all students."[2] A ninth standard concerning teachers' requirements for the profession concerned with Aboriginal histories and worldviews has been approved by the British Columbia Teachers' Council, which develops competencies and professional conduct for educators in the province of British Columbia.

    The efforts of those seeking to revise teacher education programs to include Indigenous perspectives, histories, and pedagogies have been assisted in this large-scale reform by the work of Canada's Truth and Reconciliation Commission (TRC). Reconciliation is fast becoming a vehicle for expression, concern, attention, and action in educational spheres. The TRC's *Calls to Action*[3] has inspired formalized responses at post-secondary institutions that include strategic plans, task-force recommendations, symposia, symbolic representations on campuses, Indigenous community engagement initiatives, professional learning, and required course instruction that authorizes the teaching and learning of Canada's shared colonial history with Indigenous peoples, and more specifically the legacy and impact of residential schools.[4] Specifically, the *Calls to Action* confer responsibilities for teacher education through actions that include "educat[ing] teachers on how to integrate Indigenous knowledge and teaching methods into classrooms" and "identify[ing] teacher training needs"[5] as it pertains to building pre-service teachers' capacity for intercultural understanding, best practices on residential school history, and implementing Kindergarten to Grade 12 curriculum and learning resources. As a result, teacher education has become a critical site for reconciliation in both policy and practice.

Across Canada, the number of teacher education programs embracing the TRC's *Calls to Action* continues to grow.[6] Conditions that support curriculum content aimed at enhancing the capacity of pre-service teachers to engage with the Indigenous histories, perspectives, and content occurs through specific and related approaches that include anti-racism, critical pedagogy, decolonization, and more recently, indigenization.[7] In addition, there is an increasing number of teacher education programs offering a mandatory and concentrated course in Indigenous education, while other programs integrate their commitments to the Calls to Action across the teacher education curriculum.

In this chapter, I contend that preparing settler pre-service teachers for the profession through a framework of reconciliation holds promise for fundamental shifts in Indigenous-settler relations so urgently needed in Canada. Exploring the role of reconciliation in teacher education, I present three themes that bear upon curriculum and teaching. These themes consider how teacher candidates makes sense of reconciliation, the significance of residential school history as a necessary part of curriculum, and the role of teacher educators addressing Indigenous perspectives, content, and pedagogies in their work with pre-service teachers. While each theme reveals certain tensions that exist with reconciliation approaches, the conversations also raise important elements for nurturing reconciliation efforts in the curriculum and pedagogies of teacher education. Given the increasing presence of reconciliation in teacher education inspired by *Calls to Action* that bear directly on teacher responsibilities, we need to bring the concept of reconciliation into dialogue with the policies, practices, and programs that shape our work with educators.

Making Sense of Reconciliation amid the Conceptual Confusion

Introducing reconciliation in or through teacher education forms part of a broader political and cultural agenda aimed at transforming Indigenous-settler relations in this country, beginning with teacher educators and their students. This reconciliation agenda for teacher education assumes that, by engaging students of all backgrounds in the theory and practices of Indigenous education, they will have a greater historical awareness of Canada's shared colonial history and engage in respectful relationship building between Indigenous and non-Indigenous peoples. In turn, these education students' ability to embed Indigenous perspectives and content in their practice will be enhanced in ways that extend their teaching skills and sense of professionalism. Consolidation of national and provincial policy imperatives directed at reconciliation through or in teacher education places "new pressures and responsibilities on teachers to work in extremely sensitive, knowledgeable and critical ways."[8]

A good part of the effectiveness of this consolidation strategy will depend on how reconciliation is understood by pre-service teachers in terms of pedagogies and practices. Scholars and educators have scrutinized the concept of reconciliation within Canada. It has been used to draw attention to the significant disparities in well-being between Indigenous and non-Indigenous peoples, and to concentrate efforts at reducing the gap and addressing long-standing inequities in the quality of life between First Nations and Canada.[9] It has also been considered an influential framework for raising awareness about the on-going legacies of colonialism in settler societies. For example, Clarke, de Costa, and Maddison suggest that we have not, until recently, talked in national or mainstream discussions about shared colonial histories.[10] Rather, the problems that have been identified are always located as Indigenous, limiting the exploration and responsibilities of non-Indigenous peoples' role in reconciliation. The necessary social reconstruction involved in reconciliation begins with small acts of learning about what has happened in our past.[11] Further, the ninety-four Calls to Action directed at settler Canadians serves as a rubric for social policy and roles for churches, governments, schools, and other institutions.[12] Other advocates underscore the personal and collective healing so urgently needed among Indigenous families and communities, but also healing of relationships in our larger society.[13]

Recognition of and redress for past injustices would contribute to that restoration. Within these sentiments, settlers play an important role in reconciliation.

Others responding to the TRC have been more critical, taking issue with reconciliation's focus on residential schools, rather than attention to the broader set of relationships that created policies and practices of assimilation.[14] Still, there are those who dismiss reconciliation altogether given the disconnection from decolonization movements and Indigenous land rights.[15] Kanein'kehaka scholar, Taiaiake Alfred, argues that any "notion of reconciliation that rearranges political orders, reforms legalities and promotes economics is still colonial unless it centres our relationship to the land," otherwise, "reconciliation is recolonization."[16] Anishinaabe scholar Leanne Simpson suggests that reconciliation needs to focus on Indigenous peoples' political resurgence and regeneration of languages, cultures, and traditions of governance.[17] According to these Indigenous scholars, reconciliation, if it is to be possible at all, must account for Indigenous peoples' priorities of land, resurgence, and sovereignty.

These varying perspectives on reconciliation reveal the opportunities and limitations that reconciliation holds for Indigenous-settler relations and underscore the complexities of the heightened social responsibilities that settlers have towards reconciliation. It is in the context of this "conceptual confusion"[18] created by diverse viewpoints that teacher educators and teacher candidates are currently engaging with recommendations put forward in the *Calls to Action*. Even though reconciliation implicates teacher candidates in settler colonialism, its focus on changing Indigenous-settler relations through redress and accountability motivates their participation in curricular frameworks and pedagogical practices. This is because reconciliation allows many teacher candidates to continue to be invested in their own innocence. That is, these students tend to see themselves as "being good people ... doing good things, in engaging with destructive histories or problematic power structures,"[19] and doing so in ways that protect their privilege. Such a strategy, which Tuck and Yang refer to as "settler moves to innocence," allows teacher candidates to be "relieved of feelings of guilt or responsibility without giving up land or power or privilege."[20]

Teacher candidates engage in other "moves to innocence" shaped by conceptual understandings of reconciliation. Indigenous scholar Susan Dion describes rationalizations that educators make to absolve themselves of responsibilities towards Indigenous education priorities, referring to this positioning as the "perfect stranger."[21] Grappling with settler privilege that comes from occupation of Indigenous lands, teacher candidates excuse their complicity in what it means to benefit from living on stolen and contested lands.[22] Many of them are not able to understand themselves in relationship to the settler dynamic that exists between land and colonialism. Simply allowing teacher candidates to reimagine themselves into new subject positions[23] without challenging settler consciousness or moving them towards responsibility limits reconciliation processes and practices that can occur through and in teacher education. If teacher candidates are not pointed towards action then reconciliation as a framework for transformation remains a trendy topic, as it has been cast in social media and scholarly writing.

Different Starting Positions

In accordance with the TRC's *Calls to Action*, reconciliation requires that teacher candidates learn about the history and legacy of residential schools (Call to Action no. 63)—institutions that were pervasive, systematic, and devastating in their control of Indigenous peoples, with intergenerational effects, and part of a larger colonial agenda aimed at assimilating Indigenous people into mainstream society. While knowledge of this shared colonial history may occur in teacher education coursework, the significance of how this knowledge is positioned in teacher education must be underscored. Indigenous education priorities that emphasize supporting Indigenous learners, families, and communities and incorporating Indigenous knowledges into the classroom must be understood within the larger colonial project, which includes schooling that has eroded Indigenous family structures and denigrated Indigenous traditions, languages, and cultures. It is imperative that emerging settler-educators understand how this form of colonial education is linked to the systemic barriers and inequalities inherent in the current educational system that continues to marginalize Indigenous knowledge traditions and results in significant challenges to the educational success of Indigenous learners.[24] Given that mandatory instruction in Indigenous education coursework is in its early stages of development in many teacher education programs across Canada, it is time to develop a focused and sustained attention to the history and legacy of residential schools within the curriculum.

In support of these efforts to introduce such courses into teacher education programs, I have studied teacher candidates' knowledge base, in research undertaken with students who have completed a required course in Indigenous education. In responses to a written questionnaire by 100 teacher candidates near the completion of their professional programs, more than 40 of these students indicated that they were introduced, challenged, or more informed by the topic of residential schools, which is a theme of the common syllabus for this compulsory course. They were asked to respond to a set of prompts about what they learned in the course, which included *I was surprised to learn about...*, *I felt most uncomfortable when...*, and *I wish I had learned years ago....* In their responses, residential schooling was dominant. For example, they responded to the prompt *I was surprised to learn about* ...with such comments as: "... how bad some of the histories were, like residential school"; "... the medical tests and experiments conducted on residential school children"; "... the details of residential schools"; "... how recently the residential schools were closed"; "... residential school experiences and the social, physical, emotion, and spiritual injustices that were put on Aboriginal peoples"; and "... the events that took place within residential schools. It was a very tough class to get through as it dealt with some very heavy issues."

Their lack of knowledge about the nature of the destructive policies and practices of residential schools may very well be tied to their lack of opportunity to learn about this history prior to their participation in teacher education, especially as this history has been largely ignored in national curricula.[25] This was evident in their responses to the prompt *I wish I had learned years ago...*, in which they indicated that they should have learned about residential schools and Aboriginal history in high school or post-secondary studies. An open-ended question that asked them to consider how this required course contributed to their knowledge, skills, and confidence as an emerging educator; their responses included the following comments:

- "I was amazed at how little Aboriginal education I received in my undergraduate studies. I have a minimal concentration of the history."
- "The residential schools workshop opened my eyes to the gravity and true ramifications of Canadian history."
- "The ripple effect of not knowing how to parent that residential schools caused."

Teacher candidates' responses in this questionnaire suggest that this mandatory course plays a role in shaping their knowledge about Indigenous-settler colonial history. As their knowledge of this significant history builds, the confidence of educators to plan and teach Indigenous histories and worldviews in their own classrooms can be enhanced. Milne demonstrates the role that professional learning can play in supporting the teaching of Indigenous histories, which is perceived as challenging content for teacher and student.[26] Her interviews with non-Indigenous educators who took part in a program that supported them in authentically embedding Indigenous cultures, perspectives, and histories into everyday learning in their classrooms focused on the role of an Indigenous coach. This onsite consultant shared their intimate knowledge of Indigenous cultures and history. Though limited understanding and knowledge of Indigenous cultures, as well as the history of residential schooling, was common among the thirty-five non-Indigenous educators, most felt ready by the end of their professional development to implement the curriculum directives specific to Indigenous histories, including residential schooling, in their own teaching. Teaching residential school history is an important pedagogical intervention towards the goals of reconciliation.

Conversely, what other research suggests is less clear about whether education is a deeply transformative site with regards to settler attitudes about Indigenous peoples and reconciliation.[27] Drawing from the Australian context, which has a much longer history of grappling with reconciliation, Maddison and Stastny assess various educational sites that promote engagement with Indigenous peoples, and therefore consider reconciliation practices.[28] For these researchers, reconciliation practices for settler participants in their focus groups and interviews across sites in Australia encompass two expectations. The first is to recognize privilege and structural connections to settler colonialism. The second is to yield space, voice, and power to Indigenous peoples, which requires humility and relating differently.

For participants in the Maddison and Stastny study, school- and media-based education were most discussed as sites that were problematic for reconciliation practices. In schools, including post-secondary institutions, Australia's colonial history was mostly mediated through books rather than engagement with Indigenous people. What they took away from their learning experiences only served to reproduce assumptions and stereotypes of Indigenous peoples that they already held. These historical understandings then shaped their ideas about reconciliation as a concept both debated and diversely understood. These authors surmise that knowledge of colonial harms does not instil a sense of responsibility to engage in reconciliation practices, suggesting that "reforming education sites will not be enough. Even in the very best classrooms, the responsibility to engage may remain elusive."[29]

For teacher candidates whose knowledge base of Indigenous-settler colonial histories may be limited or non-existent, there is a need for curricula aimed at teaching Indigenous-settler histories that are inclusive of Indigenous perspectives and linked to Indigenous peoples' present. Ministries of education, along with Indigenous communities, are committed to improving educational outcomes for Indigenous leaners and ensuring curriculum is inclusive of Indigenous perspectives, content, and learning approaches for all students in kindergarten through to secondary schooling. British Columbia has implemented a new curriculum that draws from Indigenous perspectives, worldviews, and histories framed through the lens of the First Peoples Principles of Learning. The fundamental precepts assert that learning is embedded in history, memory, and story, and that learning recognizes the role of Indigenous knowledge. Such principles result in varied teaching and learning approaches common among First Nations peoples and are reflected across each grade level and subject area. Ontario, Manitoba, and Alberta have also developed policy frameworks that include mandatory curricula in K–12, concerned with First Nations, Métis, and Inuit culture and history. Teacher candidates must develop knowledge and expertise for addressing the significant history of residential schooling, which is fast becoming part of school curriculum.

A focus on Indigenous-settler history as part of teacher education curriculum offers hope for reconciliation if reconciliation is weighted with the truth about the history of Indigenous-settler relations. Current approaches to reconciliation have outpaced an emphasis on truth-telling that was intended within the TRC mandate, despite prominence given to the voices of residential school survivors and education in the national process. Cherokee literary scholar Daniel Heath Justice contemplates the question: How do we learn to live together? He notes, "[I]t's telling that the singular term 'reconciliation' has become the shorthand form of what was originally conceived as the compound 'truth and reconciliation.'"[30] Reconciliation approaches in teacher education that support pre-service teachers to grapple with the truth of our difficult past that persists in to our future include conveying knowledge of racist attitudes and policies that shaped the residential school system, giving primacy to Indigenous voice and perspectives that humanize this history, identifying intergenerational impacts on families and communities, and introducing students to the growing resources (for example, children's and adolescent literature, first-hand accounts, curriculum with lesson plans and practical tools, e-kits, websites, organizations). Teacher candidates need to learn much more about Indigenous-settler history, including residential schooling told from the perspectives of Indigenous peoples, if reconciliation is to be a transformative framework. I believe there is nothing more compelling that could invoke empathy and responsibility among teacher candidates than learning about this history and the intergenerational legacy from the experiences, voices, and knowledge of Indigenous people and communities.

The Role of Teacher Educators

As we consider teacher candidates' pursuance of reconciliation, we must also attend to teacher educators' responsibilities for reconciliation through their teaching and curriculum in course instruction. This is because teacher educators must facilitate the teaching and learning of Indigenous perspectives, content, and pedagogies, which involves constructing teaching candidates knowledge of Indigenous-settler relationships and modelling for them the practices of Indigenous educational approaches. Attention to a reconciliation mandate in teacher education brings to the fore issues of pedagogy that consider the roles and experiences of differently positioned faculty and effective strategies that respond to recommendations specific to teachers in the TRC's *Calls to Action*.

Who teaches Indigenous perspectives and content and through which courses is sometimes contested. The newspaper headline, "Halifax University under Scrutiny over Residential Schools Course Assigned to White Professor,"[31] highlights the debate. There had been a social media critique of Mount Saint Vincent, a Canadian university, for permitting a non-Indigenous scholar to teach an Indigenous-focused course, describing it as historical appropriation and reinforcement of systemic oppression of Indigenous peoples.

Some claim that a non-Indigenous instructor simply does not have the life-experience to teach a course concerned with the history of residential schooling. This conflict demonstrates the need for institutions to expand their Indigenous faculty. More important, it points out the need for non-Indigenous faculty and institutions to work closely with Indigenous communities, who have the requisite knowledge and expertise to guide teaching and learning.

Non-Indigenous faculty unprepared or unwilling to engage with Indigenous perspectives, content, and learning approaches in their work run the risk of reproducing damaging stereotypes, racist ideologies, and settler privilege, while also creating unsafe environments for Indigenous students.[32] They also describe feeling vulnerable taking up Indigenous course-related material.[33] Further, they sometimes struggle to make connections to Indigenous perspectives in their courses.[34] Ally scholars and those being tasked with new teaching responsibilities in this post-reconciliation era must grapple with the challenges and opportunities that their own identities present.

Research examining the teaching and learning of Indigenous perspectives, content, and pedagogies suggest Indigenous faculty must also negotiate their own identity and culture in the colonial space of the post-secondary classroom.[35] This includes being called on to speak to the Indigenous experience or the stress associated with teaching students resistant to Indigenous content and perspectives.[36] Many Indigenous faculty who are given responsibility for mandatory Indigenous courses feel susceptible to negative teaching evaluations from resentful students. To avoid this colonial violence, Indigenous faculty will opt out of teaching Indigenous-specific coursework that enrols largely settler students. Relationships between Indigenous faculty members and local Indigenous peoples shape the former's capacity to incorporate knowledge specific to the territory.[37] Their geographic situatedness calls in to question their ability to teach Indigenous perspectives by both Indigenous and non-Indigenous students.[38] Even their identity as academics is called in to question when they are viewed as spiritual or too cultural.[39]

My previous research with instructors teaching required Indigenous education coursework describes the kinds of inspection they face from teacher candidates.[40] Instructors face questions of authenticity, whereby non-Indigenous instructors described "needing to prove themselves" to teacher candidates. Discussing a co-teaching situation with a colleague, a non-Indigenous teacher educator with years of experience in this course observed how teacher candidates responded differently to her and her Indigenous colleague. She felt she was perceived by students as not having anything to contribute to class conservations. Another ally instructor, describing how her authority is constantly challenged by teacher candidates, said, "Our bodies are texts to be read. So you'll see me and you'll say, hmmm, why is she teaching this course? She is not Aboriginal ... when I open my mouth and I am speaking with an accent and you look at my colour ... they think, is she qualified to do it?"[41]

For Indigenous instructors teaching this required Indigenous education course, they took issue with certain assumptions held by pre-service teachers, including that Indigenous instructors "knew everything" about Indigenous peoples and issues. Among the more resistant student stances, one Indigenous instructor reflects: "There are those who think ... [Aboriginal instructors] are somehow privileging [an Aboriginal] perspective" and that there is some sort of "agenda."[42] This study reveals that even though teacher educators work from across lived experiences and different identity positions to embrace Indigenous ways of knowing in their teaching, the social positions that they occupy are under constant scrutiny. However, the benefits for pre-service teachers of learning from Indigenous and ally teacher educators is described by one Indigenous teacher educator: "Our teacher candidates need to see Aboriginal and non-Aboriginal people teaching this course. A non-Indigenous person teaching role models for mostly non-Aboriginal students [shows] they can do this too."[43]

The dynamics of identity and teaching within university classrooms has implications for how institutions advance reconciliation, especially as post-secondary institutions move towards the accelerated trend to include Indigenous perspectives in coursework and are challenged to meet the demand for Indigenous faculty. Changes that include the introduction and expansion of Indigenous faculty, knowledges, and pedagogical approaches in the post-secondary classroom are both challenging and productive. We know that there are many Indigenous and settler ally scholars working together to effect change in our classroom, institutions, and relationships. Reporting on the experiences of instructors engaged in teaching for reconciliation in these spaces, Lynn Davis and her colleagues warn that this will not be easy:

> These are sites of difficult learning (Britzman, 2013) as curriculum and pedagogies engage not only intellectual, but physical, emotional, and spiritual learning as well. These are the spaces to which educators, students, and even administrators bring their individually embodied experiences and identities, structured within differently racialized collective histories of colonization and diaspora, and so there is much at stake in processes of transformation.[44]

Just as our identities shape and limit how our teaching efforts are perceived by students, colleagues, and institutions, our identities influence how we respond to the responsibilities to advance reconciliation goals in our classrooms. There is a growing body of research that helps instructors think through learning approaches to the teaching of Indigenous perspectives, content, and pedagogies and moving towards Indigenous-settler reconciliation in teacher education. Helping teacher candidates think through settler privilege and personal assumptions concerning Indigenous histories and peoples has been an important step.[45] More specifically, the works of ally scholars Bridge and Scully tie Indigenous histories to settler investments in colonialism by engaging pre-service teachers in land-based engagement with Indigenous peoples and place.[46] Others take up Indigenous education practices that involve teacher candidates holistically in Indigenous pedagogical practices.[47] Indigenous community engagement features prominently among approaches that deepen new educators' understanding of reconciliation responsibilities.[48] As reconciliation commitments continue to grow, we can expect to learn more about how reconciliation processes might inform pedagogical practices in teacher education in ways that effect social change.[49]

Moving teacher education programs closer to reconciliation also requires building Indigenous cultural competence among teacher educators, students, staff, and administrators. Drawing on the reconciliation context in Australia in the teacher education program at Charles Sturt University (CSU), Auhl, Gainsford, Hill, and Zundans-Fraser suggest Indigenous education strategies and priorities must form the mission statement and policies of the faculty.[50] In addition, they describe initiatives such as devising Indigenous immersion experience programs, establishing Elders-in-Residence, developing graduate attributes that show commitments to reconciliation, creating practicum experiences in Indigenous communities and educative settings, and increasing Indigenous staff. The authors describe a unique approach to course design that engages Indigenous and non-Indigenous faculty in developing and implementing coursework. Working collaboratively helps to resolve the difficulties associated with inadvertent inclusion of colonial perspectives, ensures a legitimate role for non-Indigenous faculty in teaching, and prevents overburdening Indigenous faculty. In addition, a Teaching Fellows program that includes Indigenous and non-Indigenous faculty and in-service teachers provides pre-service teachers with the opportunity to experience instruction from a variety of perspectives in Indigenous education coursework. This interplay of policy, professional learning, and curriculum design demonstrates the possibilities afforded teacher educators in exploring institutional responses to reconciliation movements in teacher education.

Conclusion

We're at a unique historical moment when profound change in Indigenous-settler relations in Canada is possible. Despite the debates on the meaning and goals of reconciliation, what I have come to appreciate about reconciliation is the strong and focused way this concept is taking hold in educational contexts. This can be seen in reconciliation events, pedagogical practices, policy developments, initiatives, and curriculum reform in classrooms from early childhood, K–12, through to post-secondary education. While more work still needs to be done, reconciliation is motivating change in the way educators do things in their classrooms. This has required educators to disrupt their educational practices by troubling for themselves, and teaching others to trouble, the institutional normalcy of things.[51] This can be achieved by working across difference, learning from new perspectives, and engaging with Indigenous peoples, their priorities, and their knowledge systems.

As teacher education programs account for reconciliation through and in the curriculum and pedagogy, institutions must be ready to respond to the demands that reconciliation places on Indigenous and non-Indigenous teacher educators, staff, and students. The inclusion of Indigenous perspectives, content, and pedagogies requires adequate resourcing and structural supports to ensure change across the curriculum. Resourcing and supports should contribute to professional development, Indigenous community engagement, and pedagogical practices that occur beyond traditional classroom spaces or require different approaches. While a mandatory course on Indigenous education may form part of the checklist of a faculty's reconciliation achievements, meaningful commitments must be ongoing and work across teacher education. For teacher candidates, reconciliation cannot be disconnected from other coursework. Nor can it be the work of one group of people or one course. Otherwise, pre-service teachers will only see the relevance of Indigenous education to Indigenous learners, continuing to marginalize Indigenous priorities in education and setting limits on the large scale societal goals for reconciliation.

Daniel Heath Justice tells us that "if we're serious about establishing better relations than those we've had in the past ... then we *must* return our attention to Indigenous voices, perspectives, and experiences. There is simply no other way of moving forward."[52] Reconciliation can be a productive and hopeful space for social change, especially as it is causing us to pause, reflect, and reawaken our consciousness so that we may engage in action, change, and transformation. And I believe, if reconciliation holds the moment, it holds promise.

Notes

1. Archibald et al., "Accord on Indigenous Education."
2. Alberta Education, "Professional Practice Standards' Resources: First Nations, Metis, and Inuit."
3. Truth and Reconciliation Commission of Canada, *Calls to Action*.
4. Universities Canada, "Resources on Canada's Universities and Reconciliation."
5. Truth and Reconciliation Commission of Canada, *Calls to Action*, 5.
6. Universities Canada, "Resources on Canada's Universities and Reconciliation."
7. Battiste, *Decolonizing Education*; Schick and St. Denis, "Troubling National Discourses," 28; St. Denis, "Building Alliances," 30.
8. Luke et al., "A Summative Evaluation," 108.
9. Assembly of First Nations, "Closing the Gap."
10. Clark, de Costa, and Maddison, "Limits of Settler Colonial Reconciliation," 1–12.
11. Quinn, "Cultivating Sympathy and Reconciliation."
12. Denis and Bailey, "'You Can't Have Reconciliation Without Justice.'"
13. Reconciliation Canada, "Our Story."
14. Corntassel, T'lakwadzi, and Chah-win-is, "Indigenous Storytelling, Truth-Telling, and Community Approaches to Reconciliation."
15. Alfred, "Restitution"; Coulthard, *Red Skin, White Masks*; Denis and Bailey, "'You Can't Have Reconciliation Without Justice.'"
16. Alfred, "It's All About the Land," 13.
17. Simpson, "Land and Reconciliation."
18. Maddison and Stastny, "Silence or Deafness?" 233.
19. Macoun, "Colonising White Innocence," 87.
20. Tuck and Yang, "Decolonization Is Not a Metaphor," 10.
21. Dion, "Disrupting Molded Images," 330.
22. Scully, "Unsettling Place-Based Education."
23. Smith, "Unsettling the Privilege of Self-Reflectivity."
24. Hare and Davidson, "Learning from Indigenous Knowledge."
25. In Canada, curriculum design is done by individual provinces or territories. So while there is not a national curriculum, there exists a gap in this knowledge in provincial curricula.
26. Milne, "Implementing Indigenous Education Policy Directives."
27. Phillips, "Resisting Contradictions."
28. Maddison and Stastny, "Silence or Deafness?"
29. Maddison and Stastny, 245.
30. Heath Justice, *Why Indigenous Literatures Matter*, 158.
31. "Halifax University under Scrutiny," *Globe and Mail*, May 11, 2018.

32 Davis et al., "Critical Considerations."
33 Kovach et al., "Indigenous Presence."
34 Merculieff and Roderick, *Stop Talking*.
35 Cote-Meek, *Colonized Classrooms*; Hare, "'All of Our Responsibility'."
36 Asmar and Page, "Sources of Satisfaction."
37 Kitchen and Hodson, "Living Alongside."
38 Cote-Meek, *Colonized Classrooms*.
39 Cote-Meek.
40 Hare, "'All of Our Responsibility'."
41 Hare, 109.
42 Hare, 110.
43 Hare, 110.
44 Davis et al., "Critical Considerations."
45 Cannon, "Changing the Subject in Teacher Education"; Dion, "Disrupting Molded Images"; Haig-Brown, "Decolonizing Diaspora"; Iseke-Barnes, "Pedagogies for Decolonizing"; Wolf, "Critical Citizenship."
46 Bridge, "Land Education and Reconciliation"; Scully, "Unsettling Place-Based Education."
47 Archibald, *Indigenous Storywork*; Davis et al., "Critical Considerations"; Dion, *Braiding Histories*; Kitchen and Hodson, "Living Alongside"; Schneider, "*Ucwalmicw* and Indigenous Pedagogies"; Williams and Tanaka, "Schalay'nung Sxwey'ga."
48 Hare, "'All of Our Responsibility'"; Williams and Tanaka, "Schalay'nung Sxwey'ga."
49 Hattam, Atkinson, and Bishop. "Rethinking Reconciliation."
50 Auhl et al., "Building Indigenously Culturally Competent Teacher Education Programs."
51 Cannon, "Changing the Subject."
52 Heath Justice, *Why Indigenous Literatures Matter*, 159.

Bibliography

Alberta Education. "Professional Practice Standards' Resources: First Nations, Metis, and Inuit." Accessed April 5, 2018. https://education.alberta.ca/professional-practice-standards-resources/first-nations-métis-and-inuit/everyone/applying-foundation- knowledge/.

Alfred, T. "It's All About the Land." In *Whose Land Is It Anyway? A Manual for Decolonization,* edited by P. McFarlane and N. Schabus, 10–13. Vancouver, BC: Federation of Post-Secondary Educators of British Columbia, 2017.

Alfred, Taiaiake. "Restitution is the Real Pathway to Justice for Indigenous Peoples." In *Response, Responsibility, and Renewal: Canada's Truth and Reconciliation Journey*, edited by Gregory Younging, Jonathan Dewar, and Mike DeGangé, 179–190. Ottawa, ON: Aboriginal Healing Foundation, 2009.

Archibald, Jo-ann. *Indigenous Storywork: Educating the Heart, Mind, Body, and Spirit*. Vancouver, BC: University of British Columbia Press, 2008.

Archibald, Jo-ann, John Lundy, Celia Reynolds, and Lorna Williams. "Accord on Indigenous Education." *Association of Canadian Deans of Education, 2010*. Accessed April 17, 2018. http://mediarelations.concordia.ca/pdf/Accord%20June1%202010.pdf.

Asmar, Christine, and Susan Page. "Sources of Satisfaction and Stress Among Indigenous Academic Teachers: Findings from a National Australian Study." *Asia Pacific Journal of Education* 29, no. 3 (2009): 387–401.

Assembly of First Nations. "Closing the Gap." Accessed October 12, 2017. https://www.afn.ca/uploads/files/closing-the-gap.pdf.

Auhl, Greg, Annette Gainsford, Barbara Hill, and Lucinda Zundans-Fraser. "Building Indigenously Culturally Competent Teacher Education Programs." In *Promising Practices in Indigenous Teacher Education*, edited by Paul Whitinui, Maria Rodriguez de France, and Onowa McIvor, 41–55. Singapore: Springer Nature Singapore Pte Ltd, 2018.

Battiste, Marie. *Decolonizing Education: Nourishing the Learning Spirit*. Saskatoon, SK: Purich Press, 2013.

Bridge, Christine. "Land Education and Reconciliation: Exploring Educators' Practice." Unpublished PhD dissertation, University of British Columbia, 2018.

Britzman, Deborah P. "Between Psychoanalysis and Pedagogy: Scenes of Rapprochement and Alienation." *Curriculum Inquiry* 43, no. 1 (January 2013): 95–117.

Cannon, Martin John. "Changing the Subject in Teacher Education: Centering Indigenous, Diasporic, and Settler Colonial Relations." *Cultural and Pedagogical Inquiry* 4, no. 2 (March 2013): 21–37. Project MUSE.

Clark, Tom, Ravi de Costa, and Sarah Maddison. "Non-Indigenous People and the Limits of Settler Colonial Reconciliation." In *The Limits of Settler Colonial Reconciliation*, edited by Sarah Maddison, Tom Clark, and Ravi de Costa, 1–12. Singapore: Springer, 2016.

Corntassel, Jeff, T'lakwadzi, and Chah-win-is. "Indigenous Storytelling, Truth-telling, and Community Approaches to Reconciliation." *English Studies in Canada* 35, no. 1 (March 2009): 137–159.

Cote-Meek, Sheila. *Colonized Classrooms: Racism, Trauma, and Resistance*. Halifax, NS and Winnipeg, MB: Fernwood Publishing, 2014.

Coulthard, Glen Sean. *Red Skin, White Masks: Rejecting the Colonial Politics of Recognition*. Minneapolis, MN: University of Minnesota Press, 2014.

Davis, Lynn, Jan Hare, Lindsay Morcom, Chris Hiller, and Lisa K. Taylor. "Critical Considerations and Cross-Disciplinary Approaches to Pedagogy in the Post-Secondary Classroom." *Canadian Journal of Native Education* 40, no. 1 (Spring 2017), in press.

Denis, Jeffrey S., and Kerry A. Bailey. "'You Can't Have Reconciliation Without Justice': How Non-Indigenous Participants in Canada's Truth and Reconciliation Process Understand Their Roles and Goals." In *The Limits of Settler Colonial Reconciliation*, edited by Sarah Maddison, Tom Clark, and Ravi de Costa, 137–158. Singapore: Springer, 2016.

Dion, Susan. *Braiding Histories: Learning from Aboriginal Peoples' Experiences and Perspectives*. Vancouver, BC: University of British Columbia Press, 2009.

——. "Disrupting Molded Images: Identities, Responsibilities and Relationships—Teachers and Indigenous Subject Material." *Teaching Education* 18, no. 4 (2007): 329–342.

Haig-Brown, Celia. "Decolonizing Diaspora: Whose Traditional Lands Are We On?" In *Decolonizing Philosophies of Education*, edited by Ali A. Abdi. Rotterdam, NL: Sense Publishers, 2012.

"Halifax University under Scrutiny over Residential Schools Course Assigned to White Professor." *Globe and Mail*, May 11, 2018. https://www.theglobeandmail.com/canada/article-halifax-university-under-scrutiny-over-residential-schools-course-to.

Hare, Jan. "'All of Our Responsibility': Instructor Experiences with Required Indigenous Education Courses." *Canadian Journal of Native Education* 38, no. 1 (Spring 2015): 101–120.

Hare, Jan, and Sara Florence Davidson. "Learning from Indigenous Knowledge in Education." In *Visions of the Heart: Canadian Aboriginal Issues* (4th ed.), edited by Olive Patricia Dickason and David Alan Long, 241–262. Oxford, UK: Oxford University Press, 2016.

Hattam, Robert, Stephen Atkinson, and Peter Bishop. "Rethinking Reconciliation and Pedagogy in Unsettling Times." In *Reconciliation and Pedagogy*, edited by Pal Ahluwalia, Stephen Atkinson, Peter Bishop, Pam Christie, Robert Hattam, and Julie Matthews, 1–9. New York, NY: Routledge, 2012.

Heath Justice, Daniel. *Why Indigenous Literatures Matter*. Waterloo: Wilfred Laurier University Press, 2018.

Iseke-Barnes, Judy M. "Pedagogies for Decolonizing." *Canadian Journal of Native Education* 31, no. 1 (Spring 2008): 123–148.

Kitchen, Julian, and John Hodson. "Living Alongside: Teacher Educator Experiences Working in a Community-Based Aboriginal Teacher

Education Program." *Canadian Journal of Education* 36, no. 2 (2013): 144–174.

Kovach, Margaret, Jeannine Carrier, Harpell Montgomery, M. J. Barret, and Carmen Gillies. "Indigenous Presence. Experiencing and Envisioning Indigenous Knowledges within Selected Post-Secondary Sites of Education and Social Work." Accessed February 14, 2018. https://www.uregina.ca/socialwork/faculty-staff/FacultySites/MontgomeryMontySite/Indigenous%20Presence.pdf.

Luke, Allan, Courtney Cazden, Rhonda Coopes, Valentina Klenowski, James Ladwig, John Lester, Shelley MacDonald, Jean Phillips, Paul G. Shield, Nerida Spina, Pamela Theroux, Megan J. Tones, Malia Villegas, and Annette F. Woods. "A Summative Evaluation of the Stronger Smarter Learning Communities Project: Vol 1 and Vol 2." Brisbane, AU: Queensland University of Technology, 2013. Accessed April 22, 2018. https://eprints.qut.edu.au/59535/27/SSLC_Evaluation_2013_Abridged_Version.pdf.

Macoun, Alissa. "Colonising White Innocence: Complicity and Critical Encounters." In *The Limits of Settler Colonial Reconciliation*, edited by Sarah Maddison, Tom Clark, and Ravi de Costa, 85–102. Singapore: Springer, 2016.

Maddison, Sarah, and Angélique Stastny. "Silence or Deafness? Education and the Non-Indigenous Responsibility to Engage." In *The Limits of Settler Colonial Reconciliation*, edited by Sarah Maddison, Tom Clark, and Ravi de Costa, 231–247. Singapore: Springer. 2016.

Merculieff, Larry, and Libby Roderick. *Stop Talking: Indigenous Ways of Teaching and Learning and Difficult Dialogues in Higher Education.* Anchorage, AK: University of Alaska Anchorage, 2013. Accessed October 12, 2017. http://www.difficultdialoguesuaa.org/images/uploads/Stop_talking_final.pdf.

Milne, Emily. "Implementing Indigenous Education Policy Directives in Ontario Public Schools: Experiences, Challenges and Successful Practices." *The International Indigenous Policy Journal* 8, no. 3 (2017). http://ir.lib.uwo.ca/iipj/vol8/iss3/2 DOI: 10.18584/iipj.2017.8.3.2.

Phillips, Jean. "Resisting Contradictions: Non-Indigenous Pre-service Teacher Responses to Critical Indigenous Studies." Unpublished PhD dissertation, Queensland University of Technology, 2011.

Quinn, Joanna R. "Cultivating Sympathy and Reconciliation: The Importance of Sympathetic Response." In *The Limits of Settler Colonial Reconciliation*, edited by Sarah Maddison, Tom Clark, and Ravi de Costa, 119–135. Singapore: Springer, 2016.

Reconciliation Canada. "Our Story." Accessed October 7, 2017. http://reconciliationcanada.ca/about/history-and-background/our-story/.

Schick, Carol, and Verna St. Denis. "Troubling National Discourses in Anti-racist Curricular Planning." *Canadian Journal of Education* 28, no. 3 (2005): 295–317.

Schneider, Joyce. "*Ucwalmicw* and Indigenous Pedagogies in Teacher Education Programs: Beginning, Proceeding, and Closing in Good Ways." *Canadian Journal of Native Education* 38, no. 1 (2015): 39–61.

Scully, Alexa. "Unsettling Place-Based Education: Whiteness and Land in Indigenous Education in Canadian Teacher Education." *Canadian Journal of Native Education* 38, no. 1 (2015): 80–100.

Simpson, Leanne. "Land and Reconciliation: Having the Right Conversations." *Electric City Magazine*, January 8, 2016. http://www.electriccitymagazine.ca/2016/01/land-reconciliation.

Smith, Andrea. "Unsettling the Privilege of Self-Reflectivity." In *Geographies of Privilege*, edited by France Winddance and Bradley Gardener, 263–276. New York, NY: Routledge, 2013.

St. Denis. Verna. "Aboriginal Education and Anti-racist Education: Building Alliances across Cultural and Racial Identity." *Canadian Journal of Education* 30, no. 4 (January 2007): 1068–1092.

Truth and Reconciliation Commission of Canada. *Truth and Reconciliation Commission of Canada: Calls to Action.* http://trc.ca/assets/pdf/Calls_to_Action_English2.pdf.

Tuck, Eve, and K. Wayne Yang. "Decolonization Is Not a Metaphor." *Decolonization: Indigeneity, Education and Society* 1, no. 1 (2012): 1–40.

Universities Canada. "Resources on Canada's Universities and Reconciliation." *Universities Canada*, October 2016.

Williams, Lorna, and Michele Tanaka. "*Schalay'nung Sxwey'ga*: Emerging Cross Cultural Pedagogy in the Academy." *Educational Insights* 11, no. 3 (2007). http://www.ccfi.educ.ubc.ca/publication/insights/v11n03/articles/williams.html.

Wolf, Sandra J. "Critical Citizenship, Popular Theatre, and the Social Imagination of Pre-service Teachers." In *Politics, Participation and Power Relations: Transdisciplinary Approaches to Critical Citizenship in the Classroom and Community*, edited by Richard C. Mitchell and Shannon A. Moore, 35–49. Rotterdam, ND: Sense Publications, 2012.

CHAPTER 2

Reconceptualizing Teacher Education in Ontario: Civic Particularity, Ethical Engagement, and Reconciliation

Kiera Brant-Birioukov, Nicholas Ng-A-Fook, and Ruth Kane

Getting to the truth was hard, but getting to reconciliation will be harder. It requires that the paternalistic and racist foundations of the residential school system be rejected as the basis for an ongoing relationship. Reconciliation requires that a new vision, based on a commitment to mutual respect, be developed. It also requires an understanding that the most harmful impacts of residential schools have been the loss of pride and self-respect of Aboriginal people, and the lack of respect that non-Aboriginal people have been raised to have for their Aboriginal neighbours. Reconciliation is not an Aboriginal problem; it is a Canadian one. Virtually all aspects of Canadian society may need to be reconsidered. This summary is intended to be the initial reference point in that important discussion. Reconciliation will take some time.[1]

— Truth and Reconciliation Commission

Contextualizing the Conversation

Resurgence, repatriation, remediation, reconciliation: such movements have defined an era of relations between Indigenous and Settler[2] peoples (non-Indigenous peoples who have settled on Indigenous lands) of Canada. Canada now finds itself situated within what Edmonds calls the "Age of Apology."[3] As we approach 2020, this new era of cultural redress and reconciliation has been defined by the Canadian government's willingness to make significant institutional reforms towards redressing the historical injustices committed against Indigenous and Settler citizens who constitute inter-national territories that now make up Canada. Nevertheless, such social and political movements of redress and reconciliation have not transpired within a vacuum.[4] The South African Truth and Reconciliation Commission, the Waitangi Tribunal of New Zealand, and Reconciliation Australia heavily inspired the reconciliatory movements in contemporary Canada.[5] All of these initiatives were uniquely defined by the landscapes and identities of the original peoples of these territories. Processes of Canadian reconciliation are defined by the willingness (or lack thereof) of the Canadian government to redress the appropriation of Indigenous lands, the *Indian Act*, treaties, in addition to the forced removal of Indigenous children through the Indian residential schooling system and the Sixties Scoop. After settling one of the largest civil claims that promised to bankrupt several religious institutions across Canada, the Canadian government established a commission to investigate and document the intergenerational legacies of the Indian residential school system experience.[6] The mandate of the five-year long Truth and Reconciliation Commission (TRC) concluded with the June 2015 release of the *Calls to Action*, with its ninety-four action items, and with the unveiling of the *final report* later that winter.

Without ascribing a rigid definition for the term "reconciliation,"[7] it is most commonly defined as multifaceted, reciprocal, reflexive, and continuous processes, which strive to reconcile Indigenous-Settler relationships. The TRC conceptualizes reconciliation as

> establishing and maintaining a mutually respectful relationship between Aboriginal and non-Aboriginal peoples in this country. In order for that to happen, there has to be awareness of the past, acknowledgement of the harm that has been inflicted, atonement for the causes, and action to change behaviour.[8]

Creating educational programming and a discourse for addressing reconciliation is emerging as a priority for the Canadian education system. As Commissioner Murray Sinclair reminded us in his *final report*,[9] Canadian public education will be a core component in implementing the *Calls to Action* across Canada. According to the Calls to Action numbers 62, 63, and 64, truth-telling, redressing historical harms, and a public education curriculum that acknowledges such intergenerational harm will be integral toward reconceptualizing our past, present, and future relations as Indigenous and Settler Canadians.[10] The perspectives, knowledges, and educational experiences that Canadian educators bring to their classrooms shape the school curriculum extensively. "Too many Canadians," the TRC report reminds us, "still do not know the history of Aboriginal peoples' contributions to Canada or understand that, by virtue of the historical and modern Treaties negotiated by our government, we are all Treaty people."[11] How could (and should) those responsible for preparing our nation's teachers respond to these calls? What is the role of teacher education in ensuring that graduating teachers are able to meet the calls set forth in the TRC *final report*? In response to such pedagogical questions, this chapter examines the reconceptualization of one teacher education program in Ontario as a site of inquiry into the conceptual and curricular conditions for teacher educators and candidates to live curriculum as reconciliation.

Across Canada, some universities have begun to incorporate more Indigenous histories, perspectives, and contemporary issues across their different programs. For example, the University of Winnipeg requires all undergraduate students to complete at least one Indigenous-focused course.[12] Other responses to the *Calls to Action* include the development of reconciliation task forces, such as the ones at Queens University[13] and University of Toronto,[14] or the development of special issue journals focused on reconciliation,[15] and the *Accord on Indigenous Education* put forth by the Association of Canadian Deans of Education.

Ministries of education, faculties of education, and accreditation bodies are beginning to take concrete steps in demonstrating commitment to the *Calls to Action* within their curriculum policies and accreditation requirements. Initial teacher education programs, in particular, are not only expected to educate future Canadian educators to become more aware of Indigenous histories, contemporary issues, and perspectives, but they must also ensure that graduates are prepared to teach such content across the school curriculum. In response, several Ontario faculties of education are beginning to make First Nations, Métis, and Inuit education a requirement for teacher candidates—if they haven't already done so.[16] Yet Indigenous education remains clouded by an ongoing contention and resistance to its presence within higher education.[17]

In 2012, in an effort to counter the oversupply of teachers and to bring Ontario teacher education more in line in terms of length with other provinces, the provincial government required faculties of education to restructure the then one-year (eight-month) bachelor of education programs into four-semester programs, including a longer school-based practicum, increased from forty to eighty days. While the province mandated a *restructuring* of Ontario Faculties of Education, we prioritized time within our faculty at the University of Ottawa to use current research and local relations to inform the *reconceptualization* of our teacher education program.[18]

Reconceptualization of teacher education at the University of Ottawa was guided by three key interconnected commitments. First, a priority of teacher education is the preparation of teachers with adaptive expertise—the ability to respond to each learner they encounter. Adaptive expertise was introduced by Hatano and Inagaki[19] and further developed by others.[20] Adaptive experts are teachers who "are aware of the assumptions underpinning their practice, *including their cultural positioning*, and know when these assumptions are helpful for their learners and when to question them, and if necessary, to let them go" (emphasis added).[21] Second, teacher candidates and teacher educators actively work towards an *"inquiry habit of mind,"* a mindset promoting teacher inquiry and knowledge building.[22] Third, teacher educators recognize our responsibility to address the TRC *Calls to Action* as part of our larger civic ethical commitment toward fostering and sustaining diverse, equitable, and inclusive education as a praxis of reconcilia(c)tion.[23]

Critical to the reconceptualization and restructuring of our program at the University of Ottawa was the introduction of a foundations course, PED3138 First Nations, Inuit and Métis Education: Historical Experiences and Contemporary Perspectives, which is taken in Year One by all teacher candidates. Introducing PED3138 as a foundations course not only serves to address the knowledge gaps with respect to the history and roles of Indigenous peoples in Canada but has also provided often contested opportunities to embrace ethics as a topic within the teacher education curriculum through classroom conversations focused on Indigenous histories, perspectives, and contemporary issues. As we demonstrate in a case study later in this chapter, simply introducing a new foundations course is insufficient when the classroom climate reveals teacher candidates unwilling to embrace uncertainty, reluctant to interrogate long-held versions of history, and resistant to the interrogation of their (our) own cultural positioning. We need to continue our work to find productive ways to support our predominantly Settler teacher candidates and teacher educators by creating spaces and opportunities for ethical transformation.

Teacher education can, and indeed must, be a mutually respectful, relational, empathic, and transformational site for Indigenous and Settler teacher candidates if it is to create spaces for the study a praxis of reconciliation.[24] Despite these possibilities, Phelan posits that teacher education performs an assimilative and integrative role of inducting new teachers into the familiar and stable discourse of education.[25] In Canada, new teachers continue to be introduced to a Settler teacher education discourse. In turn, Settler discourse assumes the universality of Western knowledge systems across K–12 schooling systems.[26] Without interrogating the limitations of Settler schooling, curricula fail to adequately account for the ways in which Indigenous knowledges, experiences, and identities shape contemporary conceptions of Canadian citizenship. Interrogating the universality of Settler colonial knowledge systems, however, threatens the illusion of its very stability. Canadian teachers are on the front lines of taking up with students different civic particularities of Canadian identities.[27] Teachers are recipients insofar as they inherit the discourse put forth in teacher education programs and across the school curriculum. As educators in their own right, however, they become interpreters of the curriculum who are in a position to reproduce, disrupt, or negotiate the limitations of a singular Canadian narrative and the Settler agenda, which historically sought to erase Indigenous histories and perspectives from our history books. The responsibility, therefore, is for Canadian teachers to understand the civic particularities and identities that are included (or not) in the curricular discourse of K–12 education. In what ways can teachers, teacher educators, and teacher candidates heed the *Calls to Action* towards reconciliatory education, not despite its challenges but in light of the need to re-imagine a curriculum that attends to our ethical responsibilities and civic particularities as Canadian citizens?

Creating Pedagogical Spaces for Ethical Engagement

In this chapter, we are trying to understand how Settlers and First Nations, Inuit, and Métis communities might live a praxis of reconciliation here in what some of us now call Canada. How might we address the civic particularities of living reconciliation together? How might we live a praxis of reconciliation as a form of ethical engagement? And what does such conduct look or feel like within the contexts of Ontario teacher education? At the very least, such curricular and pedagogical work involves studying questions that concern our historical consciousness as treaty people. To do so, we need to reread the historical narratives that shape our historical consciousness and, in turn, compel us to reconstruct our (mis)understandings of past and present relations with First Nations, Inuit, and Métis communities. Teacher education can perhaps, as in the First Nations, Métis, and Inuit education course (FNMI) discussed below, provide a site for teacher candidates to question the systemic Settler colonial ways in which certain historical lived experiences have been excluded from their historical consciousness. They might, in turn, learn how to juxtapose such narrative exclusions within their teachings. Such teachings, or what Pinar calls "study," involves a certain shattering of one's historical consciousness, which has been formed via the school curriculum in terms of the historical narratives that have been taught.[28] So for teacher candidates, and for ourselves as Settlers and First Nations and as educational researchers and teacher educators, part of reconciliation is about studying the past in order to deconstruct and reconstruct how different historical narratives have come to define (from a national standpoint) what it means to be (and not be) a Canadian citizen—as a grand narrative. Each of us lives the particularities of such a grand narrative differently, depending on where we grew up and who surrounded us. However, prior research carried out within teacher education illustrates the ways in which teacher candidates continue to put forth certain national Settler narratives they have learned within the school history curriculum.[29] Moreover, the research also illustrates substantial resistance toward questioning one's Settler historical consciousness or past collective lived experiences in relation to the historical harms committed and justified in the national establishment of what some of us now call Canada. How might we broach such complicated conversations within the classroom as a space and place for ethical engagement?

Creating an ethical space to address such difficult knowledge with Settler teacher candidates, therefore, makes for difficult teacher education curriculum programming.[30] For Indigenous-specific content, the resistance of pre-service and in-service teachers is well-researched and documented in Canada.[31] Carol Schick and Verna St. Denis studied the widespread resistance articulated by teacher candidates in response to mandatory Indigenous education courses.[32] Schick and St. Denis argue that student resistance stems from viewing required Indigenous education as an "infringement on their liberty even before they enter the class."[33] Additionally, Indigenous education is viewed as being undemocratic, insofar that Indigenous perspectives are being privileged over other worldviews.

Susan Dion, a Potawatomi scholar of Indigenous teacher education, further ascertains that teacher resistance stems from the fear of confronting what they know, what they do not know, and what they refuse to know about Indigenous peoples.[34] In this sense, what she terms as the "perfect stranger syndrome," Dion argues that Canadian educators are comfortable to acknowledge Indigenous injustice so long as they position themselves neither as *part of the system* that marginalizes Indigeneity nor as having any *personal responsibility* to fix it.[35] "To be a perfect stranger," Dion posits, "is to absolve oneself of responsibility."[36] In essence, perfect strangers to Indigenous peoples (un)consciously attempt to distance themselves from their particular civic responsibilities in relation to reconciliation. Such estrangement from past historical harms becomes particularly evident among Settler teachers who are asked to address First Nations, Inuit, and Métis-related education within the school curriculum. Teacher education is a site occupied by an overwhelming majority of Settler (primarily racialized "White"), middle-class female teacher candidates.[37] Consequently, when attempting to address Indigenous histories, contemporary issues, and perspectives across teacher education programs, instructors must also learn to negotiate the various pedagogies of Whiteness and privilege that in turn inform teacher candidates' racialized and social identities.[38]

Such homogenous teacher education demographics consequently point to the great need for curricula that deconstruct normalized Settler narratives and agendas.[39] A Settler colonial knowledge system not only informs the curriculum-as-planned in Ontario classrooms but also shapes the perspectives that teachers often put forth in the educational and social structures in which they teach. Indoctrination to the *way things are done here* begins with teacher education, where new teachers are quickly inducted into the dominant discourse of their respective school systems.[40] In a Settler colonial curriculum, Indigenous perspectives have often been pushed to the periphery, if not completely excluded, and therefore contribute to the reproduction of Settler citizens who continue to be unaware of First Nations, Inuit, and Métis nations' civic particularities.[41] Teacher education, therefore, has not only the opportunity but a responsibility to embrace the discomfort and conflict that it actively avoids and, instead, attend to an inclusive and renewed discourse.[42] Reconceptualizing historical narratives that challenge a Settler colonial discourse might begin to occur when new teachers are invited to reconsider their personal implications with colonization, reconciliation, and treaty relationships.[43]

Treaty education—comprising not only a lesson with treaty dates and facts but a genuine relational engagement with the treaty relationships and principles—requires the learner to re-read one's Settler or Indigenous identity as a citizen and teacher.[44] In response to the adage familiar to Canadian social studies and history curricula, "What makes Canada 'Canada'?," the uncomfortable reality is that what is now known as Canada was and is built upon broken treaties and the appropriation of Indigenous lands. Once we begin to question Settler colonial narratives, we open possibilities for a more holistic reflection of what constitutes our civic particularities and, thus, our civic responsibilities as Canadians. Considering the contentious demands of integrating Indigenous perspectives within and across teacher education programs, how might we conceptualize the curricular and pedagogical dimensions of ethics in response to the decentring of Settler identity and implementing the 94 *Calls to Action* within teacher education?

Here we draw upon the theoretical work of Cree scholar Willie Ermine to conceptualize *ethical space* as a requisite for Indigenous education. Ethical engagement, Ermine suggests, requires co-constructing a curricular and pedagogical space *in-between* Indigenous and Settler epistemologies and their respective material, social, and metaphysical realities. Within this curricular and pedagogical space, educators must seek to create and engage a "theatre for cross-cultural conversation."[45] In response to the current contexts and limitations of Canadian curriculum, Blackfoot scholar Dwayne Donald has extended Ermine's initial conceptualization of ethical space, which, as Donald suggests, can be used as a pedagogical strategy to deconstruct the perceived divisions between Indigenous and Settler epistemologies.[46] Donald's reconceptualization of ethical space within education "entertains the possibility of a meeting place … to step out of our allegiances … and enact a theory of human relationality that does not require assimilation or deny Indigenous subjectivity."[47] Enacting the kind of human relationality that Donald suggests invites learners to step outside of the ways in which education systems have conditioned us to think and, instead, to lead with the intrinsic humanness that drives us to be moral, ethical beings. Above all, the work of ethics within Indigenous education embraces the tensions and differences that arise when suspending our different worldviews while in conversation with one another. Ethical space allows room to critically juxtapose Indigenous and Settler worldviews while maintaining the integrity of each educator and learner. When one is ethical, one not only listens but truly hears the other. The case study that follows is drawn from Kiera Brant's MA thesis, which demonstrates the ways in which ethics must forefront the work of reconciliatory teacher education.

Living a Praxis of Reconciliation

As part of Kiera Brant's thesis research, she conducted a cross-comparative case study between a First Nations, Métis, and Inuit education course (FNMI course) in Ontario, Canada, and a Treaty of Waitangi education workshop (Treaty Workshop) in New Zealand.[48] Both the course and workshop were required Indigenous education training for all incoming teacher candidates in their respective universities. In-class observations were conducted through three sessions of observations, and individual interviews were held with two teacher educators and seven teacher candidates across both countries. The FNMI course was a semester-long, twelve-week course that was intended to introduce teacher candidates to First Nations, Métis, and Inuit histories, perspectives, and knowledges in Canada. In New Zealand, the Treaty of Waitangi education was a two-day workshop held prior to the commencement of courses for incoming teacher candidates. Of the seven teacher candidates interviewed, two teacher candidates had no previous Indigenous educational experiences, five had some previous Indigenous education, including three who were unsatisfied with its quality and two who felt somewhat satisfied with the Indigenous education they received. By way of investigating the curricular challenges and opportunities of the ethical praxis unique to Canada, we will unpack the Ontario context in depth here.

This cohort of teacher candidates in 2016–2017 was the first to take the FNMI foundations course as part of the new accreditation requirement. For these teacher candidates, this was their first immersive and intensive experience with Indigenous histories, perspectives, and contemporary issues. All teacher candidates were Settler Canadians, working with the course instructor, Rachel (a pseudonym), who is a First Nations doctoral candidate. According to Rachel, the FNMI curricula were primarily centred on debunking myths and stereotypes, using appropriate language and terminology, and presenting Indigenous counter-narratives that sought to deconstruct and complicate familiar narratives about Canadian history and identity. Rachel also taught the histories of the *Indian Act* and the treaties in addition to inviting Indigenous guest speakers into the classroom to speak to their realities as Indigenous peoples in Canada. Her course syllabus included Thomas King's *The Inconvenient Indian* (2012)and Chelsea Vowel's *Indigenous Writes* (2015). The realities that Rachel, her guest speakers, and the Indigenous authors spoke to were often framed in direct contradiction to the narratives that were familiar to the teacher candidates. For example, teacher candidates had to understand the ongoing intergenerational impacts of Indian residential schools in contrast to the twentieth-century history lessons learned as part of their own schooling. Nevertheless, the possibilities for ethical engagement within teacher education calls for teacher candidates to question their historical consciousness in relation to the lived experiences for First Nations, Inuit, and Métis communities that were excluded from the Ontario historical curriculum. Ethical engagement within the contexts of Ontario teacher education might therefore begin with disrupting the existing teacher education curriculum in relation to such historical exclusions. However, as we discuss through the case study below, such unprecedented educational experiences proved to be challenging (but we hope worthwhile) for these teacher candidates.

Disrupting Teacher Education Curriculum

Through the data collected in the FNMI and Treaty of Waitangi classrooms, Kiera was able to identify two different ways in which teacher education (or the person in question) sought to engage a praxis of reconciliation: (1) negotiating *resistances against a praxis of reconciliation*, and (2) creating sites of *possibility to engage reconciliation*. First, we will unpack the challenges of reconciliation, which we understand to be any barriers that limit or hinder a praxis of reconciliation in teacher education classrooms. Such challenges included teacher candidates' lack of prior knowledge of or personal experiences with Indigenous peoples, the perceived irrelevance of Indigenous-focused content and knowledge to their future profession as teachers, Settler pedagogies of resistance against mandatory Indigenous education, and an active distancing that attempted to absolve oneself of any responsibilities in relation to historical harms against Indigenous peoples.

Negotiating Resistance: Beyond Settler Pedagogies

A praxis of reconciliation is challenged by the shortcomings of teacher candidates' prior knowledge of Indigenous peoples. Teacher educators, in any subject matter within teacher education but particularly within the context of difficult knowledge, must ask and seek to understand: Where are they [teacher candidates] coming from? Any genuine attempt at employing a praxis of reconciliation must not only teach Settler Canadians something new about Indigenous peoples but must first interrogate the misconceptions that may impede genuine learning.[49] The media often promotes negative stereotypes of Indigeneity, which regularly become reinforced in the classroom;[50] so where are the opportunities not only to address the fallacies suggested by such stereotypes, but to interrogate their origins, the ideologies that they uphold, and the systems such stereotypes perpetuate?

Many of the teacher candidates were candid in their former misconceptions of Indigenous peoples. For example, one Settler teacher candidate expressed that "[her] view of Indigenous people up until university was that they were really more of a nuisance, and they smuggle, and just really negative things." Another candidate said, "Growing up, I thought that Indigenous peoples—this is very offensive—I thought Indigenous peoples were all alcoholics and drug addicts, and my only exposure to Indigenous people was at the shelters." The grand narratives in our history education are primarily reinforced by media-driven tropes of Indigenous identity.[51] Considering the presence of media-informed misconceptions about Indigeneity, teacher education must then explicitly create room to debunk such myths. Living a praxis of reconciliation entails ensuring that Indigenous histories, perspectives, and contemporary issues are thorough, integrative, and authentically represented across the teacher education program curricula.

Within public schooling in Ontario, Settler-dominant curriculum continues to reproduce such misconstrued civic particularities and grand narratives about national identity.[52] In attempts to maintain narratives of the "peaceful progress" that built Canada, grand narratives dismiss the historical harms committed against different Indigenous communities. However, the Ontario Ministry of Education recently made revisions to the Social Studies and History curriculum that seek to disrupt the pacifist narratives that have come to share our social imaginary.[53] When Indigenous perspectives are represented in the curriculum, they are often told through a Settler discourse, where Indigenous histories are reduced to narratives of marginalization, victimization, corruption, and tragedy.[54] In attempts to disrupt Settler historical consciousness, teacher education must expect new teachers to critique their positionality and debunk taken-for-granted assumptions about education.[55] Without interrogating Settler-dominant discourse, teachers cannot be expected to deconstruct the ways in which colonization and privilege actively uphold systemic discrimination in and through curriculum. As we propose here, the challenge to deconstructing such mainstream discourse is a deeply personal, demanding, and reflexive process. Decolonizing and destabilizing processes pose a threat to Settler teacher identity,[56] yet there must also be acknowledgement that Indigenous identities are inherently unsafe every day in Settler schooling systems.[57] Efforts to decentralize Settler-dominant discourse in Canadian curricula must therefore embrace such unsafeness and instability that a praxis of reconciliation requires. The deconstruction of Settler-dominant curricula has to begin with a personal responsibility to reconciliation. This personal responsibility involves a commitment to continuously deconstructing and reconstructing one's educational agenda, in a move to support ethically conscious learners and civically engaged citizens.[58]

As discussed, teacher education programs in Canada are predominately comprised of Settler teacher candidates who are, in turn, taught predominantly by Settler professors. In such cases, Indigenous-based curricula are a startling contrast not only to teacher candidates' prior educational experiences but also to their epistemological and ontological lens. This suggests that Indigenous teacher education not only concerns Indigenous content—such as studying facts—but also expects teacher candidates to unpack their ancestral and racialized identities. As Kiera's study demonstrated, it can be a particularly difficult process for racialized White teacher candidates to engage for the first time in a non-White culture, especially when the non-White culture has historically been deemed inferior.[59]

Further implicated within required Indigenous education, another impediment to a praxis of reconciliation was the perceived irrelevance of the course content, that is, irrelevance of Indigenous education to teacher candidates' future practice as teachers. Some did not see themselves as teachers of Indigenous history and content nor as future educators of Indigenous students.[60] One teacher candidate, studying towards a teaching degree in mathematics, did not perceive any relevance between Indigenous education and his role as a future math teacher:

> Kiera: On this idea of reconciliation, as an educator, do you see yourself having some sort of responsibility to teach about reconciliation?
>
> Teacher Candidate 1: Well it is an important topic, [but] maybe not in my classroom. Because people don't come to math to learn about history.
>
> *[Later in the interview]*
>
> Kiera: Do you have anything else you would like to add or expand upon?
>
> Teacher Candidate 1: Um, it feels like the [FNMI] course is laid out specifically for the more liberal arts topics. Which I understand because that's the easiest way to do it. But, on the other hand, when you walk in there with math and physics or bio and chemistry, it's just like, *Okay, I would love to, but how does this help me?*

The risk of this discourse is perpetuating an ideology that Indigeneity is an arts-and-crafts culture that holds little relevance for Western knowledge, particularly within STEM education. As a math educator, nevertheless, this teacher candidate is still implicated by the responsibilities of reconciliation—our mathematics classrooms are not immune to addressing structural inequities or teaching through a social justice agenda within mathematics education.[61] Moreover, this Ontario-based teacher candidate has a ninety-six percent chance of teaching in a secondary school with First Nations, Métis, and Inuit students.[62] Reconciliatory education involves a shift in understanding where Indigenous knowledge does not only hold value for Indigenous peoples but for all Canadians, as it has shaped the very socio-political landscape we know today.

Settler educators are implicated by the complexities of differing civic particularities and, consequently, must learn to navigate between two worlds of thought. Canadian teachers have an obligation not only to learn about Indigenous peoples, worldviews, and histories but also to assume a responsibility to uphold teaching practices that challenge the differing inequities reproduced by our (mis)understandings of certain civic particularities. For example, Indigenous peoples in Canada and, likewise, Māori peoples in New Zealand have inherent rights that are outlined in treaty. Traditional history education entertains a misinformed curriculum on the purpose, process, and outcome of Indigenous-Crown treaties. This, in turn, reproduces learners and teachers who fail to understand the significance of treaty principles and treaty relationships. Treaty education, Jennifer Tupper suggests, is an act of ethical relationality, wherein students and teachers are invited to return to the original nation-to-nation understanding of one another's worldview and history, as originally intended in the treaties.[63] Treaty education invites learners to understand their historical locatedness and civic responsibility by inviting them to both engage with an historical "past" and to (re)situate themselves in a present time that is defined by that past.

Nevertheless, treaty education continues to fall short in Canada.[64] Without meaningful Indigenous education that situates Settler and Indigenous identities as congruent to one another, teachers—and teacher candidates—are actively constructing identities that distance themselves from Indigenous people. Such "perfect stranger" discourse implies that educators do not see Indigeneity as part of their civic responsibilities in relation to their professional and personal identities as new teachers.[65] Consider the following statement made by a Settler male teacher candidate from Ontario:

> Kiera: You expressed [earlier in the interview] that, as a citizen, you feel a responsibility in the reconciliation process—
> Teacher Candidate 2: Well, not personally because my family is foreign. I'm a second-generation immigrant. So I personally—
> Kiera: Where are you from?
> Teacher Candidate 2: Italy. So I feel, personally, I had nothing to do with this. But this is like [pause] for the Canadians.
> Kiera: Okay, so you would more closely identify with being Italian than Canadian?
> Teacher Candidate 2: Well, I was born here. I live here. This is my home. But, like, I don't share their history. The history I have was World War II and Rome. I share their current culture, but I don't share their history.

Here we have a teacher candidate articulating the construction of not only his ancestry but how this ancestry informs his Canadian identity. In this sense, his Italian ancestry is used to demonstrate how he can be absolved of reconciliatory responsibilities through ancestral association. Such active distancing perpetuates a notion wherein Indigenous peoples are something of the past, and that past injustice and contemporary Indigeneity does not inform contemporary Canadian social, cultural, or political particulars.

By practicing active distancing, educators attempt to exonerate themselves from any potential guilt for historical injustices. Strategic manoeuvring in and out of collective guilt is commonly practiced by Settler Canadians who, at times, might deny their membership within the collective group that is responsible for injustice (such as not being technically Canadian), or who may outright deny that their collective group can be held responsible for any injustice or wrongdoing.[66] Rhetoric such as "moving on" or "keeping what's in the past in the past" evokes the fallacy that the colonization and systemic discrimination of Indigenous peoples has ended and has no vestigial consequence today. Such distancing, however, is sometimes fuelled by a drive to absolve oneself of guilt or shame. Yet, as Roger Simon warns, we must be cognizant of the "de-coupling of guilt and responsibility,"[67] wherein the rejection of guilt can cultivate the rejection of responsibility. Who is to accept and heal the burden of colonization? "Whereas the descendants and beneficiaries of colonization may choose to walk away from the 'burden,'" Kiera wrote in her initial analysis of this statement, "Indigenous peoples are left alone to pick up the remnants of a broken system that was designed to erase their very existence."[68] Active distancing justifies a sense of complacency in a Settler-dominated discourse—but such complacency, likewise, must be fuelled by ignorance about the past and a rejection of engaging historical consciousness.

Chinnery poignantly reminds us that critical historical consciousness is not merely learning *about* history and historical injustice. The mere acquisition of facts does not evoke ethical force.[69] Rather, history education that is informed by provoking a sense of historical consciousness is an opportunity to acknowledge one's responsibility to and for the past, and how one chooses to live in relation to the tensions that exist because of it. Disrupting the Settler-dominated curriculum implicates oneself professionally and personally, wherein teachers consider themselves to be teachers of

Indigenous and Canadian education and to be ethically engaged Canadian citizens.

Sites of Possibility: (Un)Learning and Responsibility

Despite educators' best intentions to create safe, neutral, and stable learning conditions, the classroom is already defined by uncertainty, discomfort, and risk.[70] In light of the deconstruction and reconstruction processes that are necessary for curricular reconciliation,[71] there are increasingly contentious responsibilities placed upon teacher educators (typically Settler Canadians) to facilitate these de/re-construction processes, in addition to meeting curricular standards and accountability measures for Canadian teachers. For the Ontario teacher candidates, moments of (un)learning occurred throughout the course, specifically in relation to understanding/unsettling privilege and Settler identities. When teacher candidates were asked if they could point to one particular moment in their recent Indigenous education when their thinking about Indigenous education had changed, none (at that time) could recall one specific moment. Rather, the teacher candidates alluded to many little "ah-ha" moments. Disrupting what teacher candidates know—or think they know—about Indigenous peoples involves embracing the discomfort and instability required to un/re-learn about education, Settler identity, and Indigeneity. Integral to their understandings about reconciliation was a strong sense of acknowledgement in many forms. For many of the teacher candidates, reconciliation begins with an honest and personal acknowledgement of ones' identity and ones' inherent privileges, histories, and responsibilities. Acknowledgement alone, nevertheless, does not immediately implicate one within reconciliatory pedagogies.

All teacher candidates who were interviewed acknowledged at least some sense of responsibility in remedying injustice towards Indigenous peoples. Yet the degree to which they felt personally responsible for reconciliation varied. Some teacher candidates expressed a vague sense of at least seeing value in Indigenous education, but then they would struggle to articulate the specifics ways in which they as educators will play a role in reconciliation processes. Teacher candidates, however, were eager to consider and foster transformative pedagogies in relation to their professional identities as teachers and personal identities as ethical citizens. As one Ontario teacher candidate said:

> To me, presenting *reconciliation in the classroom requires personal responsibility* as a person first. As teachers we like to think of ourselves as coming to the classroom objectively, but we never do—we can't. Like, we can try and be more objective, but we cannot remove ourselves as people from the classroom. So I have a lot of learning left to do. And, to be honest, I don't want to learn. It's exhausting, it's hard, it's emotional. *But if I want to be a responsible educator, I need to be a responsible person* [italics added for emphasis].

Here this Ontario teacher candidate spoke to the daunting and complicated conversations that reconciliatory teaching demands. As she says, one's commitment to becoming an ethical educator is deeply personal and emotional, yet such responsibility also requires engagement with *outside subjectivity*—the opportunity to engage with that which is outside our immediate (and, perhaps, taken-for-granted) subjectivity.[72] One of the many objectives of Indigenous education, in addition to re-learning histories, is to encourage teachers to "step out of our allegiances" in efforts to interrogate inherited knowledge systems.[73] To avoid rendering Indigenous peoples, cultures, histories, and worldviews as Other or irreconcilably different, inner-reform transpires when there are opportunities to oscillate between the familiar and the strange, in efforts to deconstruct what one considers relative to one's reality.[74] Such inner-reform, what Pinar[75] terms "subjective reconstruction," requires not only theory *of* or *about* the Other but demands engagement with such alterity. Towards such subjective reconstruction—such as the movement required of the teacher candidate who distances himself as a math educator towards a teacher candidate who feels personally responsible for reconciliation—demands both "solitary study as well as dialogical encounter."[76] What if teacher candidates were expected to engage with "outside subjectivity," not in attempts to learn *about* Indigenous knowledges but *through* them?

Reconceptualizing Our Civic Particularities as Ethical Engagement

In the context of Indigenous teacher education, there must be parameters where ethics and ethical relationality are concerned. In teacher education, where conversations of reconciliation, partnership, and treaties are curricular priorities, ethics need to be at the core of these conversations. Overcoming the existing tensions surrounding an inherited Eurocentric curriculum cannot be reduced to best practices but involves an honest engagement with the historical particulars that came before—whether it be residential schooling or the appropriation of land.[77] The possibility of engaging a praxis of reconciliation must also address the aforementioned challenges associated with teacher candidates' (lacking) prior knowledge; a perceived irrelevance of Indigeneity to one's practice; and an active distancing to Indigenous peoples, histories, and education. The universality of Settler pedagogies within teacher education must also be part of a discursive and recursive project to de-centre these narratives within Indigenous education and counter the assimilative and integrative role of teacher education.

In a praxis of reconciliation, we must move beyond self-invested interests and assumptions of the traditional role of the educator. The unpacking of students' assumptions—and, likewise, of teacher educators' assumptions—is a necessary facet in the work that lies ahead within a reconciliatory agenda. Towards the reconceptualization of teacher education in Ontario, including our own work at the University of Ottawa, Indigenous education must be—at a minimum—a required component of teacher preparation and also of teacher educator (our) professional learning. Commitment to reconciliation does not end there, however. As evidenced by the case study of an Ontario-based Indigenous education course, the work of Indigenous and reconciliatory education is clouded with contention, resistance, and deeply entrenched Settler pedagogies. In attempts to navigate the conflict and discomfort that reconciliatory education demands, the re-centering of ethics must be considered integral to one's curricular and pedagogical choices. As we move towards a new decade of reconciliation, we must remain critical of our reconciliation processes. To foster a teacher education agenda that destabilizes Settler-dominant narratives, ethical engagement and the nurturing of historical consciousness must be continuously re-centred at the forefront of teacher education curricula, with attention to the needs of Indigenous communities in Canada.

Notes

1. Truth and Reconciliation Commission of Canada, *Final Report*, vi.
2. "Settler" is capitalized to recognize the political and civic responsibilities of those with Settler identities in Canada. Different from the state or action of "settling" and hence being a "settler" (i.e., "my family settled in the West Coast" or "we have settled into our new home"), Settler Canadians are implicated in the history and legacy of Settler colonialism in Canada. Just as Indigenous peoples are proper nouns, to recognize their nationhood and Indigeneity, so too is Settler capitalized to acknowledge Settler histories, identities, and responsibilities that are necessary for reconciliatory relationships.
3. Edmonds, *Settler Colonialism and (Re)Conciliation: Frontier Violence, Affective Performances, and Imaginative Refoundings*, 2.
4. Henderson and Wakeham, *Reconciling Canada*, 4–5.
5. For further information: TRC of South Africa, http://www.justice.gov.za/trc/; Waitangi Tribunal, https://www.waitangitribunal.govt.nz; and Reconciliation Australia, https://www.reconciliation.org.au/about-us/.
6. Brant-Castellano, Archibald, and Degagné, *From Truth to Reconciliation*, 3.
7. Here we consciously use the term reconciliation in attempts to further the conversation put forth by the TRC, yet we recognize its limitations and criticisms. For further work on criticizing re-conciliation, see Inuk scholar John Amagoalik (Amagoalik, "Reconciliation or Conciliation? An Inuit Perspective").
8. Truth and Reconciliation Commission, *Final Report*, 6–7.
9. Truth and Reconciliation Commission, *Final Report*, 4.
10. Truth and Reconciliation Commission of Canada, *Calls to Action*, 7–8.
11. Truth and Reconciliation Commission of Canada, *Final Report*, 4.
12. University of Winnipeg, "Indigenous Course Requirement."
13. Queens University, "Committees and Reports: Truth and Reconciliation Task Force."
14. Halpern, "Truth and Reconciliation at U of T."
15. Association of Canadian College and University Teachers of English, "CFP: Special Issue."
16. Petrarca and Kitchen, "A Time of Change," 47; Ng-A-Fook, Ingham, and Burrows, "Reconciling 170 Years," 138.
17. Schick and St. Denis, "What Makes Anti-Racist Pedagogy in Teacher Education Difficult," 56–57, 61–66; Dion, "Disrupting Molded Images," 330–331.
18. Wideen, "Teacher Education at the Crossroads." According to Wideen, the *restructuring* of teacher education often suggests top-down reform

that may or may not have direct impact upon schools or teacher candidates themselves; *reconceptualization,* on the other hand, demands on-the-ground change that is accountable to the needs of teacher candidates and teacher preparation. Efforts at restructuring teacher education, therefore, also require a simultaneous reconceptualization of what it means to prepare teachers: "Old wine in new bottles does not fare well" (Wideen, 6).

19   Hatano and Oura, "Reconceptualizing School Learning," 28.
20   Feiman-Nemser, "Teacher Learning," 697–705; Soslau, "Adaptive Teaching Expertise," 768–769.
21   Timperley, *Learning to Practice in Initial Teacher Education*, 5.
22   Timperley et al., *Best Evidence Synthesis*, 203.
23   Battiste, *Decolonizing Education*, 21–22, 29–33; Tupper, "Treaty Education," 146–153.
24   Battiste, *Decolonizing Education*, 128; Ma Rhea and Atkinson, "Growing Understanding," 155–172.
25   Phelan, *Curriculum Theorizing and Teacher Education*, 62.
26   Battiste, Bell, and Findlay, "Decolonizing Education in Canada," 83; Kuokkanen, *Reshaping the University*, 1.
27   Here we use "Canadian identity" in the singular to refer to the problematic myth of being "Canadian" as a universal and homogenous identity. Whereas the nation-state of Canada comprises diverse and ever-changing nationalities, cultures, and socio-political landscapes, the narrative of being "Canadian" still often assumes a singularity whereby "identity" is static and any counter-narratives (such as being a pluralistic or multicultural society) are framed as supplementary to the one true narrative.
28   Pinar, *Gender of Racial Politics and Violence in America*.
29   Ng-A-Fook and Smith, "Doing Oral History Education toward Reconciliation," 68–70.
30   Here we understand *difficult knowledge* as used by Deborah Britzman to refer to the pedagogical and curricular implications of emotion, trauma, and uncertainty (Britzman, *Lost Subjects, Contested Objects*, 117).
31   Dion, "(Re)Telling to Disrupt," 57–59; Higgins, Madden, and Korteweg, "Witnessing (Halted) Deconstruction," 252; Schick and St. Denis, "Troubling National Discourses," 310.
32   St. Denis and Schick, "What Makes Anti-Racist Pedagogy in Teacher Education Difficult?" 56–57, 61–66.
33   Schick and St. Denis, "Troubling National Discourses," 310.
34   Dion, "Disrupting Molded Images," 331.
35   Dion, *Braiding Histories*, 178–181.
36   Dion, "Mediating the Space Between," 470.

Reconceptualizing Teacher Education in Ontario 59

37 Drawing upon critical history and the work of anti-racist scholar Timothy J. Stanley, we use the term "racialized White" to refer to peoples who are European or Europeans descendants. This distinction is to problematize the normalization of White-ness, which is not a neutral reality but a construct built upon racisms and racialized perception (Stanley, *Contesting White Supremacy*, 16). This perceived "Whiteness" is not synonymous with Settler identity although also not mutually exclusive; in other words, being Settler-Canadian does not necessarily mean one is racialized as White although one can certainly be both Settler and racialized White.
38 Kincheloe and Steinberg, "Constructing a Pedagogy of Whiteness," 178–179, 194.
39 Solomon et al., "Discourse of Denial," 149.
40 Phelan, *Curriculum Theorizing and Teacher Education*, 62.
41 Ng-A-Fook and Milne, "Unsettling Our Narrative Encounters," 95.
42 Phelan, *Curriculum Theorizing and Teacher Education*, 96; Carson and Johnston, "Difficulty with Difference," 76.
43 Tupper and Cappello, "Teaching Treaties as (Un)Usual Narratives," 571–577; Smith et al., "Deconstructing a Curriculum of Dominance," 66.
44 Tupper, "Treaty Education," 151–152.
45 Ermine, "Ethical Space," 202.
46 Donald, "Forts, Curriculum, and Ethical Relationally," 45.
47 Donald, 45.
48 Brant, "'But How Does This Help Me?'"
49 By way of example, to teach something "new" about Indigenous peoples might be an introductory lesson on the treaties in Canada (including land surveying, negotiations, signing of the treaties, and its aftermath), but such lessons become much more interrogative if they are taught tangentially to the deconstruction of the Canadian history that we are familiar with. Often, treaty history (if taught at all) plays Indigenous peoples to be gullible victims who didn't know what they were signing whereas ethical treaty education requires an un-learning and then a re-building of historical knowledge to inform one's ethical citizenry.
50 Higgins, Madden, and Korteweg. "Witnessing (Halted) Deconstruction," 261–264.
51 Dion, *Braiding Histories*, 6, 103.
52 Smith et al., "Deconstructing a Curriculum of Dominance," 54.
53 As of September 2018, the new Ontario Social Studies (Grades 1–6) and History (Grades 7–12) curriculum will be implemented throughout the province. The new curriculum was revised and developed in collaboration with First Nations, Métis, and Inuit

educators and community members in response to the *Calls to Action*. For example, by Grade 5, students are to know the short- and long-term consequences for Haudenosaunee and Anishinaabe peoples resulting from European settlement and the disruption that colonization had on Indigenous gender norms (Ontario Ministry of Education, *Ontario Social Studies [Grades 1 to 6] and History [Grades 7 and 8]*, 112–116).

54 Clark, "Toward Reconciliation," 85; Tupper, "Treaty Education," 146.
55 Phelan, *Curriculum Theorizing and Teacher Education*, 83–86.
56 Kincheloe and Steinberg, "Constructing a Pedagogy of Whiteness," 186–187; Tuck and Yang, "Decolonization Is Not a Metaphor," 9–28.
57 Barrett, "Is 'Safety' Dangerous?" 6–7; Brant, "'But How Does This Help Me?,'" 77–84.
58 Battiste, *Decolonizing Education*, 104–108.
59 Kincheloe and Steinberg, "Constructing a Pedagogy of Whiteness," 193.
60 St. Denis and Schick, "What Makes Anti-Racist Pedagogy in Teacher Education Difficult?," 57.
61 Wager and Stinson, *Teaching Mathematics for Social Justice*, 81–98.
62 Gallagher-MacKay, Kidder, and Methot, *First Nations, Métis, and Inuit Education*, 1.
63 Tupper, "Treaty Education," 148, 153.
64 Tupper and Cappello, "Teaching Treaties as (Un)Usual Narratives," 565.
65 Dion, "Disrupting Molded Images," 331; Dion, *Braiding Histories*, 178–181.
66 Caouette and Taylor, "'Don't Blame Me for What My Ancestors Did,'" 89–90.
67 Simon, "Hopeful Practice of Worrying," 138.
68 Brant, "'But How Does This Help Me?,'" 62.
69 Chinnery, "'What Good Does All This Remembering Do, Anyway?,'" 401–402.
70 Du Preez, "Irony in 'Safe Spaces,'" 59.
71 Battiste, *Decolonizing Education*, 79.
72 Pinar, "Bildung and the Internationalization of Curriculum Studies," 26.
73 Donald, "Forts, Curriculum, and Ethical Relationally," 45.
74 Phelan, *Curriculum Theorizing and Teacher Education*, 83.
75 Pinar, *The Character of Curriculum Studies*.
76 Pinar, *What Is Curriculum Theory?*, 179.
77 Ng-A-Fook, Ingham, and Burrows. "Reconciling 170 Years," 126.

Bibliography

Amagoalik, John. "Reconciliation or Conciliation? An Inuit Perspective." In *From Truth to Reconciliation: Transforming the Legacy of Residential Schools*, edited by Marlene Brant-Castellano, Linda Archibald, and Mike Degagné, 91–100. Ottawa, ON: Aboriginal Healing Foundation Research Series, 2008.

Association of Canadian College and University Teachers of English. "CFP: Special Issue: Taking Up the Calls to Action of the TRC in Teacher Education, McGill Journal of Education." Last modified on March 6, 2017. https://accute.ca/2017/03/06/cfp-special-issue-taking-up-the-calls-to-action-of-the-trc-in-teacher-education-mcgill-journal-of-education-deadline-june-15-2017/.

Barrett, Betty J. "Is 'Safety' Dangerous? A Critical Examination of the Classroom as Safe Space." *The Canadian Journal for the Scholarship of Teaching and Learning* 1, no. 1 (2010): 1–12.

Battiste, Marie. *Decolonizing Education: Nourishing the Learning Spirit*. Saskatoon, SK: Purich Publishing, 2013.

Battiste, Marie, Lynne Bell, and Len Findlay. "Decolonizing Education in Canada." *Canadian Journal of Native Education* 26, no. 2 (2002): 82–95.

Britzman, Deborah. *Lost Subjects, Contested Objects*. New York, NY: State University of New York Press, 1998.

Brant, Kiera. "'But How Does This Help Me?': (Re)Thinking (Re)Conciliation in Teacher Education." Unpublished MA Thesis, University of Ottawa, 2017.

Brant-Castellano, Marlene, Linda Archibald, and Mike Degagné. *From Truth to Reconciliation: Transforming the Legacy of Residential Schools*. Ottawa, ON: Aboriginal Healing Foundation Research Series, 2008.

Caouette, Julie, and Donald M. Taylor. "'Don't Blame Me for What My Ancestors Did': Understanding the Impact of Collective White Guilt." In *The Great White North? Exploring Whiteness, Privilege and Identity in Education*, edited by Paul R. Carr and Darren E. Lund, 77–92. Rotterdam, NL: Sense Publishers, 2007.

Carson, Terry, and Ingrid Johnston. "The Difficulty with Difference in Teacher Education: Toward a Pedagogy of Compassion." *Alberta Journal of Educational Research* XLVI, no. 1 (2000): 75–83.

Chinnery, Ann. "'What Good Does All This Remembering Do, Anyway?': On Historical Consciousness and the Responsibility of Memory." In *Philosophy of Education 2010*, edited by Gert Biesta, 397–405. Urbana-Champaign, IL: Philosophy of Education Society, 2010.

Clark, Penney. "Representation of Aboriginal People in English Canadian History Textbooks: Toward Reconciliation." In *Teaching the Violent*

Past: History Education and Reconciliation, edited by Elizabeth A. Cole, 81–122. New York, NY: Rowman and Littlefield, 2007.

Dion, Susan. Braiding Histories: Learning from Aboriginal Peoples' Experiences and Perspectives. Vancouver, BC: University of British Columbia Press, 2009.

———. "Disrupting Molded Images: Identities, Responsibilities and Relationships—Teachers and Indigenous Subject Material." Teaching Education 18, no. 4 (2007): 329–342.

———. "Mediating the Space Between: Voices of Indigenous Youth and Voices of Educators in Service of Reconciliation." Canadian Sociological Association 53, no. 4 (2016): 468–473.

———. "(Re)Telling to Disrupt: Aboriginal People and the Stories of Canadian History." Journal of the Canadian Association for Curriculum Studies 2, no. 1 (2004): 55–76.

Donald, Dwayne. "Forts, curriculum, and ethical relationality." In Reconsidering Canadian Curriculum Studies: Provoking Historical, Present, and Future Perspectives, edited by Jennifer Rottmann and Nicholas Ng-A-Fook, 39–46. Palgrave Macmillan. 2012.

———. "Forts, Curriculum, and Indigenous Métissage: Imaging Decolonization of Aboriginal-Canadian Relations in Educational Contexts." First Nations Perspectives 2, no. 1 (2009): 1–24.

———. "The Pedagogy of the Fort: Curriculum, Aboriginal-Canadian Relations, and Indigenous Métissage." Unpublished doctoral dissertation, University of Alberta, 2009a.

Du Preez, Petro. "The Human Right to Education, the Ethical Responsibility of Curriculum and the Irony in 'Safe Spaces.'" In Safe Spaces: Human Rights Education in Diverse Contexts, edited by Cornelia Roux, 51–62. Rotterdam, NL: Sense Publishers, 2012.

Edmonds, Penelope. Settler Colonialism and (Re)Conciliation: Frontier Violence, Affective Performances, and Imaginative Refoundings. London, UK: Palgrave Macmillan, 2016.

Ermine, Willie. "The Ethical Space of Engagement." Indigenous Law Journal 6, no.1 (2007): 193–203.

Feiman-Nemser, Sharon. "Teacher Learning: How Do Teachers Learn to Teach?" In Handbook of Research on Teacher Education, 3rd ed., edited by Marilyn Cochran-Smith, Sharon Feiman-Nemser, D. John McIntyre, and Kelly Demers, 697–705. New York, NY: Routledge, 2008.

Gallagher-MacKay, Kelly, Annie Kidder, and Suzanne Methot. First Nations, Métis, and Inuit Education: Overcoming Gaps in Publically Funded Schools. Toronto, ON: People for Education, 2013.

Halpern, Rachel. "Truth and Reconciliation at U of T." *U of T News*. Last modified on January 16, 2017. https://www.utoronto.ca/news/truth-and-reconciliation-u-t.

Hatano, Giyoo, and Yoko Oura. "Commentary: Reconceptualizing School Learning Using Insight from Expertise Research." *Educational Researcher* 32 (2003): 26–29.

Henderson, Jennifer, and Pauline Wakeham. *Reconciling Canada: Critical Perspectives on the Culture of Redress*. Toronto, ON: University of Toronto Press, 2012.

Higgins, Mark, Brooke Madden, and Lisa Korteweg. "Witnessing (Halted) Deconstruction: White Teachers' 'Perfect Stranger' Position Within Urban Indigenous Education." *Race, Ethnicity and Education* 18, no. 2 (2015): 251–276.

Kincheloe, Joe, and Shirley Steinberg. "Constructing a Pedagogy of Whiteness for Angry White Students." In *Dismantling White Privilege: Pedagogy, Politics and Whiteness*, edited by Nelson Rodriguez and Leila Villaverde, 178–197. New York, NY: Peter Lang, 2000.

Kuokkanen, Rauna. *Reshaping the University: Responsibility, Indigenous Epistemes, and the Logic of the Gift*. Vancouver, BC: University of British Columbia Press, 2007.

Ma Rhea, Zane, and Henry Atkinson. "Growing Understanding: Issues in Mainstream Education in Indigenous and Traditional Communities." In *Reconciliation and Pedagogy*, edited by Pal Ahluwalia, Stephen Atkinson, Peter Bishop, Pam Christie, Robert Hattam, and Julie Matthews, 155–172. New York, NY: Routledge, 2012.

Ng-A-Fook, Nicholas, Mark Ingham, and Tylor Burrows. "Reconciling 170 Years of Settler Curriculum Policies: Teacher Education in Ontario." In *Curriculum History of Canadian Teacher Education*, edited by Theodore M. Christou, 125–143. New York, NY: Routledge, 2017.

Ng-A-Fook, Nicholas, and Robin Milne. "Unsettling Our Narrative Encounters Within and Outside of Canadian Social Studies." *Canadian Social Studies* 47, no. 2 (2014): 88–109.

Ng-A-Fook, Nicholas, and Bryan Smith. "Doing Oral History Education Toward Reconciliation." In *Oral History and Education: Theories, Dilemmas and Practices*, edited by Kristina R. Llewellyn and Nicholas Ng-A-Fook, 65–86. New York, NY: Palgrave Macmillan, 2017.

Ontario Ministry of Education. *Ontario Social Studies (Grades 1 to 6) and History (Grades 7 and 8)*. Retrieved May 8, 2018 from http://www.edu.gov.on.ca/eng/curriculum/elementary/social-studies-history-geography-2018.pdf.

Petrarca, Diana, and Julian Kitchen. "A Time of Change in Ontario's Initial Teacher Education." In *Initial Teacher Education in Ontario: The First Year of Four-Semester Teacher Education Programs*, edited by Diana

Petrarca and Julian Kitchen, 1–16. Ottawa, ON: Canadian Association for Teacher Education, 2017.

Phelan, Anne M. *Curriculum Theorizing and Teacher Education: Complicating Conjunctions.* New York, NY: Routledge, 2015.

Pinar, William F. "Bildung and the Internationalization of Curriculum Studies." In *International Conversations on Curriculum Studies*, edited by Eero Ropo and Autio Tero, 23–41. Dordrecht, NL: Sense Publishers, 2009.

———. *The Character of Curriculum Studies.* New York, NY: Palgrave Macmillan, 2011.

Pinar, W. F. (2001). *The Gender of Racial Politics and Violence in America: Lynching, Prison Rape, and the Crisis of Masculinity.* New York: Peter Lang.

———. *What Is Curriculum Theory?* 2nd ed. New York, NY: Routledge, 2012.

Queens University. "Committees and Reports: Truth and Reconciliation Task Force." Last modified on August 2, 2017. http://queensu.ca/provost/committees-and-reports/truth-and-reconciliation-commission-task-force.

Reconciliation Australia. "About Us." https://www.reconciliation.org.au/about-us/.

Schick, Carol, and Verna St. Denis. "Troubling National Discourses in Anti-Racist Curricular Planning." *Canadian Journal of Education* 28, no. 3 (2005): 295–317.

Simon, Roger. "Towards a Hopeful Practice of Worrying: The Problematics of Listening and Educative Responsibilities of Canada's Truth and Reconciliation Commission." In *Reconciling Canada: Critical Perspectives on the Culture of Redress*, edited by Jennifer Henderson and Pauline Wakeham, 129–142. Toronto, ON: University of Toronto Press, 2013.

Smith, Bryan, Nicholas Ng-A-Fook, Sara Berry, and Kevin Spence. "Deconstructing a Curriculum of Dominance: Teacher Education, Colonial Frontier Logics, and Residential Schooling." *Transnational Curriculum Inquiry* 8, no. 2 (2011): 53–70.

Solomon, R. Patrick, John Portelli, Beverly-Jean Daniel, and Arlene Campbell. "The Discourse of Denial: How White Teacher Candidates Construct Race, Racism and 'White Privilege.'" *Race, Ethnicity and Education* 8, no. 2 (2005): 147–169.

Soslau, Elizabeth. "Opportunities to Develop Adaptive Teaching Expertise During Supervisory Conferences." *Teaching and Teacher Education* 28, no. 5 (2012): 768–779.

Stanley, Timothy J. *Contesting White Supremacy: School Segregation, Anti-Racism, and the Making of Chinese Canadians.* Vancouver, BC: UBC Press, 2011.

St. Denis, Verna, and Carol Schick. "What Makes Anti-Racist Pedagogy in Teacher Education Difficult? Three Popular Ideological Assumptions." *The Alberta Journal of Educational Research* 43, no. 1 (2003): 55–69.

Timperley, Helen. *Learning to Practice in Initial Teacher Education.* Wellington, NZ: Ministry of Education, 2012.

Timperley, Helen, Aaron Wilson, Heather Barrar, and Irene Fung. *Teacher Professional Learning and Development: Best Evidence Synthesis Iteration [BES].* Wellington, NZ: Ministry of Education, 2007.

Truth and Reconciliation Commission of Canada. *Canada's Residential Schools: The Final Report of the Truth and Reconciliation Commission of Canada.* Montreal, QC: McGill-Queen's University Press, 2015.

Truth and Reconciliation Commission of Canada. *Truth and Reconciliation Commission of Canada: Calls to Action.* Winnipeg, MB: Truth and Reconciliation Commission of Canada, 2015.

Truth and Reconciliation Commission of South Africa. "Welcome." Retrieved May 8, 2018 from http://www.justice.gov.za/trc/.

Tuck, Eve, and Wayne Yang. "Decolonization Is Not a Metaphor." *Decolonization: Indigeneity, Education & Society* 1, no. 1 (2012): 1–40.

Tupper, Jennifer. "Treaty Education for Ethically Engaged Citizenship: Settler Identities, Historical Consciousness and the Need for Reconciliation." *Citizenship, Teaching and Learning* 7, no. 2 (2012): 143–156.

Tupper, Jennifer, and Michael Cappello. "Teaching Treaties as (Un)Usual Narratives: Disrupting the Curricular Commonsense." *Curriculum Inquiry* 38, no. 5 (2008): 559–578.

University of Winnipeg. "Indigenous Course Requirement." Retrieved May 8, 2018 from https://www.uwinnipeg.ca/indigenous/indigenous-course-requirement/index.html.

Waitangi Tribunal. "Waitangi Tribunal." Last modified on March 14, 2017. https://www.waitangitribunal.govt.nz.

Wager, Anita A, and David W. Stinson. *Teaching Mathematics for Social Justice: Conversations with Educators.* Reston, VA: National Council of Teachers of Mathematics, 2012.

Wideen, Marvin F. "Teacher Education at the Crossroads." In *Changing Times in Teacher Education: Restructuring or Reconceptualizing?*, edited by Marvin F. Wideen and Peter P. Grimmett, 1–16. London, UK: Falmer Press, 1995.

CHAPTER 3

Accounting for the Self: Teacher Education in a Post–Truth and Reconciliation Context

Avril Aitken

Can we conceive of a practice of teacher education that is adequate for the challenges of life in the twenty-first century, in Canada, and elsewhere around the world?

***

How might a different practice of teacher education be informed by what is happening in Canada, which is currently a post-Truth and Reconciliation Commission context?[1]

In this chapter, I make the case that in a world faced by challenges that are borderless and global, where international efforts and collective responsibility are the only possible ways to respond to the range of crises facing humanity, the primary preoccupation of future teachers and teacher educators should be self-Other relationships. More explicitly, I propose that thinking with and about subjectivity—what it is, its repercussions, one's own subjectivity and that of others—must be viewed as fundamental to teacher practice and professionalism and, therefore, central to the work of teacher educators.

Subjectivity can be understood as an individual's sense of self, shaped in relation to/with/by others and experiences, as these intersect with issues of power, knowledge, and authority.[2] Subjectivity is "idiosyncratic,"[3] unlike the common notion of teacher professional identity, which can be linked to jurisdictional standards and policies, regulatory practices, and "the normalized [teacher] subject frozen within dominant professional expectations, school practices and social values."[4] It may be tempting, given escalating conflict, crises, precariousness, and human rights violations, to focus on increasing knowledge and skills related to the problems[5] that we face locally and globally. However, as Taubman suggests,

> What happens in a school has much more to do with psycho-social forces that cannot be captured by, and are much more powerful than the imagined bounded unities of individuals exchanging knowledge in a seemingly rational and intentional circuit of communication.[6]

Following Taubman, I would argue that subjectivity and the nature of psycho-social forces, while occasionally made explicit in teacher educators' accounts of their own practices,[7] are not commonly acknowledged through the normative structures of teacher education. I propose that now, more than ever, that must be changed, and I make the case by putting the spotlight on the current Canadian context.

We find ourselves at a watershed moment, with systemic human rights violations against Indigenous[8] peoples having been brought to the forefront by Canada's Truth and Reconciliation Commission (TRC). Pointing to the urgency of changing knowledge, beliefs, values, practices, and policies in many domains, the TRC proposes that education is one of the primary means through which the requisite social and structural transformation will be achieved.[9] In the words of the chair of the TRC, Senator Murray Sinclair, "[i]t is precisely because education was the primary tool of oppression of Aboriginal people, and miseducation of all Canadians, that we have concluded that education holds the key to reconciliation."[10] While there has been relatively little discussion of how we would reach a state of reconciliation, perceptions of what steps must be taken are evident in the flurry of new and possibly mandated guides, kits, and lesson plans related to teaching *about* the findings of the TRC. One organization, Kairos, has produced a "report card" on "Provincial and Territorial Curriculum *on* Indigenous Peoples" [added emphasis],[11] which provides rankings of curriculum content, targeted levels, and whether the curriculum is compulsory. The rankings are described "as a baseline to assess progress in achieving reconciliation through education in schools across Canada."[12] With such measure and materials brought to the forefront, social change is cast as the responsibility of teachers, and the product of their work. This is something that Pinar has repeatedly denounced; that is, when "the locus of responsibility—the very site of education—is the teacher, not the student."[13] With instrumental rationality influencing the predominant narrative of how education for reconciliation might be experienced in the classroom, the associated role for teacher education hinges on questions of curriculum, pedagogy, and management of learning outcomes. In this chapter, rather than arguing that such approaches are acutely inadequate to counter generations of injustice, I make the case that centring subjectivity—explicitly—is essential if we are to shape a practice of teacher education that is adequate for the challenges of life in the twenty-first century, in Canada, and elsewhere around the world.

This chapter draws inspiration from research-pedagogy carried out with my colleague Linda Radford, of the University of Ottawa. As teacher educators who inquire into our own practice, Linda and I share an interest in subjectivity, intersubjectivity, and relationality in the complex world of becoming a teacher. In my own case, this interest extends back to the questions and concerns that shaped my life as a teacher working for the Naskapi Nation of Kawawachikamach for almost two decades. Since moving from the subarctic community to an urban centre in the late 1990s for doctoral studies, I have continued to collaborate with members of the Nation as they seek to promote the place of Naskapi language in formal education.[14] Over the years, it has been possible to trace how provincial policy and the practices of non-Naskapi school staff negatively impact community members' efforts at increasing the place of Naskapi language and culture in the school.[15] These experiences have been powerful motivators to better understand the implications of teachers' subjectivity.

In our recent work considering a future teacher's sense of self,[16] we have looked at the production of digital narratives of difficult moments in practicum. What has emerged is the magnitude of the struggles the pre-service teachers face in taking on the identity of teacher, taking up a role in the school—without also having to imagine *changing school culture as well*. This last point is particularly significant given that the TRC has called for nationwide transformation. Canada is not the first to propose that educational policy, curriculum, and related teacher action are the means to counter strife, build peace, and foster reconciliation; there is much to be learned from the reconciliation-driven initiatives[17] that have already emerged across the globe in response to other cases of conflict, strife, or injustice. While studies of such initiatives reveal their limits, in what follows, I begin with a look at the Canadian context of reconciliation-focused work, and situate my own work within it.

Cracks in the Foundation of "Canada the Good"[18]

With media and news outlets constantly updating the public, there is a tidal flow of information about international conflict, economic inequity, ecological degradation, and human migration, the last of which often results from the aforementioned crises. As border restrictions make the news, we have seen the re-emergence of populist movements and manifestations of anti-cosmopolitanism. Yet, we are living in a period when a country's "goodness" and reputation are also scrutinized. For example, the Good Country Index, developed by policy advisor Simon Anholt, uses thirty-five criteria and data from the UN and international organizations "to measure what each country on earth contributes to the common good of humanity, and what it takes away, relative to its size."[19] Notably, Canada scores well in relation to global responsibility among the 163 nations for which data is collected. And, in reputational studies, Canada has repeatedly been ranked first among over 55 nations during the last eight years.[20] Nonetheless, at home, public challenges to the narrative of Canada the Good are increasingly common.[21] Indigenous scholars and activists persist in efforts to ensure that the "truth" of Truth and Reconciliation[22] remains central to any dialogue about change.[23] Lee writes that

> the real task of reconciliation ... is not in Canada waiting around to be forgiven for colonialism so business can carry on as usual; it is for Canadians to end the ongoing colonial violence that still suffocates Indigenous lives.... We are never "all in this together" while Indigenous communities are stripped to the bone for the fat to maintain Canada.[24]

Susan Dion comments, "We need to know what we're reconciling about—and at this point, Canadians aren't really sure."[25] Lee adds, "few seem to have an understanding of what it means in the face of ongoing colonialism."[26] Tuck and Yang challenge the very notion of reconciliation, emphasizing that it seems to overlook, rather than disrupt, settlers' privilege and innocence.[27] Their point is illustrated by a metaphor found on the website of the National Centre for Truth and Reconciliation: "To reconcile is to weave a stronger and more vibrant social fabric, based on the unique and diverse strengths of Canadians and their communities."[28] The image seems to capture a newer version of Canada the Good; however, hope rings hollow as it does not acknowledge the resistance, critique, and disbelief currently in circulation.

As a teacher educator, whose work is shaped by the field of curriculum studies, I have asked myself: What does it mean to seek to prepare teachers for equitable, just work in the face of the ongoing effects of colonialism, given my own and my institution's participation in this dynamic, and given the regulatory dimensions of teacher education within my jurisdiction? Jennifer Tupper, dean in a Faculty of Education, questions how we might create "curricular spaces of renewal" and how it can be accomplished "without further dehumanize[ing] Aboriginal peoples."[29] She proposes that this involves teachers "interrogat[ing] their own settler identities and invit[ing] their students to do the same."[30] Along such lines, Linda Radford and I have been looking at what emerges when future teachers read themselves with and against traumatic texts and testimony about the history of colonization, and its ongoing manifestations and impacts. We are interested in how such engagements inform future teachers' attempts at working toward decolonization and reconciliation through informal practices. We are also interested in what might be learned about resistance to such work, which is increasingly documented.[31]

Linda and I reflect in an ongoing way on the problem of centring the experience of non-Indigenous future teachers in our research and writing.[32] We ask ourselves if focusing on non-Indigenous resistance to the difficult truth of colonization will take attention away from the efforts of others to increase Indigenous voice and authority, in and out of the academy. Through conversation with Indigenous colleagues, we question the impact of our choices: Does researching the emotional impact of learning about colonialism on non-Indigenous future teachers re-centre non-Indigenous concerns, at the expense of narratives of Indigenous resilience or Indigenous suffering? Should we step back? Faced with classrooms of future teachers, who are almost exclusively settler-Canadians, we would say that—at this point—attempting to understand how to create spaces for thinking about truth and reconciliation, and encountering their own resistances to such work, appears to be an avenue of hope. This would be most notably the case, if what we learn about subjectivity can contribute to conversations about other forms of becoming teachers' resistance to equity of all kinds, in Canada and elsewhere.

Reconciliation Program and Policy in Diverse Nations, and Their Limitations

The metaphors of education as a tool of oppression and education holding the key to reconciliation have become commonplace in discussions of the TRC in Canada.[33] This is not a perspective unique to our country; in writing about post TRC initiatives in South Africa, Cappy points out, "Whereas education under apartheid promulgated racial exclusion, the new government has promoted education as a means to redress past inequalities and promote values of the new democracy."[34] There is a growing body of research that looks at the ways reconciliation agendas are being enacted through education policy and curriculum initiatives in societies that are divided by strife, human rights violations, or conflict. Canada is following on the heels of diverse countries, whose efforts have been documented, such as Australia, Cyprus, Ireland, Israel, Rwanda, South Africa, and Sri Lanka.[35]

Significantly, while "'reconciliation' cannot be easily abstracted from the very particular context in which it is rooted,"[36] and perceptions of what constitutes reconciliation can differ significantly from one setting to the next, there are common elements in the educational approaches taken up internationally. These include cross-curricular approaches to content integration, and/or cross-curricular teaching of values such as democracy, equality, peace, and respect. There is also the creation of opportunities for shared educational experiences for students from the groups in conflict. The limits of programs focusing on new knowledge and values education are acknowledged; some researchers conclude that "such initiatives cannot fundamentally alter the structural inequalities at the macro-level and micro-level" of society.[37] Intersecting with this is the recent movement to use particular pedagogical models with explicit commitments to critical pedagogy, critical multiculturalism, and antiracist pedagogies.[38] Zembylas, who has written extensively about teachers and reconciliation in post-conflict societies, explains that such critical approaches are generally taken up by individuals or small groups of teachers, who often end up limiting the work they do, based on "concerns about the potential of offending students"[39] or due to the resistance that arises from any of their efforts. While Zembylas focuses on the teacher role, it is only mentioned peripherally in the international cases mentioned previously, and in those cases, it may be directly linked to the failure of the initiatives to achieve desired results. This and other examples illustrate the scapegoating of teachers.[40] For example, in the South African case, it is suggested that teachers need to develop "a clearer conception of the possibilities of action."[41] Somewhat differently, it is claimed that Australian teachers need to be "committed to and passionate about embedding the cross-curriculum priority of integrating Aboriginal and Torres Strait Islander Histories."[42] In a review of the literature on teachers' promotion of social cohesion, the authors write that "teachers may use their agency to resist change as well as facilitate change, to promote peacebuilding and to stoke conflict."[43] Whether we look at policy, program, or pedagogy, the role of teachers in reconciliation agendas is implied.[44] As Zembylas, Charalambous, and Charalambous explain, there is an "assumption that teachers are influential in dealing with the legacy of ethnic strife and encouraging reconciliatory attitudes."[45] This taken-for-granted notion that "educators educate *in order to* produce social justice [original emphasis],"[46] or other outcomes, as Phelan explains,[47] illustrates the kind of instrumentalism that Pinar has long argued against.[48]

Encounters with Difficult Knowledge in the Teacher Education Classroom

So what might teacher education accomplish? In the preface to *Thinking and Practicing Reconciliation*, in which Schuler, Scott, and Riegert consider international examples of general post-secondary education for reconciliation, the authors underscore that professors need to "bring students to an open-ended practice, not just to 'understand' reconciliation intellectually as ongoing, but also to engage in it as such."[49] They point to the complexity of moving reconciliation forward so that it becomes a practice of living justly and equitably in relation to others.

    Let us consider this with respect to the work of teacher educators; they must be looking past their own students—the pre-service teachers—and must keep in mind that beyond the imperatives of engaging them in learning and being, the future teachers must also learn how to support their own students' engagements. Zembylas and colleagues suggest that this involves the time and space in reconciliation-focused learning for future teachers to interrogate "how their understandings are manifest in teaching practice and what pedagogical consequences they may have."[50] I quote these authors at length, because of the significance of the passage:

> Beyond simply acknowledging different ways of feeling about reconciliation, teacher educators can also encourage teachers to explore and interrogate their own emotional attachments to certain ideas and thoughts. Efforts to engage teachers in critical emotional reflexivity (Zembylas 2008) are often perceived as threatening to teachers' ontological security, since they force teachers to confront their unspoken fears, anxieties, uncertainties and resistances. For this reason, intrapersonal reflection on teachers' emotional understanding of conflict and reconciliation related issues (see McGlynn et al. 2009) has to take seriously into account the significance of emotions, beliefs, and attitudes in sustaining or dismantling normative discourses about *us-and-them* [added emphasis].[51]

In much of his earlier work, Zembylas proposes a subject that can engage rationally (albeit emotionally) in a self-directed process of critical reflection.[52] More recently, he has been looking at the significance of the psychic and the social in post-conflict contexts.[53] While the psychic life of teachers and its significance in the classroom have not commonly been taken up in educational policy and practice,[54] there has been increasing attention to encounters in the teacher education classroom with "difficult knowledge."[55] This refers to unconscious processes that arise with "the representation of social traumas and the individual's encounter with them in pedagogy."[56] In a review of uses of the concept of difficult knowledge in research on teaching and learning to teach, Zembylas describes its significance:

> A pedagogy that wishes to develop self-criticality, ethical responsibility, and the prospects of political transformation needs to create conditions in the classroom for addressing the complex psychosocial dimensions of difficult knowledge through a strategic engagement with one's affective investments in relation to social and political norms.[57]

It has been found that when future teachers are learning to teach *for* social justice at the university, their encounters with difficult knowledge may lead them to recognize the vulnerability of others and their own related responsibility.[58] Taylor writes that this "triggers defences, transference, and other responses to the loss of self-mastery, coherence, and stability."[59] In another, similar context, Mishra Tarc engages future teachers with difficult knowledge through response to literature; she describes the signs of emotional and productive engagement in future teacher "resistance, crisis, and wordlessness."[60]

In our own classroom practices with digital representations of critical moments in practicum experiences, Linda and I have drawn on Simon, who explains that encounters with "difficult knowledge" are disruptive because of what is provoked for the self: "difficulty happens when one's conceptual frameworks, emotional attachments, and conscious and unconscious desires delimit one's ability to settle the meaning of past events."[61] In working with future teachers around their critical moments, we have witnessed their struggle to "settle the meaning" of their experiences. In the face of such encounters, as Simon explains, "one's sense of mastery is undone and correspondingly one may undergo an experience that mixes partial understanding with confusion and disorientation, the certainty of another's fear and suffering with one's own diffuse anxiety and disquiet."[62] Complicating these responses is the notion that not all is within our conscious grasp. In our inquiries we have drawn on the work of Britzman,[63] who proposes that education is a form of crisis shaped by conflicted histories, one's own schooling, fantasies of the self and others, and cultural myths of teaching. In her earlier work, Britzman names these myths as, "everything depends upon the teacher, teachers are self-made, and teachers are experts";[64] however, in moving to a psychoanalytic framing of learning to teach in later writing, she proposes that the attendant anxiety around the myths can be read as: "fear of losing, being lost, lonely, and needing help, and worrying about becoming out of control."[65] In our recent reconciliation-focused study, where future teachers created augmented reality experiences for informal learning on two campuses, we witnessed vulnerability, guilt, responsibility, and desire for innocence; we traced how these emerged in the response formation of our students, and we used the psychoanalytic concept of *rapprochement* to unpack how the psychic, social, and historical collide in the current context—where teachers are called on to move reconciliation forward.[66]

Considering Psychic Processes in Classrooms with Teachers

In taking the unconscious into account when focusing on the significance of self-Other relationships in pedagogical encounters, we have found other psychoanalytic concepts to be illuminating.[67] For example, in looking at future teachers' struggles with their own privilege and implications in colonial benefits, we propose that the notion of projection can be helpful. It is a psychological process wherein one's unacceptable feelings, thoughts, behaviours, or characteristics are attributed to another.[68] This is a sign that "psychic change is happening ... as the mind tries to overcome anxiety by ridding itself of danger (by expelling it outwards). In the process of expelling the feeling outward, however, thought is in fact made thinkable, representable to the self."[69] Similarly, we have considered how the process of transference influences an individual's meaning making, when they are considering interpersonal experiences.[70] With transference, an individual unconsciously experiences people as having characteristics of others who are, or have been, significant in their lives. As Robertson explains, this is significant for educational situations, given that it happens when "feelings [occur that] represent unconscious impulses or needs that are not remembered."[71] Britzman and Pitt stress that teachers are ethically bound to learn about their own conflicts, and they warn of the significance of transferential dynamics in the classroom, given that "the re-enactment of old conflicts that [can] appear in the guise of new pedagogical encounters."[72] As Taubman would say, we all bring our "idiosyncratic subjectivities" into new "relationship[s] fraught with unconscious desires and shadows from the past."[73] Inspired by this, in our work—and in our own encounters in the teacher education classroom—we have found it essential to try to understand the *root of certain conflicts that are experienced (transference)*, as well as the ways that our own states or ways of being are *imagined as being experienced by another (projection)*.

To make the case that this has particular significance for Indigenous communities, whose teachers may be settlers, I draw in detail from a study of non-Indigenous teachers, working in a remote First Nation, who were involved with me in a project involving forms of autobiographical work.[74] The experience of teaching in the particular setting provoked deeply held and persistent feelings of either immense success or profound personal failure for the participants of the study. For some, the teaching was a career highlight that could not be matched elsewhere or later on in their lives. In contrast, the majority described reaching a point where they questioned themselves and their abilities. This appeared to be directly connected to the intersection of the teachers' sense of self and their perceptions of the students and the community as a whole.

The cases of two participants in the study illustrate this further. The first teacher described herself as the "positive" teacher, who does not give up, which she explained was a contrast to her more experienced colleagues. Casting herself as teacher-learner in the community, she considered herself a novice among her students. Through creative and collaborative encounters in and out of the classroom, her practice exemplified curriculum as "the process of making sense with a group of people of the systems that shape and organize the world."[75] Citing student expressions of their own learning and success, the teacher said that she had "realized her dream." She described this as standing out as a teacher and being remembered by her students. The case of another individual working in the same community at the same time stands in sharp contrast to the first case. The teacher repeatedly signalled the desire to be the expert helper to the needy, and underlined the importance of the problem-solving expertise she perceived that she had brought to the community. With such a potent expression of desire, an essential part of the narrative would have been a representation of neediness by students and community members. However, in explaining years of rejection and the perception that she had failed to make a difference, the teacher stated that the students and community as a whole were not "yet" able to understand the "value of education." They did not "need" her, and she explained this as their inability to recognize what she had to offer.

Beyond the challenges of subjectivities in the school setting, the second case reveals a problem of curriculum and pedagogy; the teacher appeared to be unaware of alternate purposes or approaches to education that went beyond the ones most closely associated with transmission of knowledge, and the teacher as expert. Other possible meanings that take into account the particular culture and history of the community or the competing purposes of Indigenous education were not evident. Equally, other possible ways to understand individual students or community members were not considered. Despite having a position of authority, the teacher expressed acute powerlessness. Whereas she clearly articulated a personal goal, "to go where good teachers are really needed," she appeared unable to see a relationship between her deeply felt desire and her perspective that the students and community were not ready for education. While she remained in the community for many years, the profoundly disabling conditions for the teacher and the students persisted.

The two cases underline the significance of the teaching subject and the way perceptions of what counts as curriculum reinforce (or disrupt) particular understandings of teacher identity. Brown, Atkinson, and England, who use a psychoanalytic perspective to understand how student teachers' subjectivities are formed, make the point that scholarship in the field of education that takes up psychoanalytic lenses does not often engage with "actual educational events or policies."[76] They argue that it is more likely to be used for theoretical critique. In our own attempts at working with actual events and experiences, we have drawn inspiration from scholars like Britzman and Taubman, who have made powerful cases to advance the notion of education as a psychic crisis, and to counter the disavowal of the unconscious in education.[77] The strong work of the theorists has provided a foundation for our projects, which, while small in scale, focus on application in the everyday classroom of teacher education.

When Subjectivity Becomes an Ethical Responsibility

With the significance of subjectivity and psychic processes illustrated above, I will return to the questions I posed at the beginning of the chapter: What would characterize a practice of teacher education adequate for the challenges of life in the twenty-first century? Britzman provides an important point on which to reflect in relation to this; for learning to happen, old ideas need to be disrupted; there needs to be acceptance of a state of uncertainty and a recognition that new ways of thinking exist, even if they have not yet been thought. Britzman writes, "Here is where progress is unconsciously equated with loss."[78] In our consideration of the language used by settler teachers in relation to reconciliation, our findings suggests there is the loss of the image of Canada the Good, the loss of the fantasy of becoming the good citizen teacher, and the loss of certainty that through planning and reason, they will be able to master the problems of teaching and learning—including how to foster commitment to reconciliation among students in K–12 classrooms.[79] Importantly, a psychoanalytic perspective leads us to see that this loss of certainty is a step forward;

as Farley proposes, "uncertainty [is] the very grounds of meaning making, not its opposite."[80] How teacher educators work with the disruption of ideas and support such uncertainty in the classroom has not received significant attention.

The significance of a psychoanalytic perspective has been purposefully articulated by its advocates for some time;[81] yet, there is a disavowal of psychoanalysis in the field of education. Taubman explains:

> Today's relentless push to quantify outcomes, prepare students for the global workforce, close the test score gap, and master formulaic approaches to teaching elbows aside considerations of unpredictable subjectivities in the classroom and antinomy between socio/cultural norms and psychic unruliness.[82]

Taubman comments that promises of certainty and immediate and recognizable "use value"[83] are the kind of criteria being used to make decisions about what will be addressed in teacher education classrooms. This is pertinent to our TRC-informed context, where the problems of subjectivity are writ large. If we consider "use value" in relation to the kind of issues having an impact on Indigenous peoples, such as communities with no access to safe drinking water, we would say that immediate and direct action needs to be taken. I propose that this sense of urgency is driving the emergence of prescriptive TRC-inspired curriculum packages, intended to increase the certainty of change. How do we hold in tension the need for rapid change in the lives of Indigenous peoples, while calling for space and time to think about the self in teacher education? Understandably, focusing on the self sounds indulgent. It would be, if our attention was not focused on the complexity of subjectivity as an explicitly stated lens through which we concern ourselves with what happens in teacher education.

I propose that such a change in practice would draw the eye beyond the issue of reconciliation, toward questions of what the teacher's role might be in the face of the larger global crises mentioned at the beginning of this chapter. This way of practicing teacher education, which centres ethical relationality,[84] would ask all of us implicated to consider the self in relation to others—locally, nationally, and globally, as well as all dimensions of the natural world. Such a lived curriculum would open up questions about individual and collective responsibility to humanity and the planet, yet it would not unfairly position teachers as being uniquely responsible for a particular outcome such as reconciliation, peace, eco-justice, sustainability, and so on.

While it may be the case that the spectre of mega-problems[85] will lead to more calls for outcomes-based programs, this is all the more reason to bring subjectivity to the forefront in teacher education. This is the moment to make space and time in teacher education for living with the uncertainty of the emotional situations of learning to be a teacher, for the naming and working through of conflicts, for seeking to understand and account for one's own history, and for coming to know oneself in relation to the Other.

Notes

1. Through a process of research and hearing the testimony of survivors, the judicially driven Truth and Reconciliation Commission documented the Canadian government's use of residential schooling and systemic legal processes, which had the aim of "dispossession and dismantling of Aboriginal societies" (TRC, Calls to Action, 258). The TRC traced how repercussions of assimilationist policies and related mechanisms persist, and are witnessed through evidence of disparity, racism, systemic discrimination, and "the critically endangered status of most Aboriginal languages" (TRC, *Honouring the Truth*, 183).
2. Britzman, *Practice Makes Perfect*; Pinar, "Unaddressed"; Pinar and Grumet, *Poor Curriculum*; Taubman, *Disavowed Knowledge*.
3. Taubman, *Disavowed Knowledge*, 7.
4. Phelan, Smits, and Ma, "Philosophical Issues," 232.
5. Warwick, "Climate Change."
6. Taubman, *Disavowed Knowledge*, 29.
7. Mishra Tarc, "Reparative Curriculum"; Taylor, "Feeling in Crisis"; "Inheritance."
8. In this chapter, I use the term "Indigenous" to refer to descendants of original peoples who inhabited the territory now known as Canada; this includes First Nations, Inuit, and Métis peoples. Alternate terms circulate in the Canadian context, such as Aboriginal (TRC, *Honouring the Truth; Calls to Action*). The term "settler" is used to refer those people who are not descended from Indigenous people in Canada, whether recent or earlier arrivals.
9. TRC, *Calls to Action*.
10. Sinclair, "Education," 7.
11. Kairos *Winds of Change*.
12. Kairos
13. Pinar, *Educational Experience*, 20.
14. In my post-secondary teaching, my research, and my school-based collaborations, I attempt to honour the teachings of members of the Naskapi Nation, particularly the Elders, who have always been generous teachers (Aitken, "Remembrance," 2017).
15. Aitken and Robinson, "Walking in Two Worlds"; Robinson, "Indigenous Language."
16. Aitken and Radford, "Aesthetic Archives,"; Radford and Aitken, "Digital Dreamwork."
17. Borooah and Knox, "Contribution"; Cappy "Shifting"; Duncan and Lopes Cardoza, "Reclaiming"; Exley and Chan, "Tensions"; Mogliacci,

Raanhuis, and Howell, "Becoming Agents"; Rubagiza, Umutoni, and Kaleeba, "Schools in Rwanda"; Zembylas et al., "Four Troubled Societies"; Zembylas, "Pedagogic Struggles"; Zembylas, Charalambous, and Charalambous, "Emerging Stances."

18 Paulette Regan, TRC researcher, describes the myth of "Canada the Good" as "the bedrock of settler identity" (Regan, *Unsettling the Settler*, 11).
19 Good Country, *The Good Country Index*.
20 Reputation Institute, *2017 Country Reptrak*.
21 Regan, *Unsettling*.
22 TRC, *Honouring*.
23 Vowel, *Indigenous Writes*.
24 Lee, "Reconciling in the Apocalypse," 19.
25 L. Brown, *Toronto Star*.
26 Lee, "Reconciling in the Apocalypse," 18.
27 Tuck and Yang, "Not a Metaphor."
28 National Centre for Truth and Reconciliation, *Imagine a Canada*.
29 Tupper, "Curricular Spaces," 106.
30 Tupper, 106.
31 Brant, "'But How Does This Help Me?'"; Taylor, "Inheritance"; Zembylas, "Teacher Resistance"; Zembylas, Kendeou, and Michaelidou, "Emotional Readiness."
32 Exley and Chan write about reconciliation agendas in Australian schools, and call for questioning the roots of one's commitments to related research. We keep their questions in mind: "What is my relationship to the Reconciliation agenda? and What is my interest in writing a paper about Reconciliation agendas?" (Exley and Chan, "Tensions," 55). Linda Radford and I are both settlers of European ancestry; ever-present to us are the weight and significance of the power and privilege connected to our heritage and academic status. Woven through this are the ongoing experiences of stumbling, learning, and unlearning that compel us both to act.
33 Sinclair, "Education," 7.
34 Cappy, "Shifting," 124.
35 Ben-Nun, "The 3 Rs"; Borooah and Knox, "Contribution"; Cappy "Shifting"; Duncan and Lopes Cardoza, "Reclaiming"; Exley and Chan, "Tensions"; Mogliacci, Raanhuis, and Howell, "Becoming Agents"; Rubagiza, Umutoni, and Kaleeba, "Schools in Rwanda"; Zembylas, Bekerman, McGlynn, and Ferreira, "Four Troubled Societies"; Zembylas, "Pedagogic Struggles"; Zembylas, Charalambous, and Charalambous, "Emerging Stances."
36 Zembylas, Charalambous, and Charalambous, "Emerging Stances," 24.

37   Duncan and Lopes Cardoza, "Reclaiming," 92.
38   Zembylas, "Pedagogic Struggles."
39   Zembylas, "Pedagogic Struggles," 289.
40   Pinar, *Educational Experience*.
41   Cappy, "Shifting," 137.
42   Exley and Chan, "Tensions" 72.
43   Horner et al., *Peacebuilding*, 7.
44   Rubagiza, Umutoni, and Kaleeba, "Schools in Rwanda"; Zembylas, "Pedagogic Struggles"; Zembylas, Charalambous, and Charalambous, "Emerging Stances."
45   Zembylas, Charalambous, and Charalambous, "Emerging Stances," 19.
46   Zembylas, Charalambous, and Charalambous, 27.
47   Phelan, *Curriculum Theorizing*.
48   Pinar, *What Is Curriculum Theory*; Pinar, *Character of Curriculum Studies*.
49   Schuler, Scott, and Riegert, *Thinking and Practicing Reconciliation*, xiii.
50   Zembylas, Charalambous, and Charalambous, "Emerging Stances,"33.
51   Zembylas, Charalambous, and Charalambous, 33.
52   Zembylas, "Pedagogic Struggles."
53   Zembylas, "Emotional Regimes."
54   Taubman, *Disavowed Knowledge*.
55   Zembylas, "Theorizing 'Difficult Knowledge'"; Zembylas, "Teacher Resistance."
56   Pitt and Britzman, "Speculations," 755.
57   Zembylas, "Theorizing 'Difficult Knowledge'," 404.
58   Taylor, "Inheritance"; Taylor, "Feeling in Crisis."
59   Taylor, "Feeling in Crisis," 56.
60   Mishra Tarc, "Reparative Curriculum," 352.
61   Simon, "Shock to Thought," 433.
62   Simon, 433.
63   Britzman, *Practice Makes Practice*; *Practice Makes Practice* (Revised); *Very Thought of Education*; "Between Psychoanalysis and Pedagogy."
64   Britzman, *Practice Makes Practice*, 7.
65   Britzman, "Between Psychoanalysis and Pedagogy.," 103.
66   Aitken and Radford, "Learning to Teach."
67   Aitken and Radford, "Learning to Teach."
68   Grant and Crawley, *Transference*.
69   Robertson, "Teaching in Your Dreams," 91.
70   Grant and Crawley, *Transference*.
71   Robertson, "Teaching in Your Dreams," 91.
72   Britzman and Pitt, "Pedagogy and Transference," 118.
73   Taubman, *Disavowed Knowledge*, 7.
74   Aitken, "Fragile Fixings"; Aitken, Comprendre le processus."

75 Grumet, "What Are the Basics," 19.
76 T. Brown, Atkinson, and England, *Regulatory Discourses*, 13.
77 Britzman, *Lost Subjects*; *Practice Makes Practice: The Very Thought of Education*; Taubman, *Disavowed Knowledge*.
78 Britzman, *The Very Thought of Education*, 40.
79 Aitken and Radford, "Learning to Teach"; Aitken and Radford, "When Metaphors Open a Window."
80 Farley, "Radical Hope," 551.
81 Britzman and Pitt, "Pedagogy and Transference"; T. Brown, Atkinson, and England, *Regulatory Discourses*; Pinar and Grumet, *Poor Curriculum*; Pitt, *Play of the Personal*; Robertson, "Teaching in Your Dreams."
82 Taubman, *Disavowed Knowledge*, 15.
83 Taubman, 58.
84 Donald, "Forts."
85 Warwick, "Climate Change."

Bibliography

Aitken, Avril. "Comprendre le processus de construction identitaire: Une démarche essentielle chez les enseignants." In *Approches affectives, métacognitives et cognitives de la compréhension*, edited by L. Lafortune, S. Fréchette, N. Sorin, P.-A. Doudin, and O. Albanese, 183–200. Quebec City, QC: Presses de l'Université du Québec, 2010.

———. "Fragile Fixings: An Exploration of the Self-Representations of White Women Teachers in One Isolated Northern Indigenous Community." Unpublished PhD. thesis, University of Ottawa, 2005.

———. "Remembrance as a Digitally Mediated Practice of Pedagogy." In *Oral History and Education: Theories, Dilemmas, and Practices*, edited by K. Llewellyn and N. Ng-A-Fook, 231–250. London, UK: Palgrave Macmillan, 2017.

Aitken, Avril, and Linda Radford. "Aesthetic Archives: Pre-service Teachers Symbolizing Experiences through Digital Storytelling." *Journal of the Canadian Association of Curriculum Studies* [Special issue] 10, no. 2 (2012): 92–119.

———. "Learning to Teach for Reconciliation in Canada: Potential, Resistance, and Stumbling Forward" *Teaching and Teacher Education* 75 (2018): 40–48. https://doi.org/10.1016/j.tate.2018.05.014.

———. "When Metaphors Open a Window on Narratives about Teaching for Reconciliation: Insights from an Augmented Reality Project." In *Looking Both Ways: Narrative and Metaphor in Education*, edited by M. Hanne and A. Kaal, 177–190. London, UK: Routledge, forthcoming.

Aitken, Avril, and Linda Robinson. "'Walking in Two Worlds' in the Plurilingual Classroom: Learning from the Case of an Intergenerational Project." In *Plurilingual Pedagogies: Critical and Creative Endeavors for Equitable Language (in) Education*, edited by S. Stille and S. M. C. Lau. Amsterdam, NL: Springer, forthcoming.

Ben-Nun, Merav. "The 3 Rs of Integration: Respect, Recognition, and Reconciliation: Concepts and Practices of Integrated Schools in Israel and Northern Ireland." *Journal of Peace Education* 10, no. 1 (2013): 1–20. doi:10.1080/17400201.2012.672403.

Borooah, Vani K., and Colin Knox. "The Contribution of 'Shared Education' to Catholic-Protestant Reconciliation in Northern Ireland: A Third Way?" *British Educational Research Journal* 39, no. 5 (2013): 925–946.

Brant, Kiera K. "'But How Does This Help Me?' Re(Thinking) (Re)Conciliation in Teacher Education." Unpublished master's thesis, University of Ottawa. 2017.

Britzman, Deborah P. "Between Psychoanalysis and Pedagogy: Scenes of Rapprochement and Alienation." *Curriculum Inquiry* 43, no. 1 (2013): 95–117. doi:10.1111/curi.12007

———. *Lost Subjects, Contested Objects: Toward a Psychoanalytic Inquiry of Learning*. Albany, NY: State University of New York Press, 1998.

———. *Practice Makes Practice: A Critical Study of Learning to Teach*. New York, NY: State University of New York Press, 1991.

———. *Practice Makes Practice: A Critical Study of Learning to Teach* (rev. ed.). New York, NY: State University of New York Press, 2003.

———. *The Very Thought of Education: Psychoanalysis and the Impossible Professions*. New York, NY: State University of New York Press, 2009.

Britzman, Deborah P., and Alice J. Pitt. "Pedagogy and Transference: Casting the Past of Learning into the Presence of Teaching." *Theory into Practice* 35, no. 2 (1996): 117–123.

Brown, Louise. "Teachers Need to be Educated about Residential Schools before Students, Says TDSB Official." *Toronto Star*, June 2, 2015. http://www.thestar.com/news/canada/2015/06/02/teachers-need-to-be-educated-about-residential-schools-says-tdsb-official.html.

Brown, Tony, Dennis Atkinson, and Janice England. *Regulatory Discourses in Education: A Lacanian Perspective*. Bern, Switzerland: Peter Lang, 2006.

Cappy, Christina Lane. "Shifting the Future? Teachers as Agents of Social Change in South African Secondary Schools." *Education as Change* 20, no. 3 (2016): 119–140. doi:10.17159/1947-9417/2016/1314.

Donald, Dwayne. "Forts, Colonial Frontier Logics, and Aboriginal-Canadian Relations: Imagining Decolonizing Educational Philosophies in Canadian Contexts." In *Decolonizing Philosophies of Education*, edited by A. Abdi, 91–111. Rotterdam, NL: Sense, 2012.

Duncan, Ross, and Mieke Lopes Cardoza. "Reclaiming Reconciliation through Community Education for the Muslims and Tamils of Post-War Jaffna, Sri Lanka." *Research in Comparative and International Education* 12, no. 1 (2017): 76–94. doi:10.1177/1745499917696425.

Exley, Beryl, and Mui Yoke Chan. "Tensions between Policy and Practice: Reconciliation Agendas in the Australian Curriculum English." *English Teaching: Practice and Critique* 13, no. 1 (2014): 55–75.

Farley, Linda. "Radical Hope: Or, the Problem of Uncertainty in History Education." *Curriculum Inquiry* 39, no. 4 (2009): 537–554.

The Good Country. *The Good Country Index*. Accessed October 23, 2017. https://goodcountry.org/good-country/data-treatment

Grant, Jen, and Jim Crawley. *Transference and Projection*. Berkshire, UK: Open University Press, 2002.

Grumet, R. Madeline. "The Curriculum: What Are the Basics and Are We Teaching Them?" In *Thirteen Questions: Reframing Education's Conversation*, edited by J. L. Kincheloe and S. R. Steinberg, 15–21. New York, NY: Peter Lang, 1995.

Horner, Lindsey, Laila Kadiwal, Yusuf Sayed, Angelina Barrett, Naureen Durrani, and Mario Novelli. *Literature Review: The Role of Teachers in Peacebuilding*. Amsterdam, NL: Research Consortium on Education and Peacebuilding. Accessed November 26, 2017. https://educationanddevelopment.wordpress.com/rp/outputs-research-consortium/.

Kairos. *Indigenous Rights: Winds of Change—Read the Report Card*. Accessed on October 23, 2017. https://www.kairoscanada.org/what-we-do/indigenous-rights/windsofchange-report-cards.

Lee, Erica V. "Reconciling in the Apocalypse." *The Monitor* (March–April 2016): 18–19. https://www.policyalternatives.ca/sites/default/files/uploads/publications/National Office/2016/03/CCPA_Monitor_March_April.pdf.

McGlynn, Claire, Michalinos Zembylas, Zvi Bekerman, and Tony Gallagher. *Peace Education in Conflict and Post-Conflict Societies: Comparative Perspectives*. New York, NY: Palgrave, 2009.

Mishra Tarc, Aparna "Reparative Curriculum." *Curriculum Inquiry* 41, no. 3 (2011): 350–372.

Mogliacci, Rada Jancic, Joyce Raanhuis, and Colleen Howell. "Supporting Teachers in Becoming Agents of Social Cohesion: Professional Development in Post-Apartheid South Africa." *Education as Change* 20, no. 3 (2016): 160–179. doi:10.17159/1947-9417/2016/1482.

National Centre for Truth and Reconciliation. *Imagine a Canada*. Accessed on February 1, 2017. http://nctr.ca/education_imagine.php.

Phelan, Anne M. *Curriculum Theorizing and Teacher Education: Complicating Conjunctions*. New York, NY: Routledge, 2015.

Phelan, Anne M., Hans Smits, and Ying Ma. "Philosophical Issues in Initial Teacher Education." In *Handbook of Canadian Research in Initial Teacher Education*, edited by T. Falkenburg, 227–244. Ottawa, ON: Canadian Association for Teacher Education, 2015.

Pinar, William F. *The Character of Curriculum Studies: Bildung, Currere, and the Recurring Question of the Subject.* New York, NY: Palgrave MacMillan, 2011.

———. *Educational Experience as Lived: Knowledge, History, Alterity: The Selected Works of William F. Pinar.* New York, NY: Routledge, 2016.

———. "The Unaddressed 'I' of Ideology Critique." *Power and Education* 1, no. 2 (2009): 189–200.

———. *What Is Curriculum Theory?* Mahwah, NJ: L. Erlbaum Associates, 2004.

Pinar, William F., and Madeline R. Grumet. *Toward a Poor Curriculum.* Dubuque, IA: Kendall/Hunt Publishing, 1976.

Pitt. Alice J. *The Play of the Personal: Psychoanalytic Narratives of Feminist Education.* New York: Peter Lang, 2003.

Pitt, Alice, and Deborah P. Britzman. "Speculations on Qualities of Difficult Knowledge in Teaching and Learning: An Experiment in Psychoanalytic Research." *International Journal of Qualitative Studies in Education* 16, no. 6 (2003): 755–776. doi:10.1080/0951839031 0001632135.

Radford, Linda, and Avril Aitken. "Digital Dreamwork: Becoming Teachers' Stories of Trauma." In *Provoking Curriculum Studies: Strong Poetry and the Arts of the Possible*, edited by N. Ng-A-Fook, A. Ibrahim, and G. Reis, 150–160. New York, NY: Routledge, 2015.

Reputation Institute. *2017 Country Reptrak: The World's Most Reputable Countries.* Accessed on October 23, 2017. https://www.reputationinstitute.com/country-reptrak.

Regan, Paulette. *Unsettling the Settler Within: Indian Residential Schools, Truth Telling, and Reconciliation in Canada.* Toronto, ON: University of Toronto Press, 2010.

Robertson, Judith P. "Teaching in Your Dreams: Screenplay Pedagogy and Margarethe Von Trotta's 'The Second Awakening of Christa Klages.'" *The Canadian Journal of Film Studies/Revue Canadienne D'Etudes Cinematographiques* 13, no. 2 (2004): 74–92.

Robinson, Loretto. "Indigenous Language Policy and Practice: Beliefs of Teachers from the Naskapi Nation of Kawawachikmach." Unpublished master's thesis, Bishop's University. 2017.

Rubagiza, Jolly, Jane Umutoni, and Ali Kaleeba. "Teachers as Agents of Change: Promoting Peacebuilding and Social Cohesion in Schools in Rwanda." *Education as Change* 20, no. 3 (2016): 202–224. doi:10.17159/1947-9417/2016/1533.

Shuler, Jill, Jack Scott, and Leo W. Riegert. *Thinking and Practicing Reconciliation: Teaching and Learning through Literary Responses to Conflict.* Newcastle-upon-Tyne, UK: Cambridge Scholars Publishing, 2013.

Simon, Roger. "A Shock to Thought." *Memory Studies* 4, no. 4 (2011): 432–449. doi:10.1177/1750698011398170.

Sinclair, Murray. "Education: Cause and Solution." *The Manitoba Teacher* 93, no. 3 (2014): 6–10.

Taubman, Peter. *Disavowed Knowledge: Psychoanalysis, Education, and Teaching.* Studies in Curriculum Theory Series. New York, NY: Routledge, Taylor & Francis Group, 2012.

Taylor, Lisa K. "Feeling in Crisis: Vicissitudes of Response in Experiments with Global Justice Education." *Journal of the Canadian Association for Curriculum Studies* 9, no. 1 (2011): 6–65.

———. "Inheritance as Intimate, Implicated Publics: Building Practices of Remembrance with Future Teachers in Response to Residential School Survivor Testimonial Media and Literature." *Canadian Social Studies* 47, no. 2 (2014): 110–126.

Truth and Reconciliation Commission. *Honouring the Truth, Reconciling for the Future: Summary of the Final Report of the Truth and Reconciliation Commission of Canada.* Accessed on June 3, 2015. http://nctr.ca/assets/reports/Final Reports/Executive_Summary_English_Web.pdf.

———. *Truth and Reconciliation Commission of Canada: Calls to Action.* Accessed on June 3, 2015. http://nctr.ca/assets/reports/Calls_to_Action_English2.pdf.

Tuck, Eve, and Wayne Yang. "Decolonization Is Not a Metaphor." *Decolonization: Indigeneity, Education, and Society* 1, no. 1 (2012): 1–40. http://decolonization.org/index.php/des/article/view/18630/15554.

Tupper, Jennifer. "Curricular Spaces of Renewal: Toward Reconciliation." In *Framing Peace: Thinking About and Enacting Curriculum as 'Radical Hope',* edited by H. Smits and R. Naqvi, 97–109. New York, NY: Peter Lang, 2015.

Vowel, Chelsea. *Indigenous Writes: A Guide to First Nations, Métis, and Inuit Issues in Canada.* Winnipeg, MB: Highwater, 2016.

Warwick, Paul. "Climate Change and Sustainable Citizenship Education." In *Debates in Citizenship Education,* edited by J. Arthur and H. Cremin, 132–145. London and New York: Routledge, 2012.

Zembylas, Michalinos. "The Emotional Regimes of Reconciliation in History Textbook Revision: Reflections on the Politics of Resentment and the Politics of Empathy in Post-conflict Societies." *Pedagogy, Culture, and Society* 24, no. 3 (2016): 329–342. doi:10.1080/14681366.2016.1175497.

———. "Pedagogic Struggles to Enhance Inclusion and Reconciliation in a Divided Community." *Ethnography and Education* 5, no. 3 (2010): 277–292. doi:10.1080/17457823.2010.511361
———. *The Politics of Trauma in Education*. New York, NY: Palgrave, 2008.
———. "Teacher Resistance to Engage with 'Alternative' Perspectives of Difficult Histories: The Limits and Prospects of Affective Disruption." *Discourse: Studies in the Cultural Politics of Education* 38, no. 5 (2017): 659–675. doi:10.1080/01596306.2015.1132680.
———. "Theorizing 'Difficult Knowledge' in the Aftermath of the 'Affective Turn': Implications for Curriculum and Pedagogy in Handling Traumatic Representations." *Curriculum Inquiry* 44, no. 3 (2015): 390–412. doi:10.1111/curi.12051.
Zembylas, Michalinos, Zvi Bekerman, Claire McGlynn, and Ana Ferreira. "Teachers' Understanding of Reconciliation and Inclusion in Mixed Schools of Four Troubled Societies." *Research in Comparative and International Education* 4, no. 4 (2009): 406–422. doi:10.2304/rcie.2009.4.4.406.
Zembylas, Michalinos, Panayiota Charalambous, and Constadina Charalambous. "Teachers' Emerging Stances and Repertoires towards Reconciliation: Potential and Challenges in Greek-Cypriot Education." *Journal of Peace Education* 8, no. 1 (2011): 19–36. doi:10.1080/17400201.2011.553378.
Zembylas, Michalinos, Panayiota Kendeou, and Athina Michaelidou. "The Emotional Readiness of Greek Cypriot Teachers for Peaceful Co-existence." *European Journal of Education* 46, no. 4 (2011): 524–539. doi:10.1111/j.1465-3435.2011.01498.x.

CHAPTER 4

Using Methods of Juxtaposition to Jolt Teacher Understanding: Exploring Ethical Forms of Pedagogical Practice with Counter-Stories

Teresa Strong-Wilson

William Pinar asks: "How might we teach to restore temporality—a sharp sense of the past, enabling discernment of the present and foreshadowings of the future—to the complicated conversation that is the school curriculum?"[1] His response is allegory. Allegory may not seem to be an obvious answer to what is in fact a very concrete and pressing practical problem. The problem might be articulated as follows. How do teachers understand their ethical responsibility to others and enact "ethical engagements with the other?"[2] How do they engage with potentially fraught histories brought to the curriculum table in the classroom? How do they negotiate multiple histories in relation to their own histories and understandings as teachers? Further, how do they meaningfully involve students in these complicated, "contextually inflected, phenomenologically animated" conversations with others and with one another?[3] And how do they do this given daily pressures to be accountable, increasingly in measurable ways, to principals, parents, governing boards, and ministries of education? In Canada, these pressures have not yet been felt directly in teachers' pay cheques (as tied to student outcomes on standardized tests), but south of the border, things have been going in this direction. Much like migrating birds, though, southern educational initiatives have been known to find their way north, given the right political conditions. Canadian teachers already experience an increasing anxiety about assessment, which in my home province of Quebec is manifested in trickle-down pressures from contractual agreements mandated between the Ministry of Education and school boards. Increases in student scores in targeted areas of the curriculum (Math, English Language Arts, French) are tied to funding: to neighbourhood schools remaining open or closing. So, while allegory may seem to be a term gathering dust, part of a dimly remembered high school English class, Pinar has re-invested the term with a currency germane to education, germane to Canadian contributions to the challenge of re-conceptualizing teacher education worldwide, and germane to my chapter. Pinar's allegorical approach to curriculum studies, otherwise recognizable as *currere*, provides the main support for my argument on juxtaposition.

Allegory involves telling more than one story; indeed, it tells a double story, as does curriculum, with its double entendre on the word subject: subject as the discipline or topic that is the focus of study, and subject as the person invested in such study: the student (and the teacher) who engages intellectually, emotionally, spiritually, and bodily with a subject matter.[4] "For double the vision my eyes do see, / And a double vision is always with me: / With my inward eye 'tis an old man grey; / With my outward a thistle across my way" reads the flyleaf of the book *The Double Vision*, by Canadian literary critic Northrop Frye. Double vision was an idea gleaned from his literary mentor, the poet William Blake, from whose verse Frye excerpted these lines.[5] Millions have downloaded the popular TED talk by Nigerian writer, Chimamanda Nzgozi Adichie, on the dangers of telling a single story; 13,422,366 to be exact, as of October 8, 2017.[6] Adichie's talk engages with more than double, indeed with multiple, overlapping stories involving adjacency, agency, and responsibility—thoughts in keeping with Michael Rothberg's notions of multidirectional memory and implicated subjects (notions to be developed in this chapter). Pinar specifies that allegory "tells a specific story that hints at a more general significance";[7] it is a way of *linking* past, present, and future as threaded through an individual's subjectivity. This threading act, an image that Pinar returns to often in his writings, reminds me of challenges in trying to thread a sewing needle. Curiously, though, this threading—the act of manoeuvering a string-like thing through the narrow aperture of a needle's eye—involves expansiveness; here, the expansiveness of imagination. Imagination is what allows meanings apprehended from a distant or not-so-distant past or place to "leak into our experience of the present."⁸ This is part of the subjective labour that instantiates curriculum *as* consciousness, with consciousness conceived as "worldiness"—an Arendtian ascription that Pinar borrows and that Maxine Greene would have readily assented to; Pinar situates worldiness "as 'chief' among cosmopolitan virtues."⁹

If allegory relies on juxtaposition and juxtaposition on imagination, allegory becomes "simultaneously social *and* subjective, focused on power *and* psyche, the social *and* the solitary."¹⁰ Through its "combinatory structure ... through both its internal elements (how the story that is told is told) and its positioning in disciplinary, subjective and social structures,"¹¹ allegory opens a space for "ethical self-encounter,"¹² which is the focus of my thinking in this paper with respect to teachers, students, and their conversations around literary texts. Within the subjective reconstruction that is the work of curriculum, the teacher's part is central; positioned as "an artist," "complicated conversation" is "the teacher's medium."¹³

In this paper, I develop three ways in which juxtaposition can open teachers and students to ethical self-encounters: first, by drawing on Pinar and Grumet's method of *currere*; second, Rothberg's multidirectional memory and implicated subject; and third, Sebald's idea of coincidence. All three depend on juxtaposition, a mode of bringing disparate things, people, and events into provocative relation, even as they remain distinct from one another. I then provide two examples from a research study with elementary and secondary teachers. Briefly, the study develops pedagogical approaches to social justice education through teacher (and student) discussion of post-colonial literature.¹⁴ Social justice education is a large umbrella under and with which many quite different approaches align themselves. In keeping with *currere* as well as with Sebald, I understand social justice education to be about developing a social conscience, which entails critical reflection on the relations between self and (real) others as well as subjective reconstruction: study by an individual of his or her own attitudes towards and stance on social issues close at hand and further away. Post-colonial literature (a label that is somewhat of a misnomer, as Thomas King points out, since it remains "a hostage to nationalism"¹⁵) is better understood in this study as "counter-stories":¹⁶ stories that narrate a history and an experience resistant to the dominant narrative and that may deploy strategies to make this resistance explicit, such as in Thomas King's children's picture book *Coyote*

Columbus, but may also make the counter-story an implicit structure of the narrative itself.[17] Emma Laroque counts among what she calls "resistance stories" any narratives written or published by Indigenous authors: that is, literature not written within the "civ/sav dichotomy" but by living human beings whose very presence is testimonial to their surviving colonization: "… we stand here to say, we have endured and we are not 'the Other' of White invention.… We have been dispossessed, marginalized, censored and appropriated, yes, but the message is resistance."[18] Counter-stories are often based on "counter-memories," memories of experiences produced through oppression, subjugation or silencing: "… the history of otherness," as Bouchard summarizes in his preface to Foucault's writings. Foucault helped bring previously shunned topics like violence, punishment, transgression, and sexuality into the public eye.[19] Many books used in the study are autobiographical in form (such as memoirs) or are autobiographically informed, based on post-memory[20] and the intergenerational effects of trauma. The work with teachers (all of whom are of white European descent [Italian, Portuguese, Scottish] coming from suburban or rural milieus in Quebec) implicates study of "relations of resemblances" among the stories as well as places of disjuncture:[21] Following Pinar, this involves noticing analogies between story and self, story and others, story and story, story and world. Analogy is what "links us to other beings"; however, it is also "internal to our own being—what connects the person we were yesterday with the slightly different person we are today."[22] These places and relations become marked by temporality: a "historic index" with the power to "arrest" teachers' thinking[23] even as it can provoke previously unlooked-for connections. I turn now to the three juxtaposition approaches used to open teachers to ethical self-encounters.

Methods of Juxtaposition

Currere

Currere is a method for a project of subjective reconstruction that assumes an allegorical structure by telling one story (social) by way of another (individual). Because it is both critical and personal, *currere* brings matters close (emotionally, spiritually, and so on) but in such a way as to also create a distance, allowing for critical, intellectual engagement with one's memories and stories. It does so first through the detour of story. Grumet says that "we start with narrative,"[24] travelling through "once upon a time" to arrive at the present.[25] This is a process of "appropriation":[26] of reclaiming one's stories from the vagaries of memory but also from the alienation that is often the student's (and teacher's) experience of the curriculum in which the person is often expunged—"missing in action," as Pinar has reiterated.[27] Detour happens through narratively exploring lived experiences: eliciting as much detail as possible to produce what memoirist Hampl calls a first draft,[28] this in response to Pinar's invitation to "regress" (*currere* contains four phases—regression is the first phase[29]). Grumet speaks to the function of detours in *currere*:

> Autobiography barely recaptures the past or even records it. It records the present perspective of the story teller and presents the past within that structure. It employs the past to reveal the present assumptions and future intentions of the story teller, an elaborate detour that travels through once upon a time in order to reach now.[30]

What is reclaimed is not the original experience but a version of it; the text produced is itself a detour: experience transformed into an object. It starts to act as a kind of wedge, Grumet's useful analogy to describe how the text begins to interpose itself between "layers" of experience.[31] "We read what we have written," talking about the stories with others.[32] In being shared, the drafts relocate what may have seemed to be private details to a public, shared space, where they are often divested of their privacy (although not their particularity and resonance for the person; if anything, the resonance often intensifies).

A central element in the study, then, has been the teachers' memory-work (*currere*), which starts off the day-long research workshops we have been holding together. Teachers are invited to recall their memories of storied formation in their literacy education, remember significant objects, and call to mind important places, creation myths, or explore pathways of childhood memory. What are also recalled, both in the eliciting and in the listening to one another's stories, are the ellipses: the gaps, the forgotten places, the unknowns, which as blank spaces can be as indelible as those filled-in.

In this process of "excavation," "what is returned … is hardly the original experience.… There in the interstices, the spaces where the pieces don't quite meet, is where the light comes through."[33]

Doubt and suspicion, marks of distantiation, become companions. Stories are not left to linger nostalgically. They begin to sit adjacent to one another, in intimate relation with other layers of story: the teachers' own texts (produced in previous workshops), other teachers' stories, the counter-stories, and the teachers' accounts of how they are teaching with the counter-stories in their classes, and students' responses to the counter-stories and the pedagogy. This excavation process in which multiple stories are being juxtaposed can initiate further detours, a further circling downwards, backwards and forwards. The purpose of the exercise is not to trap the teacher in the past nor to generate a vortex of perpetual detouring; it is to create momentum through critical reflection as a process of coming close and moving away, of appropriation and distantiation. "The stringing together of ... distinct narratives," Grumet explains, taking up an image reminiscent of Pinar's threading and drawing attention to the important role played by wedging and juxtaposition, "loosens our immersion in any one of them and permits us to carry the momentum of our movement between them, beyond them."[34]

How the teacher tells her story of teaching also becomes an integral part of the detour: of the bending back and the return. "*Currere* is a reflexive cycle in which thought bends back upon itself and thus recovers its volition."[35] In this paper, drawing on Sebald, I have likened this detour to a periscopic form of narration—in sections to follow, I look at periscopic narrative as an ethico-aesthetic space, exploring it through an account of two teachers' detours and travels in the study. Full appreciation of the ethical work involved in the teachers' personal and pedagogical engagements with the counter-stories, however, first entails looking at multidirectionality—the placing of multiple counter-stories on the same curriculum table.

Multidirectional Memory

Multidirectional memory is Michael Rothberg's way of putting into creative, non-reductive relation counter-histories and memories that would otherwise be competing for attention, much like real estate, in the public realm. Borders of memory and identity, he suggests, "are jagged: what looks at first like my own property often turns out to be a borrowing or adaptation from a history that initially might seem foreign or distant."[36] Multidirectional memory responds to the "complex and uncertain moral and ethical terrain" of moving between traumas.[37] In education, it also helps respond to questions about what to focus on and when and why, and where (as Rothberg articulates) the goal ought to be understanding but also solidarity among situations appreciated as distinct from one another but related. Indeed, Rothberg locates memory's powerful creativity in its juxtapositions: an "anachronistic quality" that brings together "now and then, here and there."[38]

A multidirectional approach has been very useful in the research project to help teachers imagine pedagogy when multiple histories co-exist on the table, implicitly juxtaposed. We have been using Rothberg's multidirectional memory approach to invite more explicit juxtapositions among the several histories addressed through the novels, picture books, and graphic novels: the legacies of the effects of colonialism on local Indigenous communities (Canada, New Zealand, and Latin America), especially through study of residential school stories in Canada; intergenerational legacies of slavery in the United States as well as Brazil; traumatic effects of genocides (Rwanda, the Holocaust). One of the contributions of Rothberg's multidirectional approach is to bring the Holocaust into relation with other traumas on the grounds that Holocaust memory initiated trauma research as well as contributed, as a resource, to movements of decolonization. Such juxtapositions, within as well as across histories, can open teachers to ethical self-encounters, in the manner that in the next section (on coincidences) I will develop in relation to Sebald and the periscopic narrative. Teachers often recount being brought up short, of re-directing their gaze and thinking about resemblances that they had not thought about before.

This pedagogical approach (of juxtaposing memories, texts, histories) echoes the structure of the counter-stories themselves, which often rely on juxtaposition as a literary device. Certain stories are allegorical in structure, using one narrative *by* which to tell another, the two sitting, uneasily, subversively, beside one another; *Brundibar*, for instance. Sendak and Kushner's picture book tells the story of two children who go to the marketplace in search of milk to help their ailing mother.[39] Brundibar, a local bully, does his utmost to prevent the children from accomplishing their goal. Eventually, all of the townspeople and animals gather together to assist the children and defeat their enemy. The story was an opera written by Jewish Czech composer Hans Krása, which the Germans insisted be performed for audiences by children in Theresienstadt. The Red Cross was one such audience. The opera was performed countless times. Sendak's illustrations bring out the resemblance between the bully and Hitler while the ailing mother echoes the lived situations of those who were dying from disease and malnutrition in concentration camps.

Still other books invoke juxtaposition by way of dialectical images, which was Walter Benjamin's term for pictures that jolt understanding by bringing into intimate constellation contradictory, opposing, or incongruous elements.[40] One example is Gavin Bishop's *The House that Jack Built*. This picture book juxtaposes the Maori creation myth with the story of the systematic destruction of land through colonization—the house(s) that Jack built (as per the cumulative nursery rhyme); all are on the same page.[41] The Maori creation myth encircles and symbolically permeates the main narrative (Jack's) told in the centre of the two-page spreads. Jack also corresponds with the actual Jack Bull who travelled to New Zealand from London as a new settler in 1798. As described on the New Zealand Picture Book Collection website, a collection of local books curated by faculty members at the University of Waikato and intended to support diversity in the school curriculum, in Gavin's book, "[t]he detailed contemporary illustrations using traditional Maori form tell the story from a Maori perspective—beginning with the myth of creation: Papatuanuku, the earth mother, Ranginui the sky father and their children as guardians of the land. As the story goes on and Jack's house grows, Papuatanuku is shown in the illustrations to weaken and fade."[42] The book stands as an indictment of the long-term effects of settler colonialism on Indigenous peoples in New Zealand.

Yet another example comes from residential school picture books, as in the picture of young children being carted away in a cattletruck that is often the last image that appears in stories like *As Long as the River Flows* and *Shi-she-etko*[43]—the conclusion is actually only the beginning of what many readers know will be the children's descent into the hell that was residential school[44] (although this is not depicted in the picture books, at least not in these two books). This cattletruck image corresponds to a reality (the way in which many Indigenous children were transported to residential school), but when placed as the closing image in a children's picture book, the effect is doubly jarring, confounding the happy ending of most children's books. It juxtaposes the young girl Shi-she-etko's expectations around waiting for school to begin with the discordant, disturbing image of her (and other children) being separated from their families, transported like so many cattle intended for "slaughter."[45]

The multidirectional juxtaposition of texts on the table involves the creative and critical juxtaposition of different histories and stories. The teachers' memory-work has been equally important within this multidirectional frame to evoke teachers' particular histories in relation to particular places and particular times. Rothberg points out that "despite the plentiful evidence of violence and willed oblivion that can accompany hegemonic (and sometimes even subaltern) acts of remembrance," the locus of the work *begins* with individual memory.[46] In saying this, Rothberg simultaneously suggests that the structure of memory itself is multidirectional; it participates in collective memory, through being "formed within social frameworks" while also being shared; even individual memory (which is never truly solitary) ultimately depends on the shared labour of different perspectives.[47] Teachers may discover, through this memory-work, aspects of their own histories that connect to others in ways that they did not anticipate.

A multidirectional approach, combined with *currere*, also ties in closely with cosmopolitanism when conceived, as Pinar points out, not simply as a recent global trend but as a structure of feeling linked to subjectivity—a "lived sense of self,"[48] one that (as per allegory) looks inward as it also looks outward. He says: "It is our individuality, I have long argued (Pinar and Grumet 2006 [1976]), that configures educational experience. Intellectual work is psychological labor"[49] even as, "as educators, our calling is to participate in the complicated conversation that is the curriculum"[50]—a curriculum marked by the multidirectionality of which Rothberg speaks. Conversations about social justice implicate the "presence of the individuated Other."[51] In the study that I am using by way of example in this paper, educational experiences are threaded through teachers' and students' ethical engagement with stories, individually and with one another. The project thus gives expression to the particularity of cosmopolitanism even as it addresses "implicated subject position[s]"; the ethical position, as Rothberg points out, "from which Sebald writes ... [as a] ... second generation non-Jewish German."[52]

An Ethico-Aesthetic Form: Coincidence and the Periscope

Lives, though distinct, are not separate. What happens in one place and time is not unrelated to what happens in a different place and time, even though the individuals may not know one another or be aware of the other's existence. This Sebaldian theme provides further ethical impetus for the work with the teachers. Coincidence is the literary device used by W. G. Sebald, a German literary scholar, to bring lives into juxtaposition, this by way of the figure of the walker or wanderer who is also a narrator. We might imagine the teacher—and the student—likewise as walkers. Coincidence is the *presupposition of significance* within a world in which there is no coincidence; it is an artifact of an "ethico-asthetic" form.[53] Elsewhere, drawing on Sebald, I have likened this to a process of "following one's nose,"[54] of pursuing (and being dogged by) an invisible subject: a preoccupation sensing important connections that may or may not come to full articulation.

W. G. Sebald, born on the cusp of the end of the Second World War (1944), inherited the burden of the past of his country's (Germany's) actions, this as part of a backpack that he later said he could never put down. Late in his life, he turned to prose fiction as a way to confront this past. Sebald's narrator bears an uncanny resemblance to Sebald himself, physically as well as in the particulars of his biographical history, and also closely resembles teachers in being an implicated subject. The notion of the implicated subject comes from Michael Rothberg's most recent work. Rothberg explains: "Implication draws attention to how we are entwined with and folded into ('im-pli-cated in') histories and situations that surpass our agency as individual subjects."[55] The term, as Rothberg has conceived of it, includes "bystanders, beneficiaries, latecomers of the post-memory generation and others connected 'prosthetically' to pasts they did not directly experience."[56] Consciousness of oneself as an implicated subject involves "a detour through multidirectional terrain."[57]

Like the idea of autobiography as an elaborate detour, the notion of the implicated subject involves indirectness, here of indirect responsibility or what Sebald has also called contiguity.[58] In the same year when I am being pushed in my pram amid the beautiful mountain scenery of Bavaria, Sebald says about May 1944, the month and year of his birth, Kafka's sister (Gabriele) died while being deported to Lodz. Stories are brought into relation with one another and through their juxtaposition, a larger story or allegorical structure is intimated and felt, which in an interview with Sebald, Silverblatt astutely likened to an "invisible subject"[59]—an ascription with which Sebald agreed. It is as if there is something on Sebald's/the narrator's mind that grows as a persistent, shadowy presence and concern in the reader's mind as well.[60]

The uncanny thing is that while Sebald's narrator travels to various places and hears about others' stories, he is continually brought back home—to his own place and story. Zilcosky compares the literary trope of "getting lost" to a kind of re-birth, with its offer of gaining a new perspective on one's self. What we instead find in Sebald, though, Zilcosky claims, is an *inability* to get lost. If the journeys elsewhere, to other places in which Sebald's narrator encounters others' stories, which are often heard at second- and third-hand, might be characterized as divagations and dis-orientations, Sebald's writing "demonstrates how our disorientations never lead to new discoveries, only to a series of uncanny, intertextual returns."[61] With its uncanny returns by other routes (detours), it resembles, as Sebald himself noted, borrowing from one of his literary mentors, Thomas Bernhard, "a periscopic form of narrative."[62] There are many such moments in Sebald's writing in which, in hearing someone else's story, the narrator is abruptly returned to the Germany that he had been trying "for various reasons to escape."[63]

Among the most striking of these "periscopic" instances, Zilcosky notes, occurs during the Max Ferber narrative in Sebald's *The Emigrants* when Ferber (whose first name echoes Sebald's own—Max) narrates how his life was destroyed by the Holocaust—the separation from and loss of family members. Time, recounts Ferber, "is nothing but a disquiet of the soul," as his thoughts—and his art—increasingly turn to the subject of his family's erasure and, through theirs, his own.[64] Ferber spends his days in a large room, which the narrator ("Sebald") finds through his Sunday walks. The narrator has himself recently moved (viz. been exiled) to Manchester from Germany; there, he writes. His walks (detours) take him to various parts of the city but not accidently. He explores what was once the Jewish quarter, now in ruins. Later, he ventures out of the city and comes across a former warehouse—again, not coincidentally, one that previously served as a depot for a railway company. "I could hear sighs":[65] echoes of the rails that transported Jews to their destruction under Nazism. He keeps walking, which leads him to a sign "To the Studios" and Ferber. Ferber virtually lives inside of his studio. The air and surfaces are permeated with dust, which come from his technique of drawing using charcoal sticks then erasing and scraping what he had drawn, which resulted in "a steady production of dust, which never ceased except at night."[66] The ironic echoes of the crematoria are apparent. And yet, at the end of the day, the narrator says, Ferber managed to create "a portrait of great vividness" from that which "had escaped annihilation."[67] Likewise with Ferber's life. Over time, as Ferber tells his life story, including relinquishing his mother's diaries (the only remnant of the family's past), the story has a striking effect on the narrator. Through study of Ferber's story (including visiting Kissingen, where Ferber's mother grew up), the narrator is brought back to his own history: "Although I was amply occupied … with my research and with the writing itself… I felt increasingly that the mental impoverishment and lack of memory that marked the Germans, and the efficiency with which they had cleaned everything up, were beginning to affect my head and my nerves."[68]

In Sebald's last novel, published just before he died, *Austerlitz*, the return is even more "abrupt" and dizzying, in what Rothberg has likened to an experience of the "multidirectional sublime"[69]—that "haunting sense of the fragile co-presence of histories somehow connected"[70] that is brought on by "disturbed acts of seeing" when positioned as if on the edge of a void, pit, or abyss, staring at a past that still feels very much present.[71] The narrator's return (in *Austerlitz*) occurs by way of the nauseating smell of soap in Breendonk, one of the many places in which the German SS would torture prisoners like Belgian writer Jean Améry and Italian artist Gastone Novelli, both of whom wrote about their experiences; Novelli's experience is recounted in Claude Simon's novel, *Le Jardin des Plantes*. Like Améry, Novelli had become involved in the Resistance, was captured, and experienced the same form of torture as Améry, albeit in Dachau. After the war, the letter A became a motif in Novelli's art, "rising and falling in waves like a long-drawn-out scream."[72] When, following in the footsteps of his study of Jean Améry and as the narrator descends into Breendonk, he experiences a Proust-like moment (like Rothberg's multidirectional sublime), upon encountering this particular smell of soap. The scent reminds him of a German word for a scrubbing brush, "which was a favourite of my father's and which I always disliked."[73] Sebald's father was in the German Wehrmacht; it is now well-known that the regular armies played a key role in the terrible events that unfolded during the war. Instead of a pleasant Proustian madeleine sensation, the soap triggers "black striations," which quiver in front of the narrator's eyes, setting in motion feelings of nausea and vertigo.[74] It is a moment of felt (viz. autobiographical) *implication*.

Sebald's perspective reminds us about the impossibility of exile and the inevitability of return, even as it is also apparent that return needs to *feel* uncanny, coincidental; in other words, it needs to come by multidirectional routes, through detours involving hearing others' stories. This is the ethico-aesthetic of the periscope, which relies on juxtaposition of the political with the phenomenological.[75] In the fault-lines between stories—the cracks and fissures that open as stories overlap, even as they remain inalienably distinct from one another—the sensation is profoundly disorienting. However, it is precisely this juxtaposition that contributes to a "between": a temporal space which is a space of "alterity"[76] even as it is also a space where "the human subject dwells."[77] This uneasy space of alterity/dwelling corresponds to Rothberg's implicated subject, echoing Sebald's invisible subject in being a space of preoccupation, of uncomfortable thoughts brought on by hearing others' stories and discerning their relation to the teacher's/the students' own lives through a felt ethical responsibility. As Pinar suggests, "[s]uch disquiet—that non-coincidence with what is—can engender resolve, that which is in-between hope and despair."[78]

Entering the Periscopic, Ethico-Aesthetic Space

Among the most significant moments in the post-colonial study have been those in which a teacher has turned away (detoured) and then circled back in a periscopic way. Two such examples stand out: one on the part of an elementary teacher, the other a secondary teacher; and especially in the second case, we might discern in her movements the periscope as an ethico-aesthetic form of understanding.

Andrea[79]

Andrea teaches Grades 5 and 6 (Cycle 3) although she has also taught younger grades (Grades 2 and 3). She has been teaching for nine years. Of the five elementary teachers who joined the project in December 2016, she has been among the most quiet and reticent. Her speaking turns are briefest, and are significantly shorter than those of the other teachers, even in response to the autobiographical prompts, which usually elicit winding tales. Andrea grew up in an Italian family. She said little about this history, though, thinking perhaps it was not worth recounting in any detail but also maybe feeling left out as she did not see herself as a reader; she was always more interested in when the reading would be over so that she could engage in more physical types of activity. The teachers coming to the table may be called *the converted*. They come with a clear interest in social justice issues as well as with a history of trying out social justice issues or texts in their teaching. They are also often avid readers. Andrea came with no such history. Thus her quietness, I assumed. This project seemed a detour for her, and I wondered after the second meeting if she would return or instead quietly disappear. However, she surprised all of us in the June 2017 workshop.

As mentioned, we begin our meetings with detour into memory-work. We then turn/detour to teachers' narrating what they have been trying out in their classes with the counter-stories. On this occasion, Andrea volunteered to go first, which was unusual. What she talked about was not remarkable—it is what other teachers have also done. She incorporated two residential school stories (picture books) in her classroom, as part of a unit on residential school; the unit lasted three weeks to a month. She had the support of a student teacher, which may have made a difference: she was not alone. But what was striking in her account was her keen interest in wanting to share (rather than listening and waiting), this combined with echoes of a previous conversation: a "complicated curriculum conversation"[80] we had had in a February workshop.

In that workshop, elementary teachers, paired with secondary ones, were given picture books; they were invited to juxtapose them, coming up with teaching ideas. Andrea was paired with Benjamin, a secondary teacher. Both are quiet teachers, with the difference being that Benjamin has thought deeply on social justice issues even if he is also perpetually doubting, as if he needed to be persuaded that what he was doing was sufficient, suspecting perhaps that he could be doing more or better. Perhaps this combination (awareness and reticence) proved generative for Andrea.

June was the first time Andrea had reported teaching with the counter-stories. She had been borrowing books, but never found time or occasion to actually use them in teaching. By her own account, the difference that these residential school stories (*Shi-she-etko; Shin-chi's Canoe*) made in her class were in the emotions elicited: "We have a lot of kids that just, they don't care about anything. So we try to get them to *feel* something. To connect. To relate."[81] With these stories, something shifted, she claimed. The elementary students showed evidence of being affected, personally. As did Andrea as well. This, I realize, was also what was different. It wasn't so much that before Andrea was quiet; it was that she seemed impassive, at least with respect to these stories whose connection may have seemed remote to her. The juxtaposing activity with Benjamin, followed by the complicated conversation of the group, seemed important; it was here that Andrea read, or rather re-read (since she had already borrowed them previously), the residential school picture books that she was to then use in her unit, venturing to bring them closer. What might have also proved important to Andrea was hearing Sophie, who was also in the February 2017 workshop.

Sophie

Sophie is a secondary school teacher. She teaches combined English and history in the liberal arts program at her school. She teaches various grades but her senior (Grade 11) class focuses on a course dedicated to the study of genocides through reading memoirs. Her teaching has garnered the attention of the Ministry of Education. We had been in her class to witness her literature circles in which students discussed self-selected projects on a genocide topic of their choice, culminating in 3,000-word essays. The talk was highly animated: complicated conversations à la multidirectional memory about the different books. Not long after that classroom visit to hear these critical, inquiring, passionate 11th graders, we learned that the Ministry of Education was scheduled to film her class on graphic novels. In short, Sophie's critical and creative approach is public knowledge. She is known to bring a deep commitment to teaching and to social justice issues; this was apparent from the inception of the research (November 2015). No one needed to invite her to do thus and thus; she was already there, and with books of her own. She was constantly reading, finding new counter-stories, and sharing them with the other teachers; we could barely keep up with her, with one exception. The one topic she showed absolutely no interest in, even though we did various activities with books, was Indigenous issues. This changed for her in December 2016.

Sophie attributed the change to stumbling across a book called *Barkskins*.[82] Annie Proulx is not an Indigenous writer. But Proulx's novel, in its multi-century, cross-generational organization, reminded her of another one that she had encountered in the group. I had brought it to the June 2016 meeting. Called *Homegoing*, it is written by a Ghanian first author, Yaa Gyasi, and it recounts the generational effects of slavery.[83] Sophie had read it over the summer and loved it, finding the overlapping stories deeply compelling. She had us order a class set for an extended unit, which was just taught in winter 2018. It was one of several books on the table when we visited her Secondary V class in March 2017.

Memory-work involves returning to the past, or as Pinar says, to a present over which the past hovers. Sophie had never said so, but her silence around Indigenous issues must have started to feel corrosive. Why not *this* genocide? This question became more urgent in light of growing attention newly re-awakened by Canada's Truth and Reconciliation Commission and related events (such as murdered Indigenous women). As Pinar suggests, current events are a way to bring home the significance of "historical moments" through the "pressing events of the day," which provoke "the esthetic juxtaposition of academic knowledge" with "students who may already be worldly-wise"[84].

In the February workshop, Sophie explained that while as a student and then a teacher, she was always interested in social justice, yet she "never wanted to explore anything to do with the Natives." Her new-found interest had the character of a revelation: "I am going to be completely honest and hope you'll not be too judgmental."[85] The reason she gave was that the test-driven curriculum had literally "killed" this topic for her; it not only held no interest for her but just the thought of addressing was abhorrent to her—and the same was true of her students: reflective of the "deform" of schooling into a lifeless terrain of teaching solely to the test.[86] She recounted her experience to them and asked them about theirs. "And they were, like: Exactly the way that you feel about it. I have no feelings about this subject." In an interview that took place in December 2016, Sophie had spoken about the importance of feelings—that she teaches through emotion, through having the students connect with the subject matter. She also added in the workshop, thinking aloud: "… upon reflection, [it has] made me realize how much our passion is what fuels…. Like, I mean, I already knew that, but it just became so obvious. Like, had I read, had I chosen something else, and was talking about that, they would have wanted to read THAT book."[87]

Here was teacher testimonial to how important the teacher's autobiographical, intellectual/emotional journey was in ethically teaching to a subject by "working from within."[88] She could not teach *to* the subject until she felt it herself *as* a subject, as an implicated subject. Juxtaposition played a key indirect role, prompted by the between-space created through memories and counter-memories brought into intimate adjacency and talk about juxtaposition. More juxtaposing, it was clear, also occurred outside the study: in teachers' everyday lives, in their pedagogy, in the world, and in students' and teachers' awareness of current events. The indirectness of juxtaposition in contributing to that between, allowed teachers to figure out, in their own way and time, and in relation to their own particular selves, the resemblances among and gaps between the disparate pieces of their own and others' memories and experiences: of curriculum *and* schooling; of the post-colonial texts *and* their responses to the texts; of pedagogy *and* their students' responses. "Curriculum development is not, in this sense, programmatic, but intellectual, finally an individual affair ... animated by their [teachers'] subjective interests and those of their students, attentive to the communities (local and global) in which they work and live."[89] It is an ethical undertaking. Teaching ought to be difficult, Paulo Freire reminds us, for it requires "constant vigilance":[90] awareness of our "unfinishedness" and thus "our presence in the world as ethical" and responsible for constantly searching and critically inquiring into ourselves, the world, and our students.[91]

Conclusion

Juxtaposition re-structures the recurring question of the subject and of subjective reconstruction as ethical self-encounters. Juxtaposition is allegorical, even stealthy, in its Sebaldian placing of fragments of storied experiences beside one another, like so many coincidences piling up, in wedges whose fit with one another is imprecise, and where it becomes incumbent on the teacher, in light of his or her distinctive biography, to thread the needle and confront the question, now, of what all of these disquieting coincidences add up to. "Allegory testifies to the fact that 'now' is temporal and multiply layered, that our extrication from this present moment is immanent within it."[92] A non-negotiable piece in all of this is the counter-story, which provokes feelings of disjuncture and *non*-assimilation. It is really in their pedagogy using counter-stories that the rubber hits the road for teachers; it is by this means that the needle is threaded through. As artists, they are called upon to use their judgment to decide how to engage students, as subjects, in this difficult subject matter; the process involves indirect subjectivity in the form of detours and returns. It entails entering the ethico-aesthetic space of the periscope: a process of teaching as allegorizing through telling one story by way of another, in such a way that students will feel invited, in an ethical manner, to turn towards rather than away from the material, find themselves in unfamiliar terrain, and then end up where they began—brought back to themselves. One shape that such an implicated narrative takes, I have suggested, is periscopic in Sebald's sense of a series of intertextual detours and returns. "I already knew that," Sophie said, "but it just became so obvious" that it was her teacher's passion, her communication of an invisible subject that fuelled the conversation and that opened that ethico-aesthetic space in which students would want to move with her.

Notes

1. Pinar, "Allegories," 3.
2. Pinar, *Educational Experience*, 231.
3. Pinar, 230.
4. Pinar, *Character*.
5. Northrop Frye, *The Double Vision*, vii.
6. Chimamanda Ngozi Adichie, The danger of a single story.
7. Pinar, "Allegories," 3.
8. Pinar, 4.
9. Pinar, *Worldliness*, 28–29. On the ties between curriculum and consciousness, see Maxine Greene's essay of the same name: Greene, "Curriculum and Consciousness."
10. Pinar, *Character*, xiv. Emphasis added.
11. Pinar, 7.
12. Pinar, xiv.
13. Pinar, "Allegories," 4.
14. I gratefully acknowledge support for this project provided by SSHRC (Social Sciences and Humanities Research Council, 435-2014-1225), "Developing a pedagogy of social justice in the classroom through post-colonial literature," Ingrid Johnston, PI (University of Alberta); Co-investigators: Anne Burke (Memorial), Geraldine Balser (U Saskatchewan), Teresa Strong-Wilson (McGill), Susan Tilley (Brock), Angela Ward (U Victoria), Lynn Wiltse (U Alberta).
15. King, "Godzilla," 12.
16. Smith, *Decolonizing*, 2; Thomas, "Honouring," 183.
17. Linda Hutcheon distinguishes between overt and covert forms of narcissistic narrative in the first chapter of her *Narcissistic Narrative*.
18. Laroque, "When the Other Is Me," 118.
19. Bouchard, "Preface," 8.
20. Hirsch, "The Generation of Postmemory."
21. Pinar, "Allegories," 5.
22. Silverman, *Flesh*, cited in Pinar, "Allegories," 5.
23. Walter Benjamin cited in Abbas, "On Fascination," 59.
24. Grumet, "Curriculum," 80.
25. Grumet, "Toward," 93.
26. Grumet, "Restitution," 123.
27. Pinar, *Character*, xi.
28. Hampl, *I Could*.
29. Pinar, "Method."
30. Grumet, "Poor Curriculum," 93.
31. Grumet, "Restitution," 123.

32 Grumet, "Curriculum," 87.
33 Grumet, "Restitution," 128.
34 Grumet, 127.
35 Grumet, "Psychoanalytical," 170.
36 Rothberg, *Multidirectional*, 5.
37 Rothberg, "Sebald and Kentridge," 40.
38 Rothberg, *Multidirectional*, 5.
39 Sendak and Kushner, *Brundibar*.
40 On Walter Benjamin's notion of dialectical image see Abbas, "On Fascination," as well as Simon, *Teaching*.
41 Bishop, *House*.
42 New Zealand Picture Book Collection.
43 Loyie, *As Long*; Campbell, *Shi-shi-etko*.
44 Bear Chief, *My Decade*.
45 Strong-Wilson, Yoder, and Phipps, "Going," 87.
46 Rothberg, *Multidirectional*, 19.
47 Rothberg, 15.
48 Pinar, *Worldliness*, 3.
49 Pinar, 52.
50 Pinar, 35.
51 Pinar, 35.
52 Rothberg, "Sebald and Kentridge," 46.
53 Hutchinson, "Shadow," 279.
54 Strong-Wilson, "Following."
55 Rothberg. "Trauma Theory."
56 Rothberg, "Sebald and Kentridge," 40.
57 Rothberg, 43.
58 This idea of contiguity (which is juxtaposition, essentially) is further developed in Strong-Wilson, "Phantom Traces."
59 Silverblatt, "Poem," 80.
60 The pertinence of Sebald's notion of "invisible subject" to curriculum theory is explored in Strong-Wilson, "Following."
61 Zilcosky, "Uncanny," 102.
62 Sebald in Silverblatt, "Poem", 82.
63 Zilcosky, "Uncanny," 114. Zilcosky's internal citation is from W. G. Sebald's, *The Emigrants* (Michael Hulse Books, 1989), 149.
64 Sebald, *Emigrants*, 181.
65 Sebald, 158.
66 Sebald, 162.
67 Sebald, 162.
68 Sebald, 225.
69 Rothberg, "Sebald and Kentridge," 42.
70 Rothberg, 43.

71 Rothberg, 44.
72 Sebald, *Austerlitz*, 27.
73 Sebald, 25.
74 Sebald, 25
75 Pinar, *Worldliness*. I am proposing here Sebald's elaboration of the periscopic narrative as a shape that juxtapositions tend to assume when ordered into the form of an autobiographical story. Part of what contributes to this shape is accepting that coincidences (which may initially look like Grumet's detours) may be significant. However, what drives the subject (individual) is the presence of an invisible subject. These are ideas that I continue to write about and that have been developed in part in Strong-Wilson, "Following One's Nose."
76 Both "between" and "alterity" come from Pinar, *Worldliness*, xii.
77 Radhakrishnan in Pinar, *Worldliness*, xii.
78 Pinar, *Educational*, 183.
79 All teachers' names are pseudonyms.
80 Pinar, *Worldliness*, 35.
81 June 6, 2017, Teacher Research Workshop.
82 Proulx, *Barkskins*.
83 Gyasi, *Homegoing*.
84 Seigfried cited in Pinar, *Worldliness*, 10–11.
85 February 15, 2017, Teacher Research Workshop.
86 Pinar, *What*, xiii.
87 February 15, 2017, Teacher Research Workshop.
88 Pinar, "Working." For a more recent reiteration of the contemporary pertinence of this notion of working from within, see also Pinar, *Worldliness*, 39.
89 Pinar, *Worldliness*, 43.
90 Freire, *Pedagogy*, 51.
91 Freire, 56.
92 Pinar, *Educational*, 25.

Bibliography

Abbas, Ackbar. "On Fascination: Walter Benjamin's Images." *New German Critique* 48 (1989): 43–62.

Adichie, Chimamanda Ngozi. "The Danger of a Single Story." Filmed July 2009, 18:43, TEDGlobal video. http://www.ted.com/talks/.chimamanda_adichie_the_danger_of_a_single_story.

Bear Chief, Arthur. *My Decade at Old Sun, My Lifetime of Hell*. Edmonton, AB: Athabaska University Press, 2016.

Bishop, Gavin. *The House That Jack Built*. Wellington, NZ: Gecko Press, 1999.

Bouchard, Donald F. "Preface." In *Language, Counter-Memory, Practice: Selected Essays and Interviews by Michel Foucault*, edited by Donald F. Bouchard, 7–9. Ithaca, NY: Cornell University Press, 1980.
Campbell, Nicola. *Shi-shi-etko*. Toronto, ON: Groundwood Books/House of Anansi Press, 2005.
Freire, Paulo. *Pedagogy of Freedom: Ethics, Democracy and Civic Courage*. London, UK: Rowan & Littlefield, 2001.
Frye, Northrup. *The Double Vision: Language and Meaning in Religion*. Toronto, ON: University of Toronto Press, 1991.
Greene, Maxine. "Curriculum and Consciousness." In *Curriculum Theorizing: The Reconceptualists*, edited by William F. Pinar, 295–322. Berkeley, CA: McCutchan Publishing Corporation, 1975.
Grumet, Madeleine R. "Curriculum and the Art of Daily Life." In *Reflections from the Heart of Educational Inquiry: Understanding Curriculum and Teaching through the Arts*, edited by George Willis and William Henry Schubert, 74–89. New York, NY: State University of New York Press, 1991.
———. "Psychoanalytical Foundations." In *Toward a Poor Curriculum*, edited by William F. Pinar and Madeleine R. Grumet, 142–190. Kingston, NY: Educator's International Press, 2015.
———. "Restitution and Reconstruction of Educational Experience: An Autobiographical Method for Curriculum Inquiry." In *Rethinking Curriculum Studies: A Radical Approach*, edited by Martin Lawn and Len Barton, 84–112. London, UK: Croom Helm, 1981.
———. "Toward a Poor Curriculum." In *Toward a Poor Curriculum*, edited by William F. Pinar and Madeleine R. Grumet, 84–112. Kingston, NY: Educator's International Press, 2015.
Gyasi, Yaa. *Homegoing*. New York, NY: Knopf, 2016.
Hampl, Patricia. *I Could Tell You Stories*. New York, NY: W. W. Norton, 1999.
Hirsch, Marianne. "The Generation of Postmemory." *Poetics Today* 29, no. 1 (2008): 103–128.
Hutcheon, Linda. *Narcissistic Narrative: The Metafictional Paradox*. Waterloo, ON: Wilfred Laurier University Press, 2013.
Hutchinson, Ben. "The Shadow of Resistance: W. G. Sebald and the Frankfurt School." *Journal of European Studies* 43, nos. 3–4 (2011), 267–284.
King, Thomas. "Godzilla vs. Post-Colonial." *World Literature Written in English* 30, no 2 (1990): 10–16.
Laroque, Emma. "When the Other Is Me: Native Writers Confronting Canadian Literature." In *Issues in the North* Volume 1, edited by Jill Oakes and Rick Riewe, 118. Edmonton, AB: Canadian Circumpolar Institute, 1996.
Loyie, Larry. *As Long as the Rivers Flow*. Toronto, ON: Groundwood, 2000.

New Zealand Picture Book Collection. Downloaded January 26, 2018. http://www.picturebooks.co.nz/2010/11/the-house-that-jack-built/.

Pinar, William F. "Allegories of the Present: Curriculum Development in a Culture of Narcissism and Presentism." Plenary, First International Congress on Curriculum and Instruction, Eskişehir, Turkey, October 5–8, 2011, 1–10. Downloaded June 1, 2018 from https://www.pegem.net/dosyalar/dokuman/131590-2012041217031-1.pdf.

———. *The Character of Curriculum Studies*. New York, NY: Palgrave Macmillan, 2011.

———. *Educational Experience as Lived: Knowledge, History, Alterity: The Selected Works of William F. Pinar*. New York, NY: Routledge, 2015.

———. "The Method of *Currere*." In *Autobiography, Politics and Sexuality: Essays in Curriculum Theory, 1972–1992*, edited by William F. Pinar, 19–27. New York, NY: Peter Lang, 1975/1994.

———. *What Is Curriculum Theory?* New York, NY: Routledge, 2012.

———. "Working from within." *Educational Leadership*, 29, no. 4 (1972), 329–331.

———. *The Worldliness of Cosmopolitan Education: Passionate Lives in Public Service*. New York, NY: Routledge, 2009.

Proulx, Annie. *Barkskins*. New York, NY: Simon and Schuster, 2016.

Rothberg, Michael. "Multidirectional Memory and the Implicated Subject: On Sebald and Kentridge." In *Performing Memory in Art and Popular Culture*, edited by Liedeke Plate and Anneke Smelik, 39–58. New York, NY: Routledge, 2013.

———. *Multidirectional Memory: Remembering the Holocaust in the Age of Decolonization*. Stanford, CA: Stanford University Press, 2009.

———. "Trauma Theory, Implicated Subjects, and the Question of Israel/Palestine." Presentation, from Modern Languages Association (MLA) Convention, Chicago, IL: May 2, 2014.

Sebald, W. G. *Austerlitz*. New York, NY: The Modern Library, 2001.

———. *The Emigrants*. New York, NY: New Directions, 1989.

Sendak, Maurice, and Tony Kushner. *Brundibar*. Berlin, DE: Boosey and Hawkes / Bote and Bock, 2003.

Silverblatt, Michael. "A Poem of an Invisible Subject (Interview)." In *The Emergence of Memory: Conversations with W. G. Sebald*, edited by L. S. Schwartz, 77–86. New York, NY: Seven Stories Press, 2007.

Silverman, Kaja. *Flesh of My Flesh*. Stanford, CA: Stanford University Press, 2009.

Simon, Roger. *Teaching against the Grain: Texts for a Pedagogy of Possibility*. Toronto, ON: OISE Press, 1992.

Strong-Wilson, Teresa. "Following One's Nose in Reading W. B. Sebald Allegorically: *Currere* and Invisible Subjects." *Educational Theory* 67, no. 2 (2017): 153–171.

———. "Phantom Traces: Exploring a Hermeneutical Approach to Autobiography in Curriculum Studies." *Journal of Curriculum Studies* 47, no. 5 (2015): 613–632.

Strong-Wilson, Teresa, Amarou Yoder, and Heather Phipps. "Going Down the Rabbit-Hole: Teachers' Engagements with 'Dialectical Images' in Canadian Children's Literature on Social Justice." *Changing English* 21, no. 1 (2014): 79–93.

Smith, Linda Tuhiwai. *Decolonizing Methodologies: Research and Indigenous Peoples.* London, UK: Zed Books, 1999.

Thomas, Rubina. "Honouring the Oral Traditions of My Ancestors through Storytelling." In *Research as Resistance: Critical, Indigenous, and Anti-Oppressive Approaches,* edited by Leslie Brown and Susan Strega, 177–198. Toronto, ON: Canadian Scholars' Press, 2005.

Zilcosky, John. "Sebald's Uncanny Travels: The Impossibility of Getting Lost." In *W. G. Sebald—A Critical Companion,* edited by Jonathan James Long and Anne Whitehead, 102–120. Seattle, WA: University of Washington Press, 2004.

CHAPTER 5

"Tenants of Time and Place": Teacher Education as Translational Practice

Anne M. Phelan

An Old Irish adage:
We are the tenants of time and place, not their colonizers. They possess us, not we them.

— Caterina Ricciardi[1]

A Provocation

"What has an Irish teacher educator, from a country with a grim national history, to offer Canadian teachers as we try to address our own difficult history?" A student teacher so confronted me during a course examining the role of Canadian schools in perpetrating cultural genocide, racism, sexism, and homophobia. The course also sought to understand how teachers might interrupt that difficult inheritance and work to promote social justice. While impressed by the student's appreciation of the role of history in understanding self and society in the present, I was struck by her assumption that national histories are discrete and disconnected. Most significantly, however, I felt compelled by her to respond to the question with which all newcomers must engage: *Who are you?*

In this chapter, I respond to the student teacher's demand—to "know thyself" in *this* place—and to explore further the links between Irish and Canadian histories. Inspired by Jane Urquhart's[2] allegorical novel *Away*, my chapter pivots around two historical events: Ireland's Great Famine (1845–1847), and the assassination of the Canada's first Minister of Agriculture and Immigration, Darcy McGee, in 1868. I examine their unexpected intersections with my own history: the transformative power of myth translated across societies, the "anxious hope" of exilic experience, the persistent entanglements of colonialism. I argue that if teacher educators are to resist the excessive standardization and cultural homogenization that global educational policies attempt to install, we will have to unfurl the knot of our own civic particularity.

Natality and Belatedness: Tradition and Translation

Twenty-five years after my arrival, so much suggests that I am here in Canada in the present: I hold permanent residence status, own a home, and occupy a university position. Yet, I often experience myself as not here. I am neither from this place nor of this place. This feeling of being here and yet not here reflects, in part, a growing recognition of the fact of my belatedness. As a newcomer to Canada, I am heir to a particular history yet new to it. Belatedness orients us even as it threatens to overpower our capacity for action.[3] I am positioned as a white, European, settler making a living on the unceded territory of the Musqueam people. I am an educator in a country where schools were explicitly "created for the purpose of separating Aboriginal children from their families, in order to minimize and weaken family ties and cultural linkages, and to indoctrinate children into a new culture—the culture of the legally dominant Euro-Christian Canadian society."[4] My belatedness constitutes who I can be in this place to some degree, and it influences what I do and how I impact others. Should I be weighed down by this positioning? Or, with each new encounter, do I insist on my status as a newcomer contending that I cannot be held responsible for a past I did not make? How might responses of resentment or resignation play out in the university classroom? On one account, I become a social pariah who accepts her fate as unalterable; on another telling, I become a parvenu, who rejects her social positioning and the necessity of historical sensibility.[5] Or do I linger in the gap that is the present, full of trepidation and without "a bridge of inherited concepts"[6] to guide me? While lingering, might I respond to my student's provocation, give an account of myself, and embrace my natality not as some pre-ordained fate but as a site of responsibility?

To understand one's own belatedness and to give an account of oneself requires understanding history; without a sense of the past it is impossible to have a sense of self, of one's identity.[7] It is necessary (as the student-teacher reminded me) to understand the history that haunts. "The narrative structure of action and of human identity means that the continued retelling of the past, its continued reintegration into the story of the present, its continuous re-evaluation, reassessment, and reconfiguration, are ontological conditions of the kinds of beings we are…. Who we are at any point is defined by the narrative uniting past and present…."[8]

As Margaret Atwood asserts, history is something that belongs no longer to those who lived in it but to those who claim it and are willing to infuse it with meaning.[9] What will guide and authorize such storytelling? How do I generate meaning from a past and a place that is both mine and not mine? Arendt directs us to become pearl divers who bring "precious fragments" of history to the surface for reconsideration—"but not in order to resuscitate it in the way it was and to contribute to the renewal of extinct ages";[10] rather, our purpose is one of re-narrating—translating, if you will—those "rich and strange" fragments that would otherwise have been sedimented and obscured in "layers of language and concepts" offered in historical interpretation.[11] Following Walter Benjamin, Arendt sought to selectively re-appropriate the past—moments of rupture, displacement and dislocation in history—for the sake of shedding light on present problems.[12] At such moments, language is witness to the more profound transformations taking place in human life. Such a *Begriffsgeschichte* is a remembering, in the sense of a creative act of rethinking, that sets free the "lost potentials" of the past.[13]

The knowledge that results from the "creative act of rethinking"[14] is historical in that it can help create a historical sense of one's being in the world. Such knowledge is also affective because of the "emotive quality of language"[15] as it magically and artfully makes sense by serendipitously choosing a certain word or combination of words to represent an experience. The upshot is that history is "felt" and that one gains "a feeling for history as human experience."[16] Here Benjamin reminds us that "the remembered past experience is transformed into meaningful category, an intuition, for interpreting the present"[17]; what he "qualified as an act of allegorically constructive reading."[18]

Allegory as Montage: The Past and Present in Pieces

Pinar invokes the concept of allegory to capture the reactivation of the past in the present "in order to find the future."[19] In keeping with Arendt and Benjamin, Pinar has no interest in reconstructing the past "as it was."[20] In his casting of allegories-of-the-present, he embraces translation of the past into the present and proposes that in allegory we find both "resemblance" and "difference," connoting "the particularity of history and the past's significance for the present moment."[21] Allegory offers a particular story but hints at a more general significance, he muses. Echoing Arendt's concern that we become historically sensitive, Pinar argues that when we speak allegorically "we self-reflexively articulate what is at hand, reactivating the past so as to render the present, including ourselves, intelligible"[22] for now. By engaging history in this manner, neither the past nor our subjectivity can congeal or harden but remain open to re-interpretation in the context of new encounters with texts (via study), places, and persons.

As an attempt to build passages "from the particularity of our situations to the alterity of others past,"[23] allegory underscores the intricacy of history, its representation, and its subjectivity. Rauch expresses it in the following terms: "Allegory becomes a new mode of signification that represents the past in a new, meaningful way as if to guide us in how we can sensibly live with this 'past in ruins'."[24] The past is in pieces, as Arendt and Benjamin have taught us, and there is nothing left for us to do than gather those shards and lay them alongside to see what various juxtapositions might reveal beyond established or conventional meanings. Pinar's practice of allegory as montage[25]—the selection, editing, and piecing together of fragments—integrates Benjamin's and Arendt's sentiments. He writes:

> In juxtaposing incommensurate fragments, allegory splits our attention while dissociating nothing, demanding that we discern what is distinctive in each fragment while at the same time appreciating the complexity of association that such a montage reveals.[26]

Incommensurability of fragments reflects the disjuncture between now and then, here and not here. The reader must use the imagination to discern what is significant in each fragment while conceiving the in-between possibilities—those lost potentials.

If in remembrance there is translation (*tra-ducere*), the central element here is movement, displacement, carrying over, "to conduct through, pass beyond, to the other side of a division or difference."[27] Translation is never simply a passage from one language to another; questions concerning subject, context, and historical moment asked by the linguist also apply to any work of historical interpretation.[28] Translation is a dual movement between past and present, here (in this place) and (over) there; histories cross landscapes and societies in the form of story. Any act of cultural transport has the power to generate or shut down "new images and spaces for thought" in the receiving culture or time.[29] The newcomer is neither essentially a benign nor a malign stranger.[30] It is this very realization, perhaps, that not only provoked the student-teacher's question but my own struggle, subsequently, to understand my civic particularity as it exists *in translation* in this place, Canada. So it is crucial to ask, after Ferri: *What gets translated? What does the act of translation across generations and societies entail? Who am I in translation?*[31] In what follows, I juxtapose the fragments of literature, personal story, official histories, and literary theory to explore these questions.

Away: Transformation, Exile, and Betrayal

In her striking and sombre allegory *Away*, Canadian novelist Jane Urquhart tells the stories of four generations of women—Mary, Eileen, Esther, and Deirdre—beginning with Mary's migratory journey from famine-torn Ireland to Canada in the mid-nineteenth century. The key motif running through the novel is that we are "the tenants of time and place, not their colonizers. They possess us, not we them."[32] Time and place render our lives precarious such that they lack predictability and security. The year is 1867, the time of the foundation of the Dominion of Canada, when the history of two colonies (Ireland and Canada) and their people "interweave into a tangle of passion and violence to reach a moment of great political and ideological importance, unique and extreme, like the Celtic women of *Away*."[33] Mary's daughter, Eileen, who "had ingested the stories and their darkness"—colonization, famine, exile, and betrayal—"would always look back towards lost landscapes and inward towards inherited souvenirs."[34] Eileen passes on the stories of horror and hope to Esther saying: "You have this gift in you, the ability to be where you are, but I am in you as well, and there will be times when you want to drift away."[35]

The concept of "away" connotes three important meanings: "away" as in a fairy world to which one is taken and transformed; "away," as in far away, signalling migration and exile; and, "away," as it morphed in the New World into betrayal, "colonization, embezzling the land of others, the same violent practice exerted for centuries on the Gaelic people of Ireland."[36]

Away as Transformation

Central to the novel is the Irish folk-myth about women who are away—that is, those who have been possessed or taken away to the Otherworld. In part, Urquhart changes the myth by characterizing the experience of being away as a form of madness equated to "unrequited love and the yearning for an absent lover."[37] Set on Rathlin Island off the north coast of Ireland, the novel *Away* begins with an encounter with faeries. Mary, the protagonist, encounters the body of "a dead young sailor"[38] washed up on the shore surrounded by cabbages and silver teapots—"gifts from the sea"[39]—from a shipwreck called *Moira*, bound for Halifax, Canada. Immediately drawn to the beautiful figure of the sailor, Mary lays beside him only to hear his final utterance—Moira. A while later she is found by islanders asleep beside her faery-daemon lover, as they would have it; she had been "seduced ... touched ... and she had become significant."[40] Everyone, including her mother, knew that Mary was away. The novelist uses the change of name—from the Anglo (Mary) to its Gaelic form Moire (*Máire*)—to signal the transformation that has occurred: Mary is "stronger and more beautiful than ever," singing quietly but without any "other form of speech," performing her chores as usual but "too easily ... as milk turned to butter with a few light touches of the churn."[41] Mary, the narrator tells us, is an "exact replica," and yet she has changed utterly; she is at once "here but not here."[42] To be taken seems to be some women's fate, the villagers conclude, but how to get them back? What methods could save women from such singular enchantment? Might holy water, prayer, death, or marriage be a source of the changeling's redemption? But when they bring the priest to bless Mary with holy water, nothing but "a terrible sadness" pours over her, and in refusal, she quietly utters "no."[43] The moral outrage at Mary's presumed lost virginity and the fear of the changeling's sinister powers mingle with the unspoken hope in her ability to cure women's ailments and children's diseases.

The awe and fear of women's power induced through transformation pervade the novel; they are quieted, temporarily, upon Mary's marriage to schoolmaster Brian O'Malley. On her wedding day, she is taken from Rathlin Island to the Irish mainland, and she begins to re-enter the world via the learning opportunities Brian offers her, and for some time, knowledge of the world (geography) and the English language "held her full attention."[44] Yet the feeling of some "lost thing" inside of her persists; the "old beliefs … [which] had not been completely stolen from her … had become dormant."[45] Something in Mary "wanted finishing" that could not be "completed" by abstractions taught to her in a foreign tongue.[46]

It is upon her encounter with Ojibway Chief, Exodus Crow, that she finds kinship and completion: Mary re-discovers Irish mythology through the Ojibway's stories, both being in fact earth-centred and not exploitation-centred. They learn that they not only share the Manitou (spirit) but also "dark things,… stolen lands,… [stolen children],… disease,… lost language,… empty villages,… and how the people who once sang were now silent, how the people who once danced were now still."[47] Having both suffered "the imposition of the White Anglo-Saxon Man's 'burden,'"[48] Mary and Exodus Crow long for a land "belonging to all, owned by no one" where only "short-lived traces" are evident.[49] It is while living with Exodus Crow and his tribe—away from her family—that Mary finds her Otherworld lover waiting for her under the waters of Lake Moira. The daemon-lover now resembles the Aboriginal Manitou of the Ojibways, just as Mary resembles the legendary Irish Queen, Deirdre, who "had lived happily in the forest with three warrior brothers, one of whom she loved, until a bad king killed them, and [she] … had died of sorrow."[50]

Living in the midst of the Ojibway people, Mary recoups her power of imagination and possibility offered by her daemon lover. We glimpse Mary as a desiring subject with an interior life and not merely as an object of the male gaze. Not unlike the Edward Burne-Jones[51] image of *The Evening Star* that graces the 1997 edition of the book jacket, Mary is not of this world; she is a world unto herself, having her own reality. The woman in the painting floats, giving a sense of space as a counter to entrapment; she is no longer chained to earth. She draws our eye in the direction she seems to be heading. Seductive and nurturing, passionate yet serene, she is a silent siren whose free-floating contemplation conjures up something long forgotten by men of learning. Her nature seems to be out of sympathy with the everyday struggle and political action; she is dreamer and poet.

The theme of power through transformation reverberated through my childhood, specifically in the context of my relationship with my maternal grandmother, Margaret (1899–1972). Physically disabled, she rarely left her place by the hearth; yet she was often 'away.' She filled my imagination with stories, poems, dreams, and songs about possessed women, ethereal figures called *ban sí* (pronounced: banshee) presaging death, and other ghost-like figures who could arrive unbidden at any time. She would recite lines from Yeats's melancholy poem "The Stolen Child," and recall the old custom of placing a saucer of milk on the windowsill to ward away ill-intentioned faeries (*síoga*) from the homes of newborns.

> Come away, O human child!
> To the waters and the wild
> With a faery, hand in hand,
> For the world's more full of weeping than
> you can understand.[52]

The desire for transformation via escape rendered women and children at risk in my grandmother's recitations, however. Punctuating her mythical tales were critical accounts of ill-tempered Roman Catholic priests and her resistance to church-defined *wifely* duties during the early years of the Irish Free State (1922). A wishful longing characterized her telling: the desire to live a life that was Otherworldly; to escape the patriarchal vale of tears; to be away in *Tír na nÓg*, the Irish mythical land of eternal youth and beauty, where neither her physical body nor Church doctrine could restrain her. My grandmother's seven daughters, more practical and more schooled than she, indulged her romantic, poetic (and, to them, sentimental) ways. I ingested her stories in all their enchantment and sorrow.

Not unlike the women in my grandmother's stories and in Urquhart's novel, women in teaching have long been burdened and restrained by the expectations of others; questions about what teaching does to women still resonate. In the contemporary educational climate of advanced (neo)liberalism, performativity regimes[53] are the dominant mode of regulation of teachers, teaching, and teacher education. The teacher's role is perfunctory at best, contrasting sharply with the idea of an identity "which is always contingent upon history, desires, and circumstances."[54] Teachers are required to leave their desires at home—their love of literature, art, science—to engage in a form of forgetfulness about their worldly responsibility to the newness that children introduce and to pursue "work based on the male model that emphasizes rationality, order, detachment."[55] Eros is the drive that impels human beings toward union; it contrasts sharply with the discontinuous form of life that takes root when a teacher is required to teach by numbers.[56] The desire for union and communion that manifests in spontaneous classroom moments of joy, laughter, and pleasure is replaced by a detached and means-ends oriented professionalism. During erotic moments—recall Mary's encounter with her daemon lover or my grandmother's hypnotizing mythologies—boundaries are blurred and established patterns of relations are disturbed; these are moments of exuberance and excess for teachers and students, moments that are unreserved, lavish, and joyful.[57] Georges Bataille suggests that eroticism smashes apart the self-contained character of individuals as they are in their normal lives.[58] Eroticism takes the form of a desire to break with established patterns of interacting in schools, and the result can be transformative, leading to a type of teacher autonomy that is less about self-possession and more about intimacy. By acting with and against the social rules that would determine her, such a teacher, such a woman, engenders a self.[59]

Away as Exile

In *Away*, Jane Urquhart juxtaposes the Celtic dream world and the colonial nightmare of the Great Famine of 1845–1849, the most important event in Irish history and, according to Irish historians Ó Corráin and O'Riordain, the worst catastrophe in modern European history before the twentieth century.[60] As a failure in food supplies over a prolonged period, famines were common in Ireland during the eighteenth and nineteenth centuries. Although politicians were aware of the underlying causes of food scarcity and hunger, they did little to tackle them. On July 7, 1830, the Duke of Wellington, either anticipating or predicting the Great Famine, described "those in want in the midst of plenty … with no relief or mitigation…." while their leaders, absentee landlords, "amusing themselves in the Clubs of London, in Cheltenham, or Bath or on the Continent,"[61] failed to meet their responsibilities at home. The failure of the potato crop, upon which one-third of the population depended for survival, dealt a final blow to an already fragile society. "Emigration was on a massive scale—about 100,000 in 1846, about 200,000 in 1847, almost 250,000 in 1851."[62]

Landlords, including Lord Palmerston (later to become British prime minister), notoriously shipped destitute tenants to North America. Many arrived in St. John, New Brunswick, while others made passage to Gross Île, the quarantine station thirty miles below the city of Quebec. The medical superintendent of Grosse Île described those disembarking as " the worst looking passengers" he had ever seen.[63]

> On 26 May 1847, there were 30 vessels with 1,000 emigrants waiting at *Grosse Ile*; on 31 May 1847, there were 40 vessels waiting, stretched in a line two miles long down the St. Lawrence river; there were 1,100 cases of fever in the sheds and tents of *Gross Ile*, short of bedding, sanitation, and carers, and just as many ill in ships waiting to disembark, and another 45,000 emigrants were believed to be on the way.[64]

Misled by false promises of clothing and money (the equivalent of 172 to 430 euros per family on arrival in Canada), the aged, the destitute, and helpless widows with young children flocked onto the so-called coffin ships. So miserable and ill-treated was one shipload of passengers to St. John, arriving on November 2, 1847, that Mr. Adam Ferrie, a member of the Legislative Council of Canada and of City Council of St. John, denounced Palmerston's agent as a "worthless and unprincipled hireling, in whose bosom every principle of humanity and every germ of mercy had become totally extinct."[65]

Jane Urquhart, the novelist, picks up the story of the Famine via the forced emigration of Mary and Brian O'Malley and their son, Liam, from Ireland to Canada, sponsored by landlord Osbert Sedgwick. In *Away*, emigration is a sublime experience, incorporating pleasure and pain, excitement and anxiety, inducing a kind of delightful dread. She plays on the word "away" to illustrate the depth and extent of its significance for exiles—here her understanding of exile is "capacious" ... embracing "compulsion, self-determination and flight"[66]—who cross vast oceans, becoming entangled in the lives and aspirations of distant peoples.

Born in the end of the nineteenth century, my grandmother loved to sing the old songs recounting the injuries of an Irish colonial past including famine, eviction, and exile. She would break into melancholy melodies filled with longing for home and hope for a better future. One of her favourites, taught to me at a very early age, was "The Mountains of Mourne."[67] The lyrics tell of a rather gullible Irish country boy seeking his fortune in London.

> Oh Mary, this London's a wonderful sight,
> With the people here working by day and by night.
> They don't sow potatoes nor barley nor wheat
> But there's gangs of them diggin' for gold in the street.
> At least when I asked them that's what I was told
> So I just took a hand at that diggin' for gold;
> But for all that I found there, I might has well be
> Where the Mountains of Mourne sweep down to the sea.[68]

Foolish enough to believe in treasure, exiles were infantilized (orphaned and alone), scorned (stupid and outcast), and admired not for their courage but their enduring love of Ireland. My grandmother's songs reflected the same tensions that James Joyce articulated in the character of Stephen Daedalus in *A Portrait of the Artist as a Young Man*[69]—the pull of hearth and home, love and loyalty to the place (imagined or not) that shaped him, and on the other hand the push of a debilitating conservatism and the attraction of new places and opportunities.[70] After the Great Famine, Ireland became the land of the "bold tenant farmer" whose "careful opinions, cautious politics, orthodox religious beliefs (purged of any troublesome deviant notions), mercenary marriage settlements, unbendingly conservative outlook, and that most dynamic of all desires—the desire to better himself" had a marked influence on the social, political, and religious life of Ireland.[71] This was an authoritarian nation, inhospitable to women and poets, inconvenient desires and awkward truths. Joyce believed that he could not accomplish what he wished in such an Ireland.

Of course, Irish preoccupation with exile is much older than Joyce, my grandmother Margaret, and the Great Famine. "[T]he idea of exile has an etymological, cultural and psychic history in Ireland which can be traced back to the monastic traditions of early Irish Christianity with its attendant notions of exile as a type of martyrdom."[72] Celtic values of kinship and family, including love of place and community, persisted in the Celtic-Christian monastic era, from the fifth to the tenth centuries, such that penance for monks and nuns took the form of exile—inner exile as well as missionary activity outside of Ireland—for the sake of Christ, ultimately precipitating seventh and eighth century expansion on the Continent of Europe.[73] The anchoritic or reclusive state of the hermit, "one who has retired from the world," stems from the verb ἀναχωρέω, *anachōréō*, signifying "to withdraw"; the one who retires is someone who, for religious reasons, withdraws from secular society so as to be able to lead an intensely prayer-oriented, ascetic life.

There are other reasons why exile is an equivocal concept of the Irish. She who is away is no longer a part of ordinary existence; she is otherworldly and, as such, is of ambiguous character—someone who has taken on other ways and other languages, someone not quite rooted. Home, for the Irish, suggests a "fundamental belief in rootedness."[74] In this sense, exile is less an opportunity to cultivate "a state of estrangement"[75] from taken-for-granted beliefs and norms and more of a burden to be endured, like homelessness. Yet the very experience of being in exile involved entering a liminal zone in which one not only seeks out the familiar—those places where the rules, rituals, and narratives of home can be repeated—but also where one continues to encounter the new place from within the limits of one's own framework—that is, as a stranger.[76] The exile begins to appreciate how both the familiar and the strange—as reflected by cultures and in identities—are constructed rather than natural, in flux rather than fixed. As such, exiles are afforded "a double insight" into the meanings of relationships, institutions, cultural values, and political events, and into what it feels like and means to be interpellated by both.[77]

Teachers are guardians of the experience of exile that is education. Their role is not only to accompany children on their journey from the private to the public world, from the familiar to the strange, but to furnish conditions under which that journey can be a significant opportunity for self-knowledge and self-formation. To do so requires that the teacher herself embrace both the burden and the beauty that exile brings. Increasingly restricted to the necessary and the useful, teachers find themselves "groping in madness under a low sky,"[78] their capacity for cultivating students' responsiveness to that which is "outside subjectivity"—humanity, culture, the world—through reading, relationships, and events sidelined.[79] Under such circumstances, the double insight afforded by the exilic experience and the teacher as figurative or allegorical exile is lost; the "pain of invention" that often results in a mutually influential subjective and social reconstruction is refused.[80] Home becomes equated with "possession and entitlement with precedent, territory, language and longevity,"[81] a belief, which seems unconsciously to attest to the colonial formations which shape it; education becomes an imperialist project whereby the new is a mere restatement of the old. It is to those colonial entanglements I now turn.

Away as Betrayal

Jane Urquhart's novel features the assassination of Thomas D'Arcy McGee, a Fenian and participant in the 1848 rebellion in Ireland but who had left Ireland for the Americas.[82] The "Fenians" was an umbrella term for the Fenian Brotherhood and Irish Republican Brotherhood (IRB), fraternal organizations dedicated to the establishment of an independent Irish Republic in the nineteenth and early twentieth centuries—both in Ireland and the North America. With a substantial presence in North America, the Fenians had attempted an invasion of a British territory (Canada) in 1867; their failure was laid in large part at the feet of then Canadian Minister of Agriculture and Immigration D'Arcy McGee. McGee was seen to have traded the dream of an Irish republic for the dream of an independent Canadian nation. In Canadian nationalism, McGee seemed to see "the end of all forms of colonization and, thus, an example to be set also for Ireland."[83] Ironically, perhaps, McGee embraced a form of nationalism that reflects European sensibilities—a pan-Celtic vision of Canada. It is significant that Urquhart's novel is set at the time of the foundation of the Dominion of Canada. McGee's political views cost him his life; he was viewed by the Fenians as a traitor to the Irish national cause and was ultimately assassinated—the only political assassination ever to occur in Canada. The historical record is more complex than the one that the novelist addresses—Urquhart's Fenians are "fanatics"[84] still dreaming of Oisín, the poet of the Fianna and the last Celtic hero before the arrival of St. Patrick to Ireland.

For my grandfather, James, born in 1889, the Fenians were patriots and forefathers of the 1916 Easter Rebellion.[85] A lasting memory of my grandparents' home was a large, beautifully framed print of a scene within the General Post Office in Dublin during the 1916 Easter Rebellion. As a young child, I recall being taken up in his arms while he recounted the story of the Irish fight for independence from Britain. As he pointed toward the men I would later recognize as the architects of the revolution—Patrick Pearse,[86] James Connolly, Thomas

McDonagh, Joseph Plunkett, and Thomas Clarke—he invited me to tell him of whom they reminded me: didn't Connolly on the stretcher look a lot like Joseph, his brother, teacher, and *Teachtaí Dála* (member of Irish Free State government)? Didn't Pearse bear a strong resemblance to his brother, Richard, a member of the De La Salle Order of Christian Brothers and schoolmaster in South Africa? And so it went, as intimate family relations were interwoven with a nationalist, missionary narrative, and I was invited to contour my sense of who we were as a family from that singular historical event. It was a narrative that had been absorbed by the new Roman Catholic Free State with all that it entailed in terms of "obedience, family life, and separation from the non-Catholic Irish."[87]

For the Fenians and for my grandfather, Canada was British territory pure and simple. To emigrate was a form of betrayal, a kind of anti-nationalism (much as he viewed my brother's participation in British sports such as soccer and rugby), but to emigrate to any British dominion was an act of unforgiveable betrayal. Such sentiment was evident and echoed in the Proclamation of the Irish Republic, 1916, addressing only Ireland's "exiled children in America"[88] (note again the infantilization) whose function was to fund and assist the new Irish republic but not to question or interfere with its decisions. By referencing exclusively those who went to the United States of America, the Proclamation effectively disowned those "'children' overseas in the British dominions and colonies and those thousands, if not hundreds of thousands, resident in Britain itself."[89] In so doing, argues Ward, the Proclamation in effect erased the latter from the Irish extended family and rendered them outside the representative frames available to the authors of the Proclamation. While it is broadly recognized that the text registered "an all-inclusive generosity" and gestured towards all "who would lay an affective claim to Ireland—a stake in its future and a share in its past—rejects, dispossesses, and denies those whose existence complicates and transforms simplistic, essentialist, constructions of Irishness."[90]

It is perhaps fortunate for me that my grandfather, full of Fenian vengeance and nationalist triumphalism, had long passed before I settled in Canada (albeit like McGee, I too came the circuitous route via the United States). That said, James was a remnant of the British school system imposed on Ireland in the 1830s. He had lost the native tongue of his grandparents—Gaeilge—as the English language took hold of the Irish consciousness. It was not unlike that which Urquhart's Brian O'Malley, the schoolmaster, prophesized.

> And it's the end of us, he said, with them teaching our children. There will be none of us left, you understand, in the way that we know ourselves now. The old language will disappear …; it's what they want; … they can be … starved out, and they can be silenced; … they can be educated out….[91]

Of course, in addition to the school system, the Great Famine had hastened the decline of the Irish language, in part because it was the Gaeltacht, where the Irish language was strongest, that suffered most from famine and emigration. The strong farmers turned to English because it was the language of progress and of the future, "the passport to positions in the British Empire for their sons and daughters."[92]

In Urquhart's novel, colonization travels in the form of words and actions. Mary's son, Liam, transfers past sorrows of his Irish ancestors to the Indigenous peoples; he is only interested in building a future and has little interest in preserving or engaging the past. Betrayal takes the form of "cultural amnesia,"[93] as Liam asserts that this is "good land to cultivate and colonize,"[94] ultimately to the detriment of the Ojibway people, tenants of the land he sought. Although Liam chooses survival over revenge, it means that he embodies the attitude and the language of the colonizer. His sister, Eileen, (who inadvertently gets caught up in the assassination of D'Arcy McGee) cognizant of what her brother is about, reminds him:

> The English took the land from the Indians same as they took it from the Irish. Then they just starve everybody out…. So you never would have had it in the first place if the English hadn't stolen it … and if they hadn't stolen Ireland.[95]

Nonetheless, Liam ploughs onward, seeking "the forward momentum of change and growth … the axe in the flesh of the tree and the blade breaking open new soil."[96] Liam becomes a colonizer of stolen lands and "the fossilized narratives of ancient migrations are crushed into powder" in his limestone quarry.[97] He had learned from the best. "Imperialism after all is a cooperative venture. Both the master and the slave participate in it, and both grew up in it, albeit unequally."[98] Both know it well.

Tied to the project of mass schooling and developed as part of the production of the nation state, it is almost impossible to think about teacher education outside of a state enclosure. Historically, teacher education has promoted nationalism as a culture of belonging, however, seeking clear and conclusive definitions of Canadianness or Irish-ness—multiculturalism and Roman Catholicism, respectively. As a result, democratic ideas of civilization, society, and community, which are all dependent on our ability to imagine the other—the one who is not close—are expelled to the margins.[99] Multicultural (teacher) education, for example, emphasizes cultural difference as a source of belonging, but it ignores the critical importance of race in Canada.[100] Tensions that exist between Aboriginal and immigrant societies—Francophones and Anglophones complicit in colonial domination of First Peoples—are shrouded within an ahistorical discourse of compromise. Appreciating the temporal, historical, and political character of what we do in teacher education provokes the need for "a particularistic social theory" or a grounded, critical view of the relations among politics, culture, language, and teacher education in particular places.[101] Like Urquhart's character Liam, teacher educators and student teachers need to realize that we stand not only in relation to white peoples in Canada but also in relation to Indigenous peoples and their lands.[102]

Civic Particularity: Teacher Education in Translation

Now let me return to the questions with which I began my exploration: What is revealed about the act of translation across generations and societies in the foregoing allegorical montage of historical, literary, and autobiographical fragments? What does it mean for teacher education? Who am I in translation?

The juxtaposition of history, literature, and biography reveals the essence of "translatability," that "translation serves not the original, but the liberation and release of its potential."[103] By reopening history in the present, we can begin to appreciate how selves in all their civic particularity are made and can be remade in the present. Even the new(comer) is old, constituted by the time and place in which she has grown. In our teaching and living we shape a past for ourselves, a version of history with which we grow comfortable and feel safe. Translation is multiple and dissipative: Elements of the original are left behind while others are recast or lost altogether. The student teacher's question led me to confront the traditions—"the poetic—songs, myths, folklore, a dying language—and the political—'old sorrows,' independence, and Fenian revenge"[104] with which I grew up and from which, consciously and unconsciously, I draw a sense of self and meaning in my everyday life. Perhaps she sensed in my urgency to underscore and rectify social injustice the earnest politics of my grandfather and the difficulties that arise when a teacher tries to impose the new rather than create the conditions for its emergence. One of those conditions is that teacher educators "grapple with the challenges and opportunities that their own identities present" because we all—teacher educators and student-teachers alike—bring "differently racialized collective histories of colonization" that require addressing and redressing.[105] As such, the teacher education classroom is a place of translation—where intimate, particular histories, once shared, can exceed their prior frameworks and call for different readings of subject, context, and historical moment—our civic particularity.

Casting teacher education as a translational practice underscores its potential role in fostering a double consciousness. Being in translation can be a sublime experience in that it entails unresolved contradictory feelings of pleasure and pain, joy and anxiety, exhilaration and despair. While we may wish to preserve old cultural values and identities in new places—as was the case of the Irish during the forced migration of the 1840s—we do have a choice of whether we "support misguided attempts to translate European culture onto the new world (and thereby neutralise the sublime) or whether by stressing the poetic and associative aspect of language to support the efforts of sublime deterritorialization."[106] In this, Urquhart gestures toward a rich curriculum for teacher education in which disjunctions between cultures, identities, and landscapes are foregrounded. The transformative power of myth symbolizes an embrace of disjunction and dislocation: that on being claimed a person lives in this world and in the Otherworld. "I am here but I am not here," says Mary.[107] The young *Oisín* travels to *Tír na nÓg*, the Land of Eternal Youth, only to become an old man on his return to Ireland. Myth invites simultaneous awareness of the ordinary world and the one that underpins it; it suggests the possibility of living at "the boundary of consciousness,"[108] honouring the traces of those who are no longer present while re-interpreting and re-signifying their intellectual and spiritual legacies in the present. Recall Pinar's allegory as montage as a source of double consciousness—an appropriate framework for teacher education, in my view.

Allegory embodies translation as a creative process of rethinking, relocating an object from its original site of discourse, and provoking us to consider the questions and understandings that become possible "when one sees A in terms of B, when one transports A and lets it operate in the land of B."[109] For me, this curriculum meant Irish mythology rekindled on Objibway territory; W. B. Yeats's "Stolen Child" read in light of the cultural genocide of Indigenous peoples in Canada; Irish republicanism reconsidered in the context of Celtic pan-Canadianism and its exclusions. Such allegorical juxtapositions introduce new perspectives while disrupting the familiarity of childhood texts and textures of feeling. Embracing the potential of translation as "a transformation and renewal of something living"[110] enables us to avoid imposition and instead enter a space of openness to meanings not yet considered. Refusing to lay claim to some absolute Truth, translation reminds us that strict and final interpretation would be undesirable even if it were possible.

The embrace of teacher education as a translational practice, therefore, entails due humility. This relates to the student teacher's initial gesture toward the stolen geographies of Canada and her concern that I, as a stranger, could not help her come to terms with that difficult inheritance. I would now argue, not unlike Urquhart in the novel *Away*, that my students and I must rise above geographies[111] and begin to appreciate that social issues are not confined within historical and national boundaries nor restricted in importance to those immediately affected. If we are to carry on together across the differences encountered in the teacher education classroom, and beyond, we must engage questions of history and place, rendering the voices of our respective traditions present, "not to entomb either the past or the present, but to give them life together in a place common to both in memory"[112] where they might enable our living and thinking. The father, Brian, passes this double inheritance through Eileen, the first Canadian-born of the O'Malley children. She passes on those stories to Esther O'Malley Robertson, the narrator of the novel who whispers the story of her lineage while the fate of her homestead and the history of Indigenous ancestors are being sealed by an encroaching limestone quarry. "[W]ho we are is revealed in the narratives we tell of ourselves and of our world shared with others."[113] Indeed, Urquhart assigns the power of narration to women. Urquhart reminds her readers of women's capacity to appreciate and embrace disjunction—the here and not here—and the strengths (forms of thought beyond conventional rationality) gleaned from doing so. Women, unique and extreme, she seems to be saying, and I would add teachers, evoke vision and possibility.

Narrating past events and relations in the context of teacher education, writes Ng-A-Fook, can help us "to understand that there is a longer historical trajectory to what might feel totally new in a one-off intercultural and … political event."[114] There is little doubt that knowledge of history is key to forming a political relationship with oneself and to cultivating responsiveness[115] in the present. Appreciating how my positioning as subject to and subject of British imperialism bears upon even the most transient encounters in the Canadian classroom is important. Such historical sensibility can contribute to a politics of acknowledgement, writes Patchen Markell, meaning an appreciation of one's basic ontological condition as limited "in the face of an unpredictable and contingent future" and the ever present risk of misunderstanding, hostility, and conflict that characterizes life among others past and present.[116] While contingency and plurality are sources of vulnerability and limitation, acknowledgement ironically enables our responsiveness to a world we have not made; it does so by reminding us that we are all tenants of time and place—that is complicit and responsible—while tempering our desire to set the world right once and for all. Teaching for the sake of social justice, as I was attempting to do all those years ago, requires such historical and ontological insight.

Who am I in this place? I am: woman, exile, and settler; but I succumb to none of these positionings. As an Irish teacher educator in Canada, I am in ongoing translation: "Not lost"… "just not found yet."[117]

Who are you?

Notes

1. Ricciardi, "*Away* and the Meaning of Colonization," 66.
2. Urquhart, *Away*. As a newcomer to Canada almost twenty-five years ago, I looked to literature to help me understand this vast place. It was Urquhart's writing about the Irish in Canada that challenged me, as did my student teacher, to appreciate the importance of unravelling and understanding the link between my Irish past and my Canadian present.
3. Levinson, "Teaching in the Midst of Belatedness."
4. Truth and Reconciliation Commission of Canada, *Honoring the Truth*, vi.
5. Arendt, "Introduction." See also Natasha Levinson's (1997) discussion of the pariah and parvenu in educational contexts ("Teaching in the Midst of Belatedness") and Seyla Benhabib's (1995) essay "The Pariah and Her Shadow."
6. Kohn, "Introduction." *Between Past and Future: Eight Exercises in Political Thought*, xiii.
7. Benhabib, *The Reluctant Modernism of Hannah Arendt*.
8. Benhabib, 92.
9. Ferri, "Introduction," 10.
10. Arendt, "Introduction," 51.
11. Benhabib, *Reluctant Modernism*, 92.
12. Arendt, "Introduction."
13. Benhabib, *Reluctant Modernism*, 92.
14. Benhabib, 92.
15. Rauch, *The Hieroglyph of Tradition*, 123.
16. Rauch, 123.
17. Benjamin, *Illuminations*, 139.
18. Benjamin, 143.
19. Pinar, *What Is Curriculum Theory?*, 49.
20. Pinar, 50.
21. Pinar, 50.
22. Pinar, 50.
23. Pinar, 54.
24. Rauch, *The Hieroglyph of Tradition*, 208.
25. Pinar, *What Is Curriculum Theory?*
26. Pinar, 61.
27. Bal, *Travelling Concepts*, 64.
28. Bal, 67.
29. Knott, *Unlearning with Hannah Arendt*, 32.
30. Kearney, *Strangers, Gods and Monsters*.

31 Ferri, "Introduction."
32 Ricciardi, "*Away* and the Meaning of Colonization," 66.
33 Ricciardi, 67.
34 Urqhuart, *Away*, 207.
35 Urqhuart, 355.
36 Ricciardi, "*Away* and the Meaning of Colonization," 72.
37 Boyd, "Away," 173.
38 Urquhart, *Away*, 11.
39 Urquhart, 12.
40 Urquhart, 15.
41 Urquhart, 22.
42 Urquhart, 26.
43 Urquhart, 48.
44 Urquhart, 62.
45 Urquhart, 75.
46 Urquhart, 75.
47 Urquhart, 184.
48 Ricciardi, "*Away* and the Meaning of Colonization," 73.
49 Urquhart, *Away*, 184.
50 Urquhart, 184.
51 Edward Burne-Jones (1833–1898) was a British artist associated with the Pre-Raphaelite movement.
52 Yeats, "Stolen Child."
53 Ball, "The Teacher's Soul."
54 Britzman, *Practice Makes Practice*, 25.
55 Freedman, "Who Will Care for Our Children," 7.
56 Taubman, *Teaching by Numbers*.
57 Phelan, "Between Judgment and Constraint: Understanding Autonomy in the Professional Lives of Teachers."
58 Bataille, *Eroticism*.
59 Orlie, "Forgiving Trespasses, Promising Futures," 346.
60 Ó Corráin, "The Great Famine, 1845–9."
61 Ó Corráin, 59.
62 Ó Corráin, 80.
63 Ó Corráin, 81.
64 Ó Corráin, 81.
65 Ó Corráin, 82.
66 Ward, *Exile, Emigration and Irish Writing*, 239.
67 French, "The Mountains of Mourne."
68 French.
69 Joyce, *Portrait of an Artist*.
70 Ward, *Exile, Emigration and Irish Writing*.
71 Ó Corráin, "The Great Famine, 1845–9," 84.

72   Ward, *Exile, Emigration and Irish Writing*, 235.
73   van Liere, *An Introduction to the Medieval Bible.*
74   Ward, *Exile, Emigration and Irish Writing*, 233.
75   Pinar, *Bildung*, 30.
76   Steinbock, *Home and Beyond*, 180.
77   Britzman, *Practice Makes Practice,* Revised Edition, 232.
78   Kavanagh, "Nineteen Fifty-Four."
79   Pinar, *"Bildung,"* 26.
80   Wang, *Stranger,* 135.
81   Ward, *Exile, Emigration and Irish Writing*, 233.
82   Wilson, *Thomas D'Arcy McGee*, Vols. I, II.
83   Ricciardi, *"Away* and the Meaning of Colonization," 68.
84   Urquhart, *Away,* 342.
85   The Easter Rebellion took place in Dublin, Ireland, between Monday, 24 April, and Sunday, 29 April 1916. It was an uprising against British rule in Ireland. Though defeated by the British, the event had the effect of making the majority of Irish people in favour of an independent Irish republic.
86   I would learn many years later that many of the leaders of the 1916 Rising were poets; Patrick Pearse is one example.
87   Ward, *Exile, Emigration and Irish Writing*, 234. The social policies that came to frame the Irish Free State were misogynist and served to punish women who were deemed errant (e.g., becoming pregnant outside of wedlock) or susceptible to becoming so (e.g., wilful); it is only recently that light has been shed on social institutions such as the mother and baby homes, industrial schools, the Magdalen laundries, and asylums in which women were incarcerated for decades and their children stolen and sold both at home and away. See Dan Barry's chilling article, "Exile, Emigration and Irish Writing."
88   Ward, 234.
89   Ward, 234.
90   Ward, 233.
91   Urquhart, *Away,* 73–74.
92   Ó Corráin, "The Great Famine, 1845–9," 83.
93   Smart, "Weighing the Claims of Memory," 67.
94   Urquhart, *Away,* 279.
95   Urquhart, 279.
96   Urquhart, 279.
97   Urquhart, 356.
98   Said, *Nationalism, Colonialism, and Literature,* 74.
99   Ralston Saul, *Collapse of Globalism.*
100 Schnick and Denis, "Troubling Nationalist Discourses."
101 Kincheloe and Pinar, "Introduction," 5.

102 Haig-Brown, "Decolonizing Diaspora."
103 Benjamin, *Illuminations*, 80.
104 Ricciardi, "*Away* and the Meaning of Colonization," 72.
105 Hare, "Reconciliation, 30."
106 Goldman, "Translating the Sublime," 86.
107 Urquhart, *Away*, 57.
108 Frye, *Anatomy of Criticism*.
109 Ruitenberg, "Distance and Defamiliarisation," 429.
110 Benjamin, *Illuminations*, 73.
111 Compton, "Romancing the Landscape."
112 Carruthers, *The Book of Memory*, 260.
113 Benhabib, *Reluctant Modernism*, 92.
114 Ng-A-Fook, "Autobiography," 142.
115 Schiff, *Burdens of Political Responsibility*, 2014.
116 Markell, *Bound by Recognition*, 38.
117 Atwood, "A Place: Fragments," 76.

Bibliography

Arendt, Hannah, ed. "Introduction." In *Illuminations*, translated by Herbert Zohn, 1–54. New York, NY: Schocken Books, 1969.

Atwood, Margaret. "A Place: Fragments." *The Circle Game*. Toronto, ON: House of Anansi Press Limited, 1998.

Bal, Mieke. *Travelling Concepts in the Humanities: A Rough Guide*. Toronto, ON: University of Toronto Press, 2002.

Ball, Stephen. "The Teacher's Soul and the Terrors of Performativity." *Journal of Education Policy* 18, no. 2 (2003): 215–228.

Bataille, George. *Eroticism*. San Francisco, CA: City Lights, 1986.

Benhabib, Seyla. "The Pariah and Her Shadow: Hannah Arendt's Biography of Rahel Varnhagen." *Feminist Interpretations of Hannah Arendt*, edited by Bonnie Honig, 83–104. University Park, PA: The Pennsylvania State University Press, 1995.

——. *The Reluctant Modernism of Hannah Arendt*. Lanham, MD: Rowman & Littlefield Publishers Inc., 2003.

Benjamin, Walter. *Illuminations*, edited by Hannah Arendt and translated by Herbert Zohn. New York, NY: Schocken Books, 1969 (original work published 1923).

Boyd, Colin. "*Away*." *The Canadian Encyclopedia*, edited by James H. Marsh, 173. Toronto, ON: McClelland & Stewart, Inc., 2000.

Britzman, Deborah. *Practice Makes Practice: A Critical Ethnography of Learning to Teach*. New York, NY: SUNY Press, 1991.

———. *Practice Makes Practice: A Critical Ethnography of Learning to Teach.* Revised Edition. New York, NY: SUNY Press, 2003.

Carruthers, Margaret. *The Book of Memory: A Study of Memory in Medieval Culture.* Cambridge, UK: Cambridge University Press, 1990.

Compton, Anne. "Romancing the Landscape." *Jane Urquhart: Essays on Her Works,* edited by Laura Ferri, 114–143. Toronto, ON: Guernica, 2005.

Ferri, Laura. "Introduction." In *Jane Urquhart: Essays on Her Works,* edited by Laura Ferri, 9–14. Toronto, ON: Guernica, 2005.

French, Percy. "The Mountains of Mourne." LyricsFreak. Accessed June 28, 2018 at http://www.lyricsfreak.com/p/percy+french/the+mountains+of+mourne_20662712.html

Freedman, Sarah. "Who Will Care for Our Children? Removing Nurturance from the Teaching Profession." *Democratic Schools* (Fall 1987): 7–27.

Frye, Northrop. *Anatomy of Criticism: Four Essays.* Princeton, NJ: Princeton University Press, 1957.

Goldman, Marlene. "Translating the Sublime." In *Jane Urquhart: Essays on Her Works,* edited by Laura Ferri, 83–114. Toronto, ON: Guernica, 2005.

Haig-Brown, Cecilia. "Decolonizing Diaspora: Whose Traditional Land Are We on?" *Cultural and Pedagogical Inquiry,* 1, no.1 (2009): 4–21.

Hare, Jan. "Reconciliation in Teacher Education: Hope or Hype?" In *Reconceptualizing Teacher Education Worldwide: A Canadian Contribution to a Global Challenge,* edited by Anne M. Phelan, William F. Pinar, Nicholas Ng-A-Fook, and Ruth Kane. Ottawa, ON: University of Ottawa Press, forthcoming.

Joyce, James. *Portrait of an Artist as a Young Man.* New York, NY: B. W. Huebsch, 1916.

Kavanagh, Patrick. "Nineteen Fifty-Four." In *Patrick Kavanagh: Selected Poems,* edited by Antoinette Quinn, 118. London, UK: Penquin, 1996.

Kearney, Richard. *Strangers, Gods and Monsters.* New York, NY: Routledge Press, 2003.

Kincheloe, Joseph L., and William F. Pinar. "Introduction." In *Curriculum as Social Psychoanalysis of Place,* 1–23. New York, NY: SUNY Press. 1991.

Knott, Marie Luise. *Unlearning with Hannah Arendt.* Translated by D. Dollenmayer. New York, NY: Other Press, 2015.

Kohn, Jerome. "Introduction." In *Between Past and Future: Eight Exercises in Political Thought,* vii–xxii. New York, NY: Penguin, 2006.

Levinson, Natasha. "Teaching in the Midst of Belatedness: The Paradox of Natality in Hannah Arendt's Educational Thought." *Educational Theory* 47, no. 4 (1997): 435–451.

Markell, Patchen. *Bound by Recognition.* Princeton, NY: Princeton University Press, 2003.

Ng-A-Fook, N. "Autobiography, Intellectual Topographies, and Teacher Education." In *Autobiography and Teacher Development in China:*

Subjectivity and Culture in Curriculum Reform, edited by Zhang Hua and William F. Pinar, 121–150. New York, NY: Palgrave Macmillan, 2015.

Ó'Corráin, Donnchadh. "The Great Famine, 1845–9." In *Ireland 1815–1870: Emancipation, Famine and Religion*, edited by Donnchadh Ó'Corráin and Tomás O'Riordan, 58–84. Dublin, IR: Four Courts Press, 2011.

Orlie, Melissa A. "Forgiving Trespasses, Promising Futures." In *Feminist Interpretations of Hannah Arendt*, edited by Bonnie Honig, 337–356. University Park, PA: Pennsylvania State University Press, 1994.

Phelan, Anne M. "Between Judgment and Constraint: Understanding Autonomy in the Professional Lives of Teachers." In *Key Notes in Teacher Education: CATE Invited Addresses 2004–2008*, Volume 1, edited by Alice Pitt, 83–102. 2009. Accessed June 28, 2018 at http://cate-acfe.ca/wp-content/uploads/2019/05/PolygraphVol1.pdf.

Pinar, William F. "*Bildung* and the Internationalization of Curriculum Studies." In *International Conversations on Curriculum Studies*, edited by E. Ropo and T. Autio, 23–41. Dordrecht, NL: Sense Publishers, 2009.

———. *The Character of Curriculum Studies*. New York, NY: Palgrave Macmillan, 2011.

———. *What Is Curriculum Theory?* 2nd ed. New York, NY: Routledge, 2012.

———. *The Worldliness of Cosmopolitan Education: Passionate Lives in Public Service*. New York, NY: Routledge, 2009.

Ralston Saul, John. *The Collapse of Globalism: And the Reinvention of the World*. Toronto, ON: Viking Press, 2005.

Rauch, Angelika. *The Hieroglyph of Tradition: Freud, Benjamin, Gadamer, Novalis, Kant*. Cranbury, NJ: Associated University Presses, 2000.

Ricciardi, Caterina. "*Away* and the Meaning of Colonization." In *Jane Urquhart: Essays on Her Works*, edited by Laura Ferri, 65–77. Toronto, ON: Guernica, 2005.

Ruitenberg, Claudia. "Distance and Defamiliarisation: Translation as Philosophical Method." *Journal of Philosophy of Education* 43, no. 3 (2009): 421–435.

Said, Edward. *Nationalism, Colonialism, and Literature*. Minneapolis, MN: University of Minnesota Press, 1990.

Schiff, Jade. L. *Burdens of Political Responsibility: Narrative and Cultivation of Responsiveness*. Cambridge, UK: Cambridge University Press, 2014.

Schick, Carol, and Verna St. Denis. "Troubling National Discourses in Anti-Racist Curricular Planning." *Canadian Journal of Education*, 28, no. 3 (2005): 295–317.

Smart, Patricia. "Weighing the Claims of Memory: The Poetry and Politics of the Irish-Canadian Experience in Jane Urquhart's *Away*." *International Journal of Canadian Studies* 10 (Fall 1994): 63–70.

Steinbock, Anthony J. *Home and Beyond: Generative Phenomenology after Husserl*. Evanston, IL: Northwestern University Press, 1995.

Taubman, Peter Maas. *Teaching by Numbers: Deconstructing the Discourse of Standards and Accountability in Education*. New York, NY: Routledge, 2009.

Truth and Reconciliation Commission of Canada. *Truth and Reconciliation Commission of Canada: Honoring the Truth, Reconciling the Future: Summary of the Final Report of the Truth and Reconciliation Commission of Canada*. Accessed June 28, 2018 at http://nctr.ca/reports.php.

Urquhart, Jane. *Away*. Toronto, ON: McClelland and Stewart, 1993.

van Liere, Franciscus A. *An Introduction to the Medieval Bible*. Cambridge, UK: Cambridge University Press, 2014.

Wang, Hongyu. *The Call from the Stranger on a Journey Home: Curriculum in a Third Space*. New York, NY: Peter Lang, 2004.

Ward, Patrick. *Exile, Emigration and Irish Writing*. Dublin, IR: Irish Academic Press, 2002.

Wilson, David. A. *Thomas D'Arcy McGee, Volume I: Passion, Reason, and Politics, 1825–1857*. Montreal, QC and Kingston, ON: McGill-Queen's University Press, 2008.

———. *Thomas D'Arcy McGee, Volume II: The Extreme Moderate, 1857–1868*. Montreal, QC and Kingston, ON: McGill-Queen's University Press, 2011.

Yeats, W. B. *The Collected Poems of W. B. Yeats*. London, UK: Macmillan, 1933.

CHAPTER 6

From Africa to Teacher Education in Ontario[1]

Phyllis Dalley

I organized a panel discussion, in February 2017, on the socio-professional inclusion of Francophone immigrants from sub-Saharan Africa, focusing on those who were living in French communities in Alberta, Ontario, and New Brunswick. The discussion detailed the particular difficulties of inclusion for these immigrants within the professions (education, nursing, medicine, management, engineering, and the like). Likewise, at the University of Ottawa, other professional faculties or departments have had experiences similar to those I chronicle here. The purpose of this chapter is to bring the conversation about these painful struggles into the open: Whisperings of these experiences can be heard on campus, but they are not openly broached. Yet the practice of inclusion requires that those of us in positions of power have the courage to voice the inequalities that silence others. I have come to realize that while I strive for inclusion, I participate in the silencing of some students. I "write to right"[2] that wrong and to look to ways to improve inclusive practices in teacher education.

As a professor in the French Teacher Education program (*Programme de Formation à l'enseignement,* hitherto *Formation)* at the University of Ottawa, I have struggled with ways to undo the monochromatic mosaic that is my classroom: students from North Africa, Sub-Saharan Africa, Ontario, Quebec, and Haiti form distinct groups in class. I have found it challenging to break this pattern. As director of the same program, I have found my office to be a space of tension between the needs and expectations of schools and those of our immigrant and new Canadian students.[3] I have felt caught in this tension as I attempt to practice inclusion and to save practicum placements.

In this chapter, I grapple with the tension between inclusion and conformity to practices-already-there through the storying of two of the program's teaching-practicum-linked practices. Although I will report on things said by teacher candidates, professors, and coordinators, this telling is my own. The research problem at which I arrive at the end of the chapter is shaped by my autobiographical narration. "This autobiographical narrative inquiry that [I] engage in allows [me] to shape [my] research puzzle.... [This] autobiographical narrative inquiry is an inquiry starting point."[4] In fact, this chapter marks the first step of my reflective journey.[5] In the following sections of this chapter, I will define "inclusion"[6] as an ideal to be striven for and interpret or retell my story through that prism. But first I offer a word on the institutional and linguistic context in which I work.

Institutional and Linguistic Context

The University of Ottawa houses two teacher education programs: one in French and one in English. The French program, *Formation à l'enseignement*, prepares teacher candidates for employment in the twelve French language school boards of the province of Ontario, whereas its English counterpart, Teacher Education, does the same for the English language school boards of Ontario. While the English program is only offered on campus in Ottawa, *Formation* is offered online and on three physical campuses: Ottawa, Toronto, and Windsor. Although this article highlights issues related to *Formation* in general, it draws exclusively from events experienced at the Ottawa campus, where my work life unfolds. My knowledge of happenings on other campuses is built through yearly on-site visits and weekly meetings with their coordinators. My familiarity with the Ottawa campus is deeper, built as it is upon daily interactions with students, professors, practicum coordinators, and other staff members. I will clarify my directorship role and responsibilities in the methodology section of this chapter.

In 2015, the duration of both French and English teacher education programs in all of the province of Ontario was doubled, from two to four trimesters. Although this change removed pressure from the English language school system, with its overabundance of certified teachers, it brought the teacher shortage experienced by the French system to a crisis level: More and more individuals teach with a Letter of Permission,[7] and it has become increasingly difficult for teachers to leave their classrooms for professional development or for personal reasons. For example, an invitation to our partner French language school boards to allow twenty teachers to participate in a day-long conference on equity was refused because the participating teachers would need to be replaced in class by colleagues willing to give up their preparation time. A similar invitation by my English counterpart was accepted to varying degrees by English language school boards. Furthermore, as director of *Formation* over the past three years, I have felt growing pressure to allow teacher candidates to fill long-term supply teacher positions concurrently with their practicum, a practice that would counter our program's terms of accreditation with the Ontario College of Teachers.[8] This practice would also privilege some of our students for permanent employment over others: principals only request teacher candidates of whom they have previous knowledge, either as students in their schools or as occasional supply teachers. Hence, as a long-term contract is a precursor to permanent employment in Ontario, those candidates already privileged by their knowledge of the culture of schooling in Ontario would be further privileged. Finally, pressure is also felt to increase the number of teacher candidates accepted into *Formation*.

As our student numbers increase, so too does the expectation that practicing teachers, with as little as two years' classroom experience, will become associate teachers and mentor a teacher candidate during an eight-week practicum in their classrooms. Considering that the majority of our associate teachers are Canadian-born and at least 50 percent of our teacher candidates are immigrants or new Canadians, it follows that the mentoring role of the associate teacher often takes on an important intercultural dimension. Questions of race have also come to the fore: In 2018, three of our over two hundred Black student teachers have suggested that their White associate teacher ended their practicum for racial reasons, and one student has initiated an official complaint with the teachers' union against his associate teacher. Half of our students are Black, and the great majority of associate teachers are White. Furthermore, associate teachers generally present as female while our immigrant and new Canadian candidates are often older than their associate teachers and generally present as male.[9] Just as some teacher candidates accuse associate teachers of racism, a perceived refusal on the part of a Black immigrant or new Canadian male student teachers to follow a female associate teacher's instructions is likened to arrogance or sexism by faculty advisors and associate teachers.

Linguistically, our associate teachers and teacher candidates are also diverse: All speak French, but they speak different varieties of that language, and have varying cultural language practices—for example, deciding when it is appropriate to take a turn in conversation or determining what physical distance to maintain with one's interlocutor. Their relationship with the French language also varies—for example, deciding whether French is a first, second, or third language; a language of identity; a language of colonization; or a high or low status language. The following stories point to how these differences follow the same lines as those that separate my classes into place-of-origin groupings.

As part of the *Formation* admissions process, candidates must write a French-language proficiency examination. In one of my classes, a student from Quebec mentioned that this exam was very easy, to which I responded that this might not be a welcomed comment by the 80 percent of her colleagues who received only a partial pass on the test. These students must successfully complete a French refresher class with a grade of 80 percent to obtain their diploma.[10] From the same class at the end of term, a student from Africa exclaimed that he had understood that Québécois French is not bad French, it is simply a different French from the one he speaks. In schools, teacher candidates from African countries are told that they need to adapt their vocabulary or simplify their language to be understood by the children. In one case, a school board superintendent reported to me that he had received complaints from parents because their children could not understand the French spoken by our candidates from Africa. Where what is called Franco-Ontarian French is often judged as anglicised, the criticism of African French is that it is too elaborate, almost too French, and too accented for Franco-Ontarian children in public education. The variety known as Québécois French is often marked as Canadian Standard French, but some nonetheless view it as deficient. The underlying language ideology is that there is only one right way to speak and write French. Hence, relations between associate teachers and teacher candidates and among students in university classes are layered in gendered, cultural, racial, linguistic, aged, and geographical complexity.

Professors and the director of *Formation* are also implicated in these relations, and any one of these layers could be at the centre of a discussion on inclusive practices in teacher education. I have chosen to speak of the socio-professional inclusion of our immigrant and new Canadian students since, during my term as director, it is their inclusion and exclusion that has been acted upon the most explicitly: Their inclusion was the impetus for the creation of one of our practicum linked practices, and sixty[11] of these students saw their first practicum cancelled either the day before or within a week of its beginning. In Gumperz's terms, practicum can therefore be understood as an intercultural "key situation" in which issues at stake (passing practicum, gaining permanent employment, social status, and so on) increase the negative effect of differences in linguistic practices such as those mentioned above;[12] these differences become the basis on which speakers are included or excluded. Our immigrant and new Canadian students' exclusion was foregrounded by the cancellation of their practicum.

Within this complex situation, I have become aware of a discourse on the need to protect and need to behave. Our practicum office is currently unable to place all teacher candidates before the slated beginning of practicum, and an associate teacher who chooses not to accept other candidates after a reportedly difficult or bad experience is seen as a lost placement. Hence, during their pre-practicum seminar, students are told that they are to behave as visitors while in their respective associate teachers' classrooms. As will become clear in later sections of this chapter, I have found myself wishing that students would just keep quiet and do as they are told so that I may have time to act upon the broader situation. This wishing has, at times, become coercive action, an act of assimilation.

Immigrant and New Canadian Students

Approximately 50 percent of students at *Formation*'s Ottawa campus have completed their initial bachelor's degree in Canada and 50 percent in other countries. It is on the basis of this information that I have characterized students as either Canadian born or Immigrant/New Canadian in this chapter. Although it would be helpful to be able to compare and contrast these groups in order to detect patterns of success in the University and professional realms, it is impossible to give more accurate details about the makeup of our student body because the University does not keep such statistics, and an empirical study of our demographics has not been carried out. This section can therefore only partially address a group that is too often taken to be homogeneous.

While some have had previous careers, Canadian-born teacher candidates are generally in their early twenties, having transitioned directly from high school to university and on to *Formation*. The opposite is true of our African- and Haitian-born students. Most arrived in Canada as adults with professional degrees and are pursuing teacher education as part of their pathway into Canadian society. Thus, they have knowledge of the Ontario school system either through their children or some form of volunteer or temporary work, or they have no knowledge of it at all. Their past professional certification is normally not recognized in Canada or is hard to ascertain due to difficulties in obtaining original documents from their degree or certificate granting institutions. Added to that, according to the faculty's undergraduate secretariat, prospective candidates, having received their teacher education in other countries, often lack the prerequisites necessary to teach at the high school level in Ontario, namely with respect to having received sufficient undergraduate credit in two teachable subjects. As a result, candidates wishing to teach in high school are redirected toward the primary or junior grades or, if they have credit for one teachable subject, the junior and intermediate grades. These institutional constraints place candidates with little experience or desire to work with younger children at a higher risk of experiencing difficulties during their practicum.

Indeed, while African and Haitian students are generally successful in university classes, transition into practicum is more difficult. To address this issue, a series of transformative workshops were developed by Professor Claire Duchesne in 2008 to help immigrant and new Canadian teacher candidates build their understanding of Franco-Ontarian school culture.[13] It had been found that teacher candidates' conceptions of teaching were markedly different from those valued at the faculty.

> Les conceptions de l'enseignement centré sur l'enseignant et sur les contenus d'apprentissage construites par ces étudiants immigrants peuvent devenir problématiques lors du stage en milieu scolaire dans la mesure où le modèle d'enseignement valorisé à l'université et pratiqué dans les écoles de la province est essentiellement centré sur l'élève et sur le développement de ses processus d'apprentissage. (Immigrant students held conceptualizations of

teaching as centred on the teacher and on subject matter that could be problematic during a school-based practicum, in that the model of teaching practice put forward by the university and practised in the province's schools was centred essentially on the students and the development of their learning processes).[14]

Duchesne reported[15] that the candidates felt the workshop objectives had been met but also noted that some workshop participants went on to fail their practicum. Furthermore, these workshops were tied to direct funding by the Ministry of Education and were ultimately dropped when the funding was no longer available. It is therefore clear, both from the standpoint of this experience and by the definition of inclusion proposed in the next section, that *Formation* must look inward to its own practices to identify ways to include a response to the needs of all our students in our everyday practices. Add-ons seem more likely to derive from a view to assimilate or to integrate into a pre-existing mode of being a teacher candidate whereas inclusion requires that the program director, the professorial, and administrative bodies accept the responsibility to change our practices and programmatic structures to ensure the construction of a space of and for all. As will be made clear, such a change must take into account the needs of associate teachers who welcome our students into their classroom and who are expected to mentor them in the practice of teaching during a practicum.

In what follows, I explore two current practices in *Formation* that directly impact immigrants and new Canadians experiencing the greatest difficulties during their teacher education program: a school integration practicum (*Stage d'insertion scolaire* or SIS) and a professional ethics committee. The SIS is more akin to an inclusive practice than is the Professional Ethics Committee.

Thinking about Inclusion

In this chapter, I take inclusion to be a process by which a new discursive space is constructed by differently positioned groups or individuals within specific structures of power. This definition is drawn from a framework developed in 2014, on the basis of data I had collected since 1995, through different research projects at different times and in different Francophone or Acadian communities of Canada. The impetus for the creation of this framework was the growing polysemy of the term "inclusion" in educational policy and practice. In a final analysis, I proposed the following diagram (Figure 1) to illustrate the differences between assimilation, integration, and inclusion.

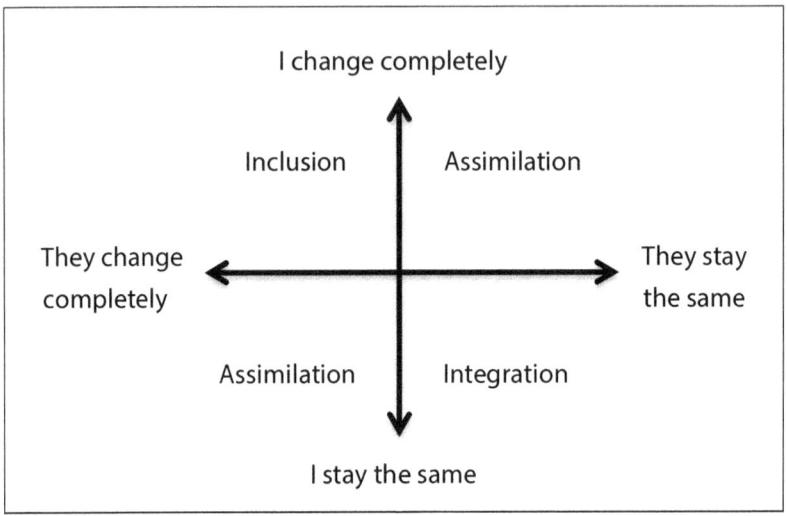

Figure 1: Inclusion as a change process. Translated from Dalley 2014.

Within this framework, "I" signifies the person or group of persons in a position of greater power, and "they" the person or group in a position of lesser power. Assimilation was chosen as a key term due to its place within French Canadian discourse: to assimilate is to stop speaking French in favour of English. Assimilation can happen at an individual or at a generational level, and much has been done both within the research community and the educational community to identify ways to counter it; the vitality of French in Canada is at stake. My intention at the time had been to point to ways in which, as Francophones, our desire to fend off assimilation has led to assimilative practices of our own.[16] Assimilation is implicated in relations of power, as it is a process by which *I* use either symbolic or physical power to coerce *them* into becoming like *me*. Should *they* be unable or unwilling to assimilate, *they* are excluded. Assimilation, then, is a homogenizing force.

On the other hand, integration can be seen as a neutral process, as the host society is accepting of the differences others bring. Indeed, these differences can be the source of celebrations and festivals. In Canada, the mosaic is an emblematic representation of integration, where all cultural groups are seen to be equal partners in its creation. Yet, in practice, an English *I* is, in most provinces of Canada, the host community into which *they* must integrate. A French *I* also exists and is host within Quebec, and in Francophone communities and schools.[17] Hence, if Francophones wish to integrate into the English workforce in Canada, *they* must accept to play by the rules of the majority and keep their Frenchness as a personal marker only.[18] Likewise, if immigrants wish to integrate into a French school, *they* must play by the rules of the Francophone host community. Hence, integration is different from assimilation in that *they* are encouraged to keep and transmit their culture and identity in the private realm but not while in *my* space. It is the same as assimilation, however, in that *I* have the power to define the rules of *their* belonging. Integration, then, is a social process that hides and reproduces power relations behind a celebratory discourse that reproduces differences between *I* and *them*. In this sense, integration is an essentializing force.

Finally, as mentioned by Plaisance, Bellmont, Verillon, and Schnider in the context of the schooling of students with particular needs, inclusion is most difficult because it requires that *I* change.[19] According to these authors, the *I* is a teacherly *I*. Within the framework I proposed, the *I* is any person or group of people in possession of the most power. In the story retold in this chapter, I, along with my colleagues, the associate teachers, and the faculty advisors share the power to (dis)qualify teacher candidates. As I retell the contradictions between my pedagogical ideal that is inclusion and my contribution to the reproduction of unequal relations of power, I attempt to take on the challenge to change. Although the aim of inclusion is to change relations of power, those relations cannot simply be denied as they are in practices of integration. Inclusion is a process of co-construction, based on interdependence between *I* and *them*, that calls on *all* to change, to see how *we (I and they)* are implicated in relations of power, and to use *our (mine and their)* power to create safe and equitable spaces for all. Inclusion is a force of recognition.

Methodology

As a White woman, I chose not to speak of my own or of my students' experiences in *Formation* at the February 2017 panel discussion that I organized. A participant told me that this was a wise decision: as a White woman, I could not legitimately speak to the experiences of my Black students.

As then, I will not attempt to replace their voices with my own. Instead, this chapter is written in my own voice, as an autobiographical narrative inquiry of a program director's struggles with inclusion in a context of heightened diversity. I recognize that this is a story retold from the perspective of an *I*. As with any narrative of experience, it can only be partial because it is already an interpretation of experiences, lived in a certain time and in a certain place, storied and retold in other times and places by one particular human being.

"Narrative inquiry is a way of understanding and inquiring into experience. It is nothing more and nothing less."[20] Narrative inquiry takes a Deweyan view of experience as relational and as the source of change in social actors. As Clandinin continues, "The regulative ideal for inquiry is to generate a new relationship between a human being and her environment—her life, community, world—one that 'makes possible a new kind of experienced object, not more real than those which preceded but more significant, and less overwhelming and oppressive.'"[21] Far from being asocial, however, narrative inquiry does not end with the stories lived by individuals; it also concerns itself with the social world in which those stories evolve and are told. Thus, narrative inquiry as methodology allows me to see the individual as an agent in her own life and in that of the world around her while also seeing that world as shaping that agency. In a sense, narrative inquiry allows me to interpret my story as one in which I interact relationally with other humans but also with the narratives of my institution, French language education, and the role of director of *Formation*. "Narrative inquiry is relational in all the ways that our Dewey-inspired view of experience make visible; that is, it is relational across time, places, relationships."[22]

At the outset, I attempted to tell this story from a distance, as though something objectively real had happened out there. I spoke of ethics, of justice, and of care. My voice was not clear. Then I struggled, not having a clear foundation in ethics, justice, or care; I got entangled, trying to make sense of what I was saying. I returned to my past wonderings about difference and language, and chose to retell my story as part of that inquiry into experiences past and present. I returned to autobiographical narrative inquiry, as I had entered into it many years ago, to struggle with my story of striving for inclusion in an institution not structured for it—this time, though, as a member of the power structure.

An important step in the process of this inquiry is to trace the lines of the story backward in time. My previous work on inclusion is an important part of both my personal and researcher story. I have left the assimilation/integration/inclusion framework as a trace of that story. It is from this point that I dive into the retelling that is this chapter. To accomplish this, I enter into a conversation with the first telling of the story. Retelling my story through the kaleidoscope of inclusion entails choosing, selecting stories, as all researchers select data, to share with readers. As researcher, I accept the responsibility to look for counter-stories to my initial interpretations. I relive many of these counter-stories as I write, re-write, and read storied moments first included in this chapter. Others add themselves to the picture, as this writing has made me more aware of the need to see instances of inclusion, integration, and assimilation in interaction with colleagues and school partners. This second reading accomplishes two things: It brings about a more nuanced interpretation of experience, and it contributes to the identification spaces of action. To repeat Dewey once again: it makes for a "less overwhelming and oppressive" experienced object.[23]

It is as director of *Formation* that I was privy to the workings of practicum and of the associated practices I will retell. It is also as director that I met with students to explain the decisions of the Professional Ethics Committee. These meetings gave me the opportunity to delve further into the students' stories of practicums gone wrong, to hear a different story from that told by associate teachers in practicum reports and by the students themselves in meetings with the Professional Ethics Committee. As director, I was also responsible for the public face of "my" program and developing positive relations with school boards and schools, our partners in the field. Finally, it also falls on the director to put faculty and university regulations into practice where warranted, on the one hand, and to propose changes to regulations and practices, on the other. The multifaceted position that was my directorship enables and colors my stories. Their retelling is a moment to pause, reflect, and interpret them again.

In the following sections I retell what I witnessed, did, and said as I struggled with inclusion at a time when *Formation*'s Pandora's box was opened.

The Professional Ethics Committee Narrative

Similar to the functioning of the Ontario College of Teachers at the provincial level, in relation to teachers' misconduct and incompetence, *Formation* has established a professional ethics committee at the university level, to treat complaints about pre-service teachers' professional misconduct and incompetence. When a teacher candidate's practicum is terminated prematurely, or if the candidate is reported to be unable to meet expectations, the Professional Ethics Committee convenes to discuss the situation with the candidate and their faculty advisor. (The faculty advisor acts as supportive liaison between the faculty, the student teacher, and the associate teacher.) Following the meeting, the Professional Ethics Committee either (a) gives the student a failing grade for their practicum, (b) adds extra time to the practicum to give the student a chance to improve and receive a passing grade, (c) cancels the current practicum and approves a new placement or a different placement in a more suitable environment, or (d) approves a SIS for the student. Of the teacher candidates seen by the faculty's professional ethics committee during my term as *Formation* director, all but one were enrolled in our program as a means to facilitate their transition from undervalued immigrant to member of the professional work force. Most were men who had taught in their home countries on the African continent or in Europe before immigrating to Canada. Hence, most teacher candidates called to the Professional Ethics Committee following difficulties experienced during practicum have been racialized male teachers from Africa, strange(rs) to the Franco-Ontarian classroom setting.

Associate teachers and faculty advisors have reported that the issue of greatest concern with these teacher candidates is their poor attitude: When they are asked to modify their planning or to build relationships with students, they do not. As a result, these student teachers are seen as lacking initiative, arrogant, and sexist. Because they stay at the back of the classroom until the associate teacher tells them to circulate and help the students, they are said to lack initiative. Because they do not accept criticism or direction, they are deemed to be arrogant or sexist when the associate teacher is a woman. Other criticisms heard by the Professional Ethics Committee are that they lecture rather than teach and that they discipline rather than manage the classroom, even when asked explicitly to use the same management techniques as their associate teachers. Furthermore, since they have taken classroom management and teaching method courses and do not ask for clarification when told to modify their practice, it is assumed that they understand what is asked of them. Such situations often lead to a belief that the student has a bad attitude: they *choose* not to change.

As a result, the associate teacher and faculty advisor file what is termed a "notice of difficulty," which the teacher candidate must sign as an attestation to having received it. Some refused to sign, as they had not been made aware of being in difficulty beforehand. To the contrary, the encouragement and support received from their associate teacher both orally and in their progress reports led them to believe that everything was going well. As director, I often received messages from these students stating that they do not understand what has happened to them and that their health has been negatively impacted by the situation. Some believe that "vous seule pouvez m'aider" (only you can help me). I tell them I must follow procedure and call a meeting of the Professional Ethics Committee.

In meeting with the Committee, teacher candidates are asked to explain the situation from their point of view: Committee members are aware that the reports they have on hand tell only part of the story. They ask teacher candidates questions and refer back to progress reports filled out by the associate teacher as well as the notice of difficulty in an attempt to understand the situation. Teacher candidates often state that their associate teacher didn't tell them what they wanted them to do or that they did not receive feedback. They may also report that the class was a difficult one, with many behavioural issues, that the teacher did not have good discipline and did not have proper control over their class. "How can a teacher candidate be expected to do what a teacher cannot do?" the candidates ask. Furthermore, the candidate may put forward that their associate teacher did not give them the teaching materials, did not engage in co-teaching but rather interrupted them while they were teaching—a practice which could be framed as co-teaching in other teacher candidate/associate teacher relationships. Often, the student will state that it is to be expected that they will make mistakes as they are learning, that this is what the practicum is about: learning. They seem to have the sense that they are expected to know how to be a teacher before beginning the practicum. Other stories suggest the contrary.

I have heard immigrant and new Canadian candidates speak about how they told their associate teachers that they are blank slates: I do not know how to teach; I am here to learn from you. These candidates report meeting with success during practicum, and they do not appear in front of the Professional Ethics Committee. Interestingly, I am not aware of similar practicum stories concerning Canadian-born students. This may be due to previous knowledge of how classrooms work in Canada, including the role of students and of teachers. Further research into practicum experiences is therefore needed. Should deference be a key to success for immigrant and new Canadians only? Should assimilation or integration be the expectation for *them*, not inclusion? An inclusive practicum would be a safe space for the bringing forward of all forms of knowledge about teaching and learning, from the teacher candidate as well as from the associate teacher and the faculty advisor. The recognition of all participants as knowing subjects is important to the construction of a professional space for all. Under my direction, the Professional Ethics Committee has encountered difficulty in honouring this principle.

When a progress report, a notice of difficulty, and a student viewpoint proved contradictory, the Professional Ethics Committee was faced with a he said/she said situation and often attempted to find a middle ground, to build a consensus between the teacher candidate's point of view and that of the associate teacher. If the candidate accepts that they are experiencing some difficulty and must make changes to move towards good teaching practice, they are most often allowed to continue their practicum or receive a new placement without any penalty. Indeed, time spent in practicum is often marked as SIS. On the other hand, should the teacher candidate refuse to concede to any fault on their part or to show "willingness to come to agreement with consensus with [the Professional Ethics Committee] about what is right,"[24] the Committee spends much time in camera discussing our sense that the candidate does not understand what is expected of them or that the adjudicators' expectations of the teacher are not clear.

Teacher candidates use the words we have included in the progress report forms, such as co-planning, co-teaching, and participative classroom management. Yet I am left feeling that these terms lack shared meaning. I do not know how these terms have been defined, or by whom and in what context. I am not sure that associate teachers and faculty advisors have explicit procedural definitions of these practices. Nor did the Professional Ethics Committee ask teacher candidates what they mean by co-planning, for example. If there is indeed a definitional void surrounding mentoring practices, this could be a zone of action towards inclusion.

Practicums are *key situations* in which different communicative conventions—such as how to gain attention from students, how to show learning, when to ask a question, who can ask questions, who can circulate in the classroom—can lead to the exclusion or assimilation of the less powerful *they*, teacher candidates. Negotiating common definitions would be an important first step in reducing the risk of misunderstanding expectations for our teacher candidates and for associate teachers. Indeed, both associate teachers and teacher candidates need help in bridging the gap that separates them. The Professional Ethics Committee is another *key situation* in which immigrant or new Canadian teacher candidates encounter a White Canadian panel having the power of the faculty behind them.

Two tendencies have emerged from the Professional Ethics Committee discussions: to be conciliatory and provide accompaniment for the teacher candidate, or to return to an examination of facts and base our decisions on them. In brief, the Committee realizes that something is amiss but has difficulty in finding a solution to the exclusion of our students from the teaching profession. As has been mentioned often by committee members, part of this difficulty stems from the absence of the associate teacher at our meetings. Their voice is heard through the progress reports, but these can be read from different perspectives and found to be either positive or negative in their meaning. Once again, the negotiation of meaning through dialogue, an important aspect of the process of inclusion, is lacking in depth: We allow time for the storying of the practicum experience, but we have not established protocols by which shared understanding of the stories might be achieved.

Typically, if responsibility could not be ascertained to the satisfaction of the Committee, the student was assigned a new placement. However, if the candidate showed anger rather than surprise, was accusatory towards the associate teacher or the faculty advisor rather than conciliatory, they were given a failing grade on their practicum. They were thus required to retake their practicum and pay additional tuition fees. Along with these punitive measures, the student might be asked to write a letter of apology to the teacher, to take an additional course, or to write a reflective piece on their practice.

The meetings of the Professional Ethics Committee were rife with tensions. One colleague proposed an analogy between our practices and that of repentance in the Catholic Church: Sins had to be admitted before repentance could be attained. Another found that we were not dealing with questions of ethics but with issues surrounding intercultural communication. Still another, that we need to give our students the benefit of the doubt when making judgments. I felt caught between my ideal that is inclusion and saving practicum placements: If we did not support the associate teacher's and the faculty advisor's decision, the faculty might be accused of not supporting associate teachers. I had heard this accusation from a principal who explained that his teachers did not want to accept immigrant or new Canadian teacher candidates because they did not feel supported by the faculty when things went wrong. One of his teachers, for example, reported that when she had attempted to fail a teacher candidate, she was told by the faculty advisor to give him a chance as he had only just arrived in Canada. The great success of the SIS in making space for associate teachers and teacher candidates to move forward together suggests that a change in our procedures is necessary to create an inclusive environment able to address the intercultural learning of both our student body and associate teachers.

The *Stage d'insertion scolaire* [School Integration Practicum, SIS] Narrative

Recognizing that a student from Africa was having great difficulty adapting to the classroom during practicum, a past practicum coordinator, Camile Paradis, proposed that he be given a four-week *Stage d'insertion scolaire* (SIS, School integration practicum). The student in question had arrived from Africa during the summer months and had never set foot in a Canadian school prior to his practicum. His SIS was approved as a stopgap measure to allow him the time to familiarize himself with a new school culture before beginning a regular, evaluated practicum. This practice was successful and repeated informally with other students from Africa. It was formalized with the move from a one-year to a two-year *Formation* program in 2015.

Starting from an inclusive perspective that opposes deficit models of education, I proposed that the SIS should not be reserved for a specific category of student—immigrants and new Canadians—but that it should be offered to any student needing extra time to transition from the university classroom to the practice of teaching in French Ontario. Nor should the decision to allow for this extra time be solely that of the practicum coordinator. Therefore, to ensure greater transparency and equity, the process for identifying students eligible for and offering them a SIS was recently reviewed.

The practicum coordinator, associate teacher, or faculty advisor can make the request for a SIS. The possibility of inviting students to self-identify as SIS candidates is also being considered, and discussions about the criteria to be used to determine eligibility for a SIS has highlighted the need to move away from criteria based on place of origin to ones based on knowledge or familiarity with current pedagogical practices in Ontario schools. The easy part of this review process has been to formalize procedures.

Whereas in the past no clear procedure existed and students could be offered a SIS at any point in their practicum, the directorship of *Formation* (director, assistant director, practicum coordinator in Ottawa as well as those in Windsor and Toronto, and our online program coordinators) has determined that a SIS should only be made available during the first of the two eight-week practicums. Furthermore, this offer must now be made within the first three weeks of the practicum as a component of a progress report and notice of difficulty. Henceforth, the notice of difficulty can lead to a professional improvement plan or to a SIS. The difference between these two options is that the improvement plan must be implemented immediately with progress evaluated on a weekly basis. If the teacher candidate does not meet the objectives of the plan, the practicum is failed. The eight-week practicum must be retaken at a financial cost to the student, and a second failed mark leads to exclusion from the program. On the other hand, the SIS is not evaluated and is more flexible in allowing for more time to negotiate learning and performance. Although a regular practicum must be completed successfully following the SIS, the student is not billed for the extra session, and no failing mark appears on the student's transcript. The SIS student has twenty-four weeks, rather than the regular sixteen, to pass their first practicum. The length of the SIS is also variable from four to eight weeks. In other words, the SIS is student-centred and organic in its organization, where the practicum is systematized and performance/competence-centred. This review has brought me full circle to a consideration of the intention of the SIS: Is it a way to allow teacher candidates more time to understand what *they* must change to assimilate, integrate, or be included into a teaching profession that *I* know?

Developing criteria for identifying students eligible for an SIS based on principles of inclusion has not been simple. The definition I proposed for inclusion places the impetus for change on all the actors involved in a social situation, rendering it necessary for *Formation* to engage with teacher candidates, associate teachers, and other partners to develop criteria for the identification of candidates and appropriate practicum sites. In a truly inclusive SIS, all involved would be expected to change their practices rather than only the student.

Making the SIS available to all who have limited familiarity with actual schooling practices rather than only to immigrants and new Canadians has changed our definition of the source of difficulty: having completed previous university study in a foreign country is no longer seen as the problem, and the need for Canadian-born students pursuing a second career, for example, to profit from an extended stay in practicum is recognized.

It has been more difficult to avoid labeling students as deficient; as outlined on *Formation*'s web page, associate teachers are expected to do a formative assessment of their teacher candidate's performance at the end of the third week of practicum, at which time the possibility of a SIS may be discussed, but only as it pertains to the needs of the student:

> *Suite à l'évaluation de progrès 1 et selon les besoins du ou de la stagiaire, le personnel enseignant accompagnateur en consultation avec la ou le professeur conseiller, la coordonnatrice ou le coordonnateur des stages, la direction du programme ou son délégué, s'il y a lieu, peuvent discuter du besoin d'approuver un stage d'insertion scolaire qui viserait à pallier un manque de familiarité avec le contexte scolaire francophone ontarien.* (Following the first progress report and according to the needs of the teacher candidate, the associate teacher, in consultation with the faculty advisor, the practicum coordinator, the program director, or her delegate, as necessary, can discuss the need to approve a SIS to address/palliate a lack of familiarity of the Franco-Ontarian schooling context.)
>
> ***
>
> *Ce stage ne sera pas évalué mais aura comme objectif de faire vivre la même expérience de la pratique de l'enseignement à la ou au stagiaire*

selon un rythme et des attentes personnalisées. (This practicum will not be evaluated, but its objective is to give the student the same experience of teaching but following an individualised rhythm and expectations.)

***

Le stage sera repris à la fin du programme régulier. (The [regular] practicum will be postponed till the end of the regular program.)[25]

Problems experienced during practicum are therefore attributed to the teacher candidate rather than contextually situated at the crossroads between socially constructed norms and values. In this sense, the teacher candidate is to assimilate into a pre-existing culture of schooling and leave behind *their* conceptions of teaching, learning, and good pedagogical practice.

In fact, the needs of the first SIS student are echoed in the Professional Ethics Committee's discussions with other immigrant and new Canadian students: understanding the difference between child-centred and academics-centred teaching and between discipline and classroom management. I suggest that these differences refer back to social norms and values, as demonstrated in the following story. During the filming of video clips about the Ontario College of Teachers' ethical standards, one of our students explained to me: "J'ai compris que le respect ici, c'est aller vers l'autre. Chez nous, c'est laisser une distance" ("I have understood that here, respect is expressed by going towards the other. At home, it is expressed by the keeping of distance").[26] Hence, "l'empathie n'a pas de place en enseignement quand le respect c'est la distance." ("If respect is the keeping of distance, empathy does not have a place in teaching.") An inclusive attitude would translate into a willingness to engage in sense-making of shared values. Such sense-making could render the tension between child- and academic-centred pedagogies more explicit and available to all for examination during teacher-candidate training. Such knowledge about the social construction of norms of practice could aid in deconstructing the belief that one is objectively better than the other. This is important, as Canadian-born students who refuse to work with their immigrant or new Canadian colleagues have said of their colleagues: *They* do not know how to work, but it is not *their* fault because *they* come from a third-world country and have not had the chance to be educated as *we* have. In practicum, these same immigrant or new Canadian teacher candidates are seen as having traditional, as opposed to modern, teaching methods.

Inclusive practices would also entail being attentive to the needs of associate teachers that we ask to accompany students with a different worldview from their own. After supervising twenty practicums, one faculty advisor shared with me what she learned from associate teachers. According to her, most wanted to support immigrant teacher candidates but felt incompetent in doing so; they could not grasp the source of their struggles. Similarly, when a number of teachers refused to accept immigrant teacher candidates into the classrooms, the practicum coordinator and I discussed reasons given for their refusal to be an associate teacher. Some stated that their position had changed within the school—teaching a new grade level or taking on leadership duties—so they didn't have the time, and others stated they had never agreed to be associate teachers. A few did confirm that they would only accept Franco-Ontarian teacher candidates. I spoke directly to one teacher who explained that she couldn't give our student what he needed due to her increased workload for the term: he was too far from the mark and would require more support then she could give him. She further explained that, upon seeing her, the student teacher—a man in his 40s—exclaimed, "Mais vous êtes toute jeune et pimpante, je croyais que vous seriez bien plus vieille!" ("Oh, but you are so young and charmingly bubbly, I thought you would be older!"). The associate teacher saw this as inappropriate, and she felt too uncomfortable in his presence to work with him for eight weeks.

Both student and associate teacher perspectives point to a need to create safe spaces for the building of intercultural relationships and for sense-making between teacher candidate and pupils as well as between associate teacher and teacher candidate. In other words, *Formation* needs to be seen as a space of transition from immigration to inclusion for all involved. It would seem that, free from pressures of evaluation, the SIS could be such a space in which it is possible to listen, hear, and recognize. For this to be so, both faculty and associate teachers must be willing to acknowledge and question taken-for-granted assumptions about what constitutes acceptable or unacceptable teaching practices. Both groups need to appreciate how such assumptions impact on judgments about teacher candidate performance and suitability for a career in teaching. Beyond willingness, providing both university and school-based teacher educators time to reflect, discuss, and question is of great importance.

Unfortunately, the French language education system in Ontario is hard-pressed to resolve an important shortage of teachers and is unable to grant release time to those teachers who are willing. Until conditions are such that we are able to engage with our partners in the process of inclusion and collective sense-making, some of our students will continue to meet with difficulty in their practicums; and associate teachers will continue to be frustrated with not knowing how to help, or they may become impatient with having to help a student who does not correspond to their image of a good teacher. In the meantime, and as a result of this initial narrative inquiry, I have chosen not to wait for ideal conditions and have begun to work with *Formation's* team to build a safer space for our students.

Moving towards More Inclusive Practices

As the winter term of 2018 ended, eight teacher candidates either failed or saw their last practicum terminated prematurely by their associate teacher. All were immigrants or new Canadians from Africa. I felt the need to be better at leading the Professional Ethics Committee. I was feeling overwhelmed and getting angry with students during our meetings because they would not simply accept their associate teacher's evaluation of their performance. I was moving away from my ideal of inclusion. My colleagues also seemed to want change, as they asked if some of these cases could not be resolved at another level. The very context of our discussion, a disciplinary hearing, was problematic for the resolution of this type of situation: The Professional Ethics Committee is a space in which students are meant to be heard, but it is also a space in which they are to be judged. However, when I brought my colleagues' proposal forward, a superior explained that it is paramount that three tenured or tenure-track professors make an official decision so as to protect us from possible student appeals to the University's Senate. Learning from one student's actions, we were nonetheless able to take steps to make our processes more inclusive and respectful of student voices.

Following a meeting with the Professional Ethics Committee, one female African student searched out resources she could call upon at the University to come to her aid. She communicated with the Student Rights Centre of the Student Federation, and they with me. I was unaware of their existence before this incident. From then on, I made it a practice to inform teacher candidates of their right to be accompanied to the meeting of the Committee by a person of their choosing and to recommend that they contact the Student Rights Centre.

The Student Rights Centre also became a resource for me as I developed new processes for the Professional Ethics Committee. The Committee has accepted that a timeline be put in place that would see students informed quickly of the reasons they are called to the Professional Ethics Committee, receive an e-copy of all documents to be studied by the Committee, and be informed of their rights and of the decisions that the Committee has the power to make on behalf of *Formation*. Our next step is to include our students in this dialogue in spaces other than in Committee meetings. In other words, we are attempting to bridge the divide between inclusion and institutional practices.

In order to reduce the tension during meetings with teacher candidates, the Professional Ethics Committee has also added a pre-meeting discussion to its procedures. During this time, all documents shared with the teacher candidate are examined, and any questions about the progression of the practicum are put to the coordinator or faculty advisor. In all cases thus far, this step has allowed the Committee to arrive at a proposal to be discussed with the student in session. We still take the time to listen to the teacher candidate, but the ability to propose next steps in their progress through practicum has made it possible for them to participate in this decision-making process. I have seen students' shoulders drop as tension was eased, heard voices lose their edge, and seen smiles reappear on faces. One teacher candidate refused the proposed two-week extension to their practicum, stating that three weeks seemed more realistic. My shoulders drop, my voice softens. A colleague proposes a site for this practicum.

The assistant director to *Formation,* the practicum coordinator, and I have also worked with an inclusion specialist from the Human Rights Centre of the University. Working with the inclusion specialist, we have redefined the role of the faculty advisor as one of enabling the development of a healthy relationship between associate teacher and the teacher candidate. The hope is that, given the impossibility of providing a course or workshop for associate teachers, faculty advisors better educated in the practice of intercultural mentoring will be able to enable inclusive practicum practices. Our first step in guiding faculty advisors towards their new role has been to organize two half-day workshops on unconscious biases. Although professor and lecturer collective agreements does not allow for mandatory training, most advisers did take time out of their days to participate in these workshops. More is to be done, but seeds have been planted.

I have also modified my own practices: I no longer pretend racism doesn't exist in schools or that all associate teachers do what we expect of them. I am aware that I cannot write such beliefs in letters of decision. Instead, I speak in private to students who have brought up the issue of racism. I tell them that I realize they are likely to encounter racism in Canada, but that I cannot know if racism is in fact what they encountered on practicum as I was not there. I propose that they see themselves as opening doors for the next cohort of immigrant and new Canadian teacher candidates from their countries. To do so, they need to find ways to develop strategies to surmount the barriers that will be put in their way. I have begun to identify organizations led by French African Canadians who can help them develop these strategies. Through this process, I have come to more fully understand that, beyond legitimizing the professional knowledge of our teacher candidates, an inclusive practice in *Formation* must also bring an appreciation of the limits on the use of that knowledge within the current educational system. Such knowledge would be important to the immigrant and new Canadian teacher candidate's successful passage through an important *key situation*: in the province of Ontario, teachers are expected to demonstrate competence in certain types of teaching practices during their first years of employment by a school board, be it as a supply teacher or as a teacher in a permanent position. Should they not demonstrate such competence during this probationary time, they are said to be in "performance deficit,"[27] and their contracts may be terminated. For our teacher candidates, *Formation's* inclusive practices need to be as much as about what we do from within as about how we facilitate our teacher candidates' coming to know how to navigate institutions not yet ready for them.

Conclusion

If those in power did not have to change to make inclusion a possibility, inclusion would likely be a more widespread practice. Inclusion is difficult because it calls on all to change. This chapter has relates stories of practices as they have been lived in teacher education by a director of a program offering training to a very diversified student population. Within this programme, racialized immigrants and new Canadians meet with important challenges during practicum and have been the object of exclusions both in schools and within the processes put forward by *Formation*. This writing has allowed me to acknowledge that we are moving reflexively to modify practices of exclusion in *Formation*, but that we need to go beyond and mentor students in ways to overcome barriers to their success. This story—necessarily partial in its truth and incomplete in it's telling—provides a snapshot in time of our journey along a sinusoidal path from difference to inclusion. More work is necessary to fully theorize our journey. In fact, this autobiographical narrative into inclusion has led me to view inclusion-as-lived to be an important research puzzle. I am left in wonderment over how the story of inclusion is told by those social actors I have included here. I am struck by the impossibility of arriving at my goal in the absence of dialogue about that goal. This is the road I will follow on the next step of my journey as researcher, teacher, and human.

Notes

1. I wish to thank reviewers for their comments on an earlier version of this chapter; their comments help make my story more complete. I am also grateful to Ari Black and to Josée Lebel who helped make my French expressions more familiar to English readers. Finally, I wish to thank Anne M. Phelan for her patience and encouragement. Research and writing are relational enterprises indeed.
2. Bolen, 2012, as cited in Holman Jones, Adams and Ellis, "Introduction," 36.
3. In proposing this dual categorization, I look to disrupt the construction of "immigrant" as a homogeneous and othering social category. Although I have not as yet delved into the literature in this field or done extensive research myself, I know from discussions with students that some have been in Canada for less than a year while others have been Canadian citizens for a few years. My sense is that the students' trajectory has an impact on their success in practicum.
4. Clandinin, *Engaging in Narrative* Inquiry, 43–44.
5. As I move through this narrative, I will point to other threads of the story that will need unpacking.
6. One of the threads of this autobiographical narrative that I will need to tell is that of the death of my husband and my ensuing struggle to make it back into legitimacy as a member of a university faculty. As I write this text, I am aware that it is my first attempt at reintegrating into the world of publishable research. It is laced with tears and anxiety.
7. "The Minister of Education may grant a Letter of Permission to a school board authorizing it to employ an individual who is not a member of the Ontario College of Teachers—that is, an individual who is not a teacher—to teach in an elementary or a secondary school for a period not exceeding one year, if the Minister is satisfied that no teacher is available." Ontario Ministry of Education, Policy/Program Memorandum No. 147.
8. The Ontario College of Teachers, a body governed by Ontario teachers, is responsible for the accreditation of teacher education programs and courses in Ontario and the certification of teachers. The College investigates and hears complaints about teachers and may suspend or revoke their certification. Once candidates complete a teacher education program, their university submits a recommendation to the College and, if the candidate has met all requirements, the College issues the teaching certificate. Teachers educated outside Ontario must submit a request for certification

directly to the College. Between 1998 and 1999, the College developed ethical standards and standards of practice for the teaching practice. Ontario College of Teachers, About the College.

9   Through the process retold in these pages, I have been mentored by Carole Bourque, a member of the University of Ottawa's Human Rights Centre. Following her example, I use the term "present" rather than assuming people would ascribe to the identities I am pointing to.

10 Aligning the language competency test and the refresher course with principles of inclusive evaluation was a personal-professional objective at the time I accepted the directorship of *Formation*. Although steps have been made in that direction, the objective has yet to be met. The inclusion of our immigrant students in practicum took precedence over this original concern. The inclusion of students othered by the language competency test is one as yet untold thread of my autobiographical narrative.

11 All told, their cohort consisted of 220 students. Immigrant and new Canadian students account for approximately 50% of that number (110). Hence, more than 50% of this group of students was turned away from practicum. No White, Canadian-born or foreign-born, student was turned away.

12 Heller, "Gumperz et la justice sociale," 44.
13 Duchesne, "L'apprentissage par transformation."
14 Duchesne, 36.
15 Duchesne, 46.
16 The first version of this framework was developed as part of a conference on "la francization" or the practice of teaching French to those students who enter French language schooling with limited knowledge of the French language (Dalley, "Francisation."). This context is too complex to detail further; suffice it to say that for many *francization* teachers see it as their task to bring children into the fold of *la francophonie*.
17 Ricento, "The consequences of official bilingualism."
18 Gerin-Lajoie and Jacquet, "Regards croisés sur l'inclusion des minorités."
19 Plaisance et al., "Intégration ou inclusion?"
20 Clandinin, *Engaging in Narrative inquiry*, 13.
21 Clandinin, 14, quoting Dewey, 1981, p. 175.
22 Clandinin, 19.
23 Dewey, *The Later Works*, 175.
24 Tronto, *Moral Boundaries*, 87.
25 Université d'Ottawa, Faculté d'éducation, *Quoi faire en cas de difficulté*.
26 All translations are by the author unless otherwise indicated.

27   This term was used in a recent conversation about the difficulties encountered by a supply teacher.

Bibliography

Clandinin, D. Jean. *Engaging in Narrative Inquiry*. Walnut Creek, CA: Left Coast Press, 2013.

Dalley, Phyllis. "Assimilation, intégration ou inclusion. Quelle vision pour l'éducation de langue française en contexte minoritaire?" In *La francophonie dans toutes ses couleurs et le défi de l'inclusion*, edited by L. Carlson-Berg, 13–34. Laval, QC: Presses de l'Université Laval, 2014.

———. "Francisation, communication orale et construction identitaire." In *Actes du forum sur la francization*. Alberta, Consortium provincial francophone pour la formation professionnelle. (2009): 33–42. https://education.alberta.ca/media/3272635/actesforumfrancisation.pdf

Dewey, John. *The Later Works, 1925–1953: Vol. 4. The Quest for Certainty: A Study of the Relation of Knowledge and Action*, edited by J. A. Boydston. Carbondale, IL: Southern Illinois University Press, 1981.

Duchesne, Claire. "L'apprentissage par transformation en context de formation professionnelle." *Éducation et francophonie* 38, no.1 (2010): 33–50.

Gerin-Lajoie, Diane, and Marianne Jacquet. "Regards croisés sur l'inclusion des minorités en contexte scolaire francophone minoritaire au Canada." *Éducation et francophonie* 36, no 1 (2008), 25–43.

Heller, Monica. "Gumperz et la justice sociale." *Langage et société* 4, no. 150 (2014): 41–53.

Holman Jones, Stacy, Tony Adams, and Carolyn Ellis. "Introduction: Coming to Know Autoethnography as More than a Method." In *Handbook of Autoethnography*, edited by Stacy Holman Jones, Tony E. Adams, and Carolyn Ellis, 1–47. Walnut Creek, CA, Left Coast Press, 2013.

Ontario College of Teachers. About the College. https://www.oct.ca/about-the-college.

Ontario Ministry of Education. Policy/Program Memorandum No. 147: Applications for Letters of Permission. May 21, 2008. http://www.edu.gov.on.ca/extra/eng/ppm/147.html.

Plaisance, Éric, Brigitte Bellmont, Alliette Verillon, and Corelia Schnider. "Intégration ou inclusion?" *La nouvelle revue de l'adaptation et de la scolarisation* 1, no 37 (2007): 159–164.

Ricento, Thomas. "The consequences of official bilingualism on the status and perception of non-official languages in Canada." *Journal of Multilingual and Multicultural Development* 34, no 5 (2013), 475–489.

Tronto, Jane C. *Moral Boundaries: A Political Argument for an Ethic of Care.* New York, NY: Routledge, 1994.

Université d'Ottawa, Faculté d'éducation. *Quoi faire en cas de difficulté.* Accessed May 11, 2018. http://education.uottawa.ca/fr/quoi-faire-cas-difficulte.

CHAPTER 7

Unknowing the Child: Toward Ethical Relations with the Precarious Other

Melanie D. Janzen

I was constantly overwhelmed by the assessments. I didn't believe in it philosophically and, honestly, sometimes it felt more like the district was assessing me. It was ridiculous—I just wanted to spend time being with the kids. And so I was just done.

— Faye

Large-scale assessments diminish teachers' capacities to respond ethically to children. Faye's narrative illustrates the ways in which her attempts to build relationships with children were undermined by the system's incessant desire to know students through testing them, frustrating Faye and culminating in her early departure from the profession. Sadly, Faye's narrative is similar to many stories we heard during our interviews with teachers, and reflects an education system rooted in Kantian conceptions of static knowledge, which is determined to *know* children. The responsibility for this agenda falls to the teachers who are expected to know the curriculum and children in contracted ways. In turn, children are expected to be recognizable and passive objects receptive to being improved according to so-called generalizable standards. When education's epistemological foundations are based on technical discursive regimes seeking to *know* children, teachers' capacities to read and respond to the differences or "otherness" of the children who present themselves in our classrooms is diminished. The violence of seeking standardization and turning otherness into sameness is amplified in the current neoliberal climate of increased managerialism and accountability, eroding spaces for the teacher's judgment, responsiveness, and relationships, and affecting the subjectivities of both the teacher and the student.

This chapter is drawn from data from a larger research study, which explores the emotional toll of teachers' obligations to children and teachers' disengagement from the profession. Within the study, my research collaborator and I each conducted twelve interviews with teachers in two different Canadian provinces. The interviews sought to explore the idea of obligation, how teachers experience obligation, the emotional toll it takes on teachers, and how this emotional toll manifests in teachers' disengagement from the profession.[1] Within this research, obligation is conceptualized as a visceral response to the child.[2] Obligation is an urgent sense the teacher may have when faced with the child's anger, fear, sadness, inquiry, or joy. It is a "feeling that comes over us when others need our help, when they call out for help, or support, or freedom, or whatever they need."[3] Importantly, obligation is central to the project of teaching; it gives teaching its moral integrity in that the teacher feels obligated to respond to the child in moments of ethical possibility. However, at the same time, obligation takes an emotional toll on the teacher because the teacher's response to the child is unavoidably fraught with questions of judgment, responsibility, and uncertainty. Importantly, what our research demonstrates is that although the obligations of teaching accumulate and weigh on the teacher, the tensions arising from moments of obligation are not a problem of teaching; rather, they are "the unremarkable occurrences in the lives of teachers."[4] In other words, although obligation creates an emotional burden for the teacher, it is also the pedagogical site from where the teacher derives a sense of ethical integrity. The importance of understanding the concept of obligation in teaching is that it affords us pedagogical opportunities to (re)orient the emphasis of teaching from the neoliberal discourses of managerialism and standardization, toward the ethical relation between the teacher and the child.

My purpose in this chapter is to centre the emotionality of teachers' obligations to the Other and to consider the tensions teachers experience within educational systems that valorize technocratic conceptions of knowledge, teachers, and students. Drawing on interview data from the larger study, I will begin by illustrating the effects that education's technocratic efforts to *know* children have on teachers' subjectivities, and to consider the ways in which discourses that privilege knowledge construct the teacher as expert (the one who must *know*) and concomitantly construct the child as object (the one to be *known*). In the second section, I will enlist Judith Butler's work on framing [5]—an operation of power that determines the recognizability of others and the precarity of those deemed unrecognizable—to consider the ways in which education's most vulnerable children become unrecognizable within a system that should be designed to welcome and serve them. Finally, drawing on Sharon Todd,[6] I will illustrate the efforts made by teachers to apprehend children beyond the frames of precarity. I conclude that teaching as an ethical relation with the Other is possible but not without risk.

Schooling as Mastery *over* the Other

The project of schooling is premised on particular epistemologies. Traditionally, schools have been transmitters of knowledge (via the sanctioned curriculum) but also generators of knowledge—mining bits of knowledge about students from test scores, inventories, and norms; assessing and measuring students; and then sorting and categorizing them. When the knowledge generated indicates that students do not measure up, the education system also presumes to know how to intervene and which remedies to impose in order to fix, catch up, remediate, close the gap, segregate, or discipline the learner. These processes reflect the education system's reverence for knowledge that is authorized, objective, fixed, and void of context, revealing education's "institutionalized fantasy of mastery."[7] An epistemology of mastery is a discursive regime of truth, infusing, constructing, and reifying all aspects of schooling. Within this discourse that privileges mastery, teachers are required to be masters of curriculum and children, and children are expected to master what is taught.

Discourses of mastery have both epistemological and ontological implications. Epistemologically, the curriculum becomes a tool of knowledge transmission rather than a pedagogical site of knowledge co-creation and transformation. Ontologically, the implicitly power-laden and hierarchical teacher-student relationship, premised on knowledge transmission and knowing the Other, constitutes and reiterates particular teacher and student subjectivities. The teachers become responsible for transmitting and assessing seemingly neutral knowledge; and the children—like objects—become sorted, identified, categorized, and disciplined according to their capacities to acquire knowledge according to predetermined norms and standards. Importantly, when the teacher-student relationship is premised on the requirement of *knowing* the Other—a mastery of the teacher over the student—it undermines the complexities of attending and responding ethically to the complicated lives of children, creating tension for the teacher between the prescribed ways of being a teacher and a sense of obligation to the student. Therefore, to seek to *know* the Other is a rational—not relational—view of the Other and constitutes the subjectivity of the teaching subject as *expert*, responsible for knowing curriculum and children, while framing the child as one who is defined by standards and deviations from them.

Teacher as Expert

As per the Latin meaning of obligation, "to bind" illustrates the seemingly physical sense of obligation as that of being tied to the Other through promise or duty. To respond to the Other requires that teachers are receptive to the disruptions by the Other (a child's questions, outbursts, or tears), and subsequently means that they are open to the undecidability of how to respond to the Other, and remain uncertain in their judgements.[8] Yet education's epistemological presuppositions of *knowing* the child have ontological effects. That is, education's desire to know charges the teacher not just with defining *what* the child knows, but also with determining *who* the child is and can be. There is an assumption that if the teacher knows the child and knows about the child—background and broader experiences—that the teacher will be better equipped to teach the child.[9] These discourses of *knowing* create a "teacher as expert" discourse that subjugates the teacher—an identity subjected and constituted by discourses that come before the teacher.[10] As Butler theorizes, subjection is "the process of becoming subordinated by power as well as the process of becoming a subject,"[11] both dominated but also activated or formed as the subject.[12] In other words, "what I can 'be' is constrained in advance by a regime of truth that decides what will and will not be a recognizable form of being."[13] The teaching subject then, discursively determined as expert, requires compliance with the particular norms that precede it. Thus, the teacher's identity becomes framed in such a way, as expert, that the teacher's sense of obligation to the Other is undermined in that the *uncertainty* required in responding ethically is not the recognizable form of being the teaching subject. As expert, the teaching subject's ability to be uncertain and undecided is constricted and yet the teacher remains tied to the obligation to respond to the child, creating an ontological tension between being recognizable as teacher—as expert—and responding ethically (with uncertainty and undecidability) in the face of the Other.

Consider Michelle, a teacher of eight years and teaching grade six, who described herself as "feeling pretty confident with knowing the curriculum, and understanding children of this particular age group," and as "having a really good rapport with families." Yet, Michelle also described feeling incredible pressure for implementing the district's prescribed math and reading programs and the additional district-imposed assessments. She explained:

> We have to do all of this online reporting to the district—*on top of* report cards. We could save ourselves a whole lot of work here and use our professional judgment instead of filling in all these forms. But that's not what we are supposed to be doing. If we got audited for our assessment stuff, right, like we could be in trouble if we don't have documentation to back it up.

Michelle complained that the prescribed approaches "don't align with my beliefs" and that they diminished her "freedom to teach." Yet, Michelle's ability to be recognizable as a teacher is dependent on her performance as expert, a form of being decided in advance.[14] Thus, for Michelle to be recognizable as a teacher, she must comply with the narratives in which implementing assessment protocols is prescribed and valued over her professional judgment. These expert discourses of the teacher precede her, authorizing an identity that requires her to "know" children through predetermined and standardized assessments.

Additionally, Michelle explained that part of her recognizability as a competent teacher carries the enormous weight of being judged by her colleagues, the school's parents, and the district administrators. She described colleagues questioning her if she left the school before five o'clock at night, insinuating that she had likely not completed her work. She worried about "the parents [who] are out front of the school watching from their cars." Michelle scorned the incessant surveillance, stating that she felt as though "Big Brother is always watching." She explained, "They have a lot of power. I could be fired if they're not happy with the way I'm doing things." Michelle attempted to shore up her confidence and demonstrate her competence as a teacher by doing schoolwork (planning and marking) every night and on weekends so that she "can be prepared" and hopefully avoid being so harshly judged. Under constant scrutiny, she tried to alleviate her worries that people will think that she was "not doing as much" as she could be.

Ball reminds us that in the current educational era of standardization and accountability, these technologies of managerialism prescribe the teacher's performativity. As Ball explains, "performativity is a technology, a culture and a mode of regulation ... [where teachers'] performances (of individual subjects or organizations) serve as measures of productivity or output, or displays of 'quality'."[15] Thus, the performativity of the teaching subject comes to represent what is valued within the system, "where commitment, judgment and authenticity within practice are sacrificed for impression and performance."[16] Because of the increased surveillance and constant judgment, where outputs represent what is worthwhile, we see the ways in which Michelle was required to perform "teacher" in particular ways. Thus, the teaching subject becomes regulated through technologies of surveillance, shifting teachers' attention from people to performance and from students to standards.

The teaching subject is also regulated through the internalization of discourses of surveillance. That is, although Michelle opposed the imposed programming and testing, as well as the heightened district demands of accountability, she had (unwittingly) internalized these regulatory discourses. For example, when the principal told Michelle to use her judgment on some of the assessments, encouraging her to complete the forms based on her previous knowledge of the child, Michelle worried about being "audited" and then "getting in trouble for not have the documentation to back up" the students' scores. She seemed to discount her own knowledge of the child and reified the district's position, stating, "Are you kidding me!? We went to all this in-servicing. Millions of dollars were probably spent on this and now you're saying, 'Use your professional judgement.'" While, on the one hand, Michelle saw the large-scale assessments as problematic and as interfering with her own beliefs about teaching and with her relationships with children, on the other hand, she regulated her own judgment, complying with the demands imposed out of fear, thereby, illustrating the ways in which these expert discourses regulate the subject in particular ways.

Michelle's narratives illustrate the ways expert discourses—through incessant regulation and surveillance—threaten the teacher who might not do, know, or be enough. Teachers feel compelled to comply with the constant—and often implicit—demands; the late night planning seeking to fulfil the fantasy of the perfectly planned and executed lesson, the continual testing and tracking of progress, the marking and reporting that seeks to sort and identify students' transgressions from the predetermined trajectory, and compliance with the expectations of the accumulative and regulatory gaze of others. Expert discourses, regulated through technologies of surveillance, come to bear on the teacher's subjectivity—who and how the teacher is allowed to be—and help to illuminate what teaching does to teachers. Teachers, like Michelle, feel torn between wanting to teach with a sense of moral integrity and complying with the normative discourses of expert that precede her. Michelle, although only in her early thirties, complained about being "emotionally exhausted and constantly stressed." She said, "I can't take a sick day. I just drag myself out of bed. I constantly feel like I need to be giving more." But what more can she give? Michelle did not say. The incessant surveillance she experienced created a sense of needing to do teaching right, while at the same time reduced what is right about teaching.

Child as Object

The hierarchically dominant teacher, seeking recognizability as expert, is subsequently expected to have expert knowledge about the child—to *know* the student in particular ways. Enlisting large-scale tools of evaluation and assessment, teachers are required to determine what knowledge the child has or has acquired in order to determine in what regard—and to what extent—the child is deficient. As Sharon Todd reminds us, to assume to *know* the Other induces a violent erasure of the particularities and differences of the Other, where the Other becomes reduced to norms.[17] Further, to know the Other presumes both that the Other *can* be known, and also that this is a pedagogical and ethical endeavour in the first place.[18] Such assumptions devalue the Other, diminishing the ethical relations between the teacher and the child that require the teacher's questioning, indecision, and judgment. When the teacher is supposed to *know* the Other in particular ways, the educator must collect and collate that information in order to determine the child, reducing the child to an object, void of context and subjectivity. Consider Faye, a teacher for sixteen years, who became so disenchanted with her school district's mandatory testing regime that she resigned from teaching.

> It's tough because I had to judge my students, and yet, I didn't feel like what I was doing was right. I was in the trap because I didn't want it to be this way, and yet I had to be. The district had us create this snowball of papers and reports and it all took so much time. Then it all got filed—which was ridiculous because we didn't have anywhere to keep it, and no one ever read it anyway! And then, in Grade 7, the kids leave the school and it all got tossed—shredded.

The educational system's requirement to *know* the child operates discursively through language while also inscribing language, pedagogies, policies, and practices, manifesting materially in benchmarks, outcomes, standards, and other measurement regimes. The time-consuming demands of the constant evaluating and testing of students, the subsequent administrative task of collecting and compiling the data, the enormous paper trail that was created, and the files that were compiled, illustrates the assumptions that the education system makes about the knowability of the students. It has a dehumanizing effect on children in that they become "known" through and as their scores, rankings, and grades.

Like Michelle, Faye described the frustrations she felt in participating in the school district's effort to *know* children through the large-scale testing as an onerous and time-consuming process, objectifying children and minimizing teachers' relationships with them. Faye explained her frustration: "The district wanted to know where kids are *at*, but we need to respond to what these kids need and to who they *are*." We see in Faye's account the tension she experienced in being compelled to do something that diminished her obligation to respond ethically to her students; foregrounding the difference between a rational and relational way of being with children.[19] Faye said:

> We've completely lost sight of the kids in all of this! I didn't believe that what I was doing was right. I didn't—I wasn't able to be present with them. I felt awful because I felt like I was treating these children like objects—and I felt complicit. I was not myself. I was not the teacher I wanted to be, and so I resigned.

Ultimately, Faye's complicity in doing something that she did not feel was right became burdensome and led to her resignation.

As we see with both Michelle and Faye, their experiences of the tensions between the demands of the education system to *know* children and their own sense of obligation *to* children manifested in feelings of guilt, fear, and frustration. The expert discourses inscribe the teaching subject, requiring them to *know* the Other and have a constitutive and regulatory effect on them. The teaching subject must enact expert as one who knows curriculum (in advance and without destiny) and also as one who *knows* the students (in rational not relational ways). In presuming to *know* the Other, a violence is enacted through "shrouding the Other in my totality."[20] Stated differently, the Other becomes that which can be claimed by me, becoming "the object of my comprehension, my world, my narrative, reducing the Other to me."[21] To claim to *know* the Other is a violent subsuming of the Other, an erasure of the Other's difference, and effectively undermines a capacity to share in an ethical relationality with an Other. As with Fay and Michelle, they are regulated to comply with the normative identities of expert in order to be recognizable as a teacher, and, in doing so, objectify children, compromising their relationships with them, and eschewing what that they "believed was right." Thus, they described feeling "caught," "trapped," and "complicit"; wedged between a system that constructs—and requires—them to be experts seeking rational *knowledge about* the Other, while at the same time, induced their sense of neglect in responding to their felt obligation to children.

The Child as Precarious

Although an education system premised on *knowing* defines and delineates the teaching subject in particular ways, it also has detrimental effects on the subjectivities of children, already Othered and, therefore, assuming a diminished status. As Gaile S. Cannella explains, children

> are the ultimate Other than the adult—those who must have their decisions made for them because they are not yet mature—those who must gain knowledge that has been legitimized by those who are older and wiser—those whose ways of being in the world can be uncovered through the experimental and

observational methods of science—those who can be labeled as gifted, slow, intelligent, or special.[22]

Within the education system (and reflective of the larger society generally) children are always Othered; deemed lesser, deficient, and knowable, which presumably justifies the surveillance and regulation imposed upon them. The education system's desire for mastery over the Other frames the student in particular ways, reinforcing normalized ideals of the student and then excluding, punishing, and disciplining those who exceed the frames. Frames are politically informed and reflect operations of power and, according to Butler, "become part of the very practice of ordering and regulating subjects according to pre-established norms."[23] Therefore, frames, while determining who counts as a student, also determine who does not. Frames matter particularly for those who are deemed precarious, that is, those whose lives are in the hands of others, "a dependency on people we know, or barely know, or know not at all."[24] Children are precarious because of their Otherness and their reliance on adults for their safe and healthy existence. Reciprocally, this means that teachers are obligated to these children as their students. Importantly, children with greater social and economic disadvantages have exacerbated precarity. That is, their precarity is magnified through the persistent and pervasive categorizing, identifying, labelling, psychologizing, and pathologizing, which further marginalizes them. Because frames determine the child's recognizability, the children who are more precarious are at risk of being less recognizable as students, or worse, not recognizable at all. Those children who present with greater deficiencies, and particularly those who demonstrate behavioural noncompliance within the school system, are often further scrutinized and marginalized through legal, medical, and psychological discourses.[25] Let's consider Stacey's account of her time teaching in middle years.[26]

> I had this one boy, Chris ... He was just—he had so many barriers in his life that made it really hard for him to be successful. He had no chance because the teachers before had bad mouthed him and said that "he's never going to amount to anything but a criminal." He hated school and it was an awful situation for him—really bad. So when he arrived in my class, the other teachers tried to warn me about him, but I just made it my mission to not be that teacher. Instead I wanted to be somebody that Chris would look

back on and would know that I loved him—even if [he] had other horrible experiences in his life. He had so many things working against him, but I saw all of these qualities in him.

We see in Stacey's narrative, the ways in which Chris, a boy already Othered because of his status as a child, falls outs of the frame of "student" and so becomes unrecognizable, by some of the teachers. When students cannot, do not, or will not conform to the frames that determine the student, they become labelled, cast out, and disregarded. The other teachers deemed Chris unrecognizable and determined that, "he had no chance." Thus, we see how the frames regulate "which subjects become possible at all or, rather, how they become impossibilities."[27] Chris, although only a child, was already an impossibility.

Gary Thomas and Andrew Loxley criticize the authorized—and socially constructed—discourses that frame children as

> displaced by a morass of half-understood ideas about disturbance, a jumble of bits and pieces from psychoanalysis, psychology, and psychiatry, a bricolage of penis envy and cognitive dissonance, of Freudian slip and standard deviation, of motivation and maternal deprivation, regression and repression, attention seeking and assimilation, reinforcement and self-esteem—ideas corrupted by textbook writers and mangled by journalists and the writers of popular culture.[28]

In other words, the means through which education attempts to *know* children is epistemologically, empirically, and ethically fraught, drawing on dissonant disciplines, resulting in superficial and simplistic elucidations of children. As Thomas and Loxley warn, once children's behaviour becomes identified as a psychological or social disorder, the need for moral judgement and response is interrupted. The educational purpose morphs from a child's education to the school's need to keep the child in order and illustrates the operations of power at work.

Butler helps us to understand that "lives are supported and maintained differently.... Certain lives will be highly protected ... [while] other lives will not find such fast and furious support."[29] Thus, not all lives are grievable, and the aggressive assessment sorting and labelling machines make some children's lives more precarious than others.[30] Chris's precarious existence made him unrecognizable as a student by the other teachers. The norms that circulate "produce certain subjects as 'recognizable' persons and make others decidedly more difficult to recognize."[31] As with Chris, some children's precarity is magnified by factors of their differences and their deviations from the norms, exceeding the frames of recognizability. Particular social and political conditions in which some children exist—like the numerous barriers of poverty and inequity we see in Chris' situation—exacerbate precarity, making these subjects more vulnerable.[32] As Butler warns, "If certain lives are not considered lives from the start, not conceivable as lives within certain epistemological frames, then these lives are never lived or lost in the fullest sense."[33] Chris, exceeding the frames of recognizability, is unrecognizable as a student—as a vulnerable child—by the other teachers. His destiny is already determined: "He won't amount to anything." Left up to the teacher to be seen and acknowledged, while at the same time rendered unrecognizable,[34] the child does not count in the school's accounting of the child.

The frames that exist within education are the norms by which students' subjectivities are recognized. They are the norms that operate, regulate, and categorize, constituting who is and is not recognizable. At best unnoticed and at worst actively ostracized, these students, who are already precarious, become more vulnerable when they do not measure up. Determined as deviant or deficient by an education epistemology that presumes to *know* them, they are often assumed pre-destined "to end up in jail or dead before he's eighteen," as one of our participants flatly stated. As Butler explains, "if violence is done against those who are unreal, then, from the perspective of the violence, it fails to injure or negate those lives since those lives are already negated."[35] We can dismiss these children and their futures because these lives are already deemed lost.[36] Yet, Stacey and Faye sought to apprehend the child beyond the frames of recognizability, to acknowledge the child's vulnerability exacerbated by social and political forces.[37] They demonstrated a willingness to be in relation with these precarious Others, and to engage in the risk of relationality even when these children appeared beyond recognition as students.

Teaching as an Ethical Relation

Many teachers in our study often spoke about the tensions they felt between what the system of education required of them (that is, to *know* the Other) and their desire for more ethical relations with children; that is, to apprehend children beyond the dominant epistemological and technical frames of schooling. Consider George, a resource teacher in middle school, and his frustrations: "Teaching needs to be more inspirational and more creative and more about the kids. It can't just be about the numbers on the tests." Like Faye and Michelle, George expressed his frustration with the education system's persistent attempts at quantifying children, and wishing for the valuing of other (not quantifiable) attributes of children, such as creativity and curiosity. In identifying these tensions between rationality and relationality, we see in teachers like George attempts to engage ethically with their students, attempts to *learn from* the Other; that is, to engender an encounter between the self and the Other as a "profoundly ethical event"[38] premised on openness and an exposure of one's vulnerability.

But what does it look like to *learn from* the Other? What qualities, dispositions, or practices do teachers enlist in order to enliven such ethical relations with the Other? In order to respond to these questions, it is important to be reminded of Todd's distinction between the self and Other. As Todd interprets Levinas, she reminds us that, the "encounter between the self and Other is the time and place of responsibility."[39] Although George asserts that teachers need to be focused on rapport and relationship, Todd cautions that this relationship required to *learn from* the Other cannot be constituted through pity or sympathy.[40] As Todd explains, "the mystery here is the radical alterity of the Other, and so the encounter must always refuse reducing the Other to a common ground with the self."[41] Thus, although feelings of empathy and sympathy may be important and even inevitable, an ethical engagement with the Other must maintain the distinction between the self and the Other. In other words, in order to maintain the alterity of the Other—the distinction between the self and the Other—the ethical engagement is not an attempt to seek a common ground, but rather to maintain a divide; to remain attentive and receptive to the differences of the Other.[42]

In order to create relationships where difference is valued, one must maintain a disposition of curiosity about and an openness to the Other, resisting knowing the Other through simplistic assumptions, and instead being interested in what is *unknown*, what lies beyond the frames of recognition. George relays a story about one particular middle years student, Destiny:

> The other teachers thought she was lazy. They said, "She's dull. She's this. She's that." And her foster parents—she was a kid in care—thought she was a good kid too, but she wasn't their child; so she was good money and wasn't causing trouble for them. So we have a kid getting low grades and yet no one cared about that. But I think we need to stand up for these kids. That's what we signed up for as teachers. I was fortunate to have the time to just sit with Destiny—to talk with her. It was a chance to work with a kid who was a mystery to me.

George resisted the easy labels such as "lazy" and instead wanted to engage with Destiny and to consider the aspects of her that were a mystery to him. With George, we see a teaching relation where *learning from* the Other requires an openness to the unknown, a disposition of wonder. An ethical relation with the Other requires a resistance to assumptions that the Other can be known and instead demands a desire to consider the mysteries of and remain curious about the Other. In doing so, one maintains the radical alterity and unknowability of the Other.[43]

In maintaining a stance of openness toward the Other, the teacher resists *knowing* or relying on what is *known about* the Other. We see this when George rejects the dismissive descriptors of Destiny, refusing to assume to *know* her, thereby rejecting the frames that risk making her unrecognizable. George, similar to Stacey, is not satisfied with what is presumed to be known about the student—the rationalized labels that arrive before the child, underscoring the child's precarity and reducing her human-ness. Instead, George and Stacey both have a deep interest in *learning from* the student, maintaining an openness to the ambiguity of the Other.[44] Here we see that the ethical relation between the teacher and the student, and the ethical possibility of education, is only conceivable when *knowing about* the child (assessing, judging, identifying) is not the objective of the relationship.[45] One must be able to resist the rational and limiting labels of education's epistemological hegemony, and rather, cultivate "an eagerness to inquire … a willingness to suspend judgment and bracket existing—potentially limiting—ways of thinking, seeing, and categorising."[46] Thus, in order to foster ethical relations and to *learn from* the Other, one must suspend judgments about the Other and attempt to apprehend the child beyond the existing frames of recognizability.

We see the importance of the suspension of judgment in Doug's account of working with a "difficult" high school student, Jeanine. Although Jeanine was "getting by," there was something about her that worried Doug. Doug explained, "I spent years developing a relationship with Jeanine. At first she wouldn't even speak to me." According to Doug, her other teachers described her as "fairly smart" but they also complained that, "she was not a hard worker and rarely did her homework." Doug continued, "One day, she told me everything: her Dad was an alcoholic with terminal cancer who did not live with her and her Mom. Her Mom was also addicted to alcohol and spent her welfare money on her addiction. Turns out, Jeanine was working three jobs so she could pay the mortgage on the house!" Doug's efforts to develop a relationship with Jeanine took years and perhaps she finally talked to him simply because he was open to listening to her.

Doug did not seek to *know about* Jeanine, to categorize or diagnose her, and he resisted the easy labels assigned by others. Instead, Doug attempted to engage in a relationship with Jeanine without knowing if she would ever even speak with him. The moment of listening illustrated Jeanine's trust in Doug, as well as Doug's tolerance for uncertainty in the listening relationship. In suspending judgment, being patient, and demonstrating openness, Doug eventually earned her trust.

In his relationship with Jeanine, Doug was both "passively open and exposed"[47] to the alterity of the Other. Put simply, he was rendered vulnerable and susceptible to the unforeseen effects of the relationship.[48] Doug helped Jeanine to apply for and receive a $25,000 scholarship for university, and yet it troubled him. He worried about his role in Jeanine's success, vacillating between guilt that perhaps he had pushed her to apply for the scholarship and hope that she had an opportunity that she could not have previously imagined. He was pleased for her because "Jeanine was so over-the-moon happy that she was going to university because no one in her family had even graduated from high school before." And yet his guilt remained: "I worried that I hadn't done my job correctly." Doug doubted his decisions and worried that Jeanine felt pressure to apply for the scholarships because of his encouragement. These are the risks of ethical relations; when "I am exposed to the Other, I can listen, attend, and be surprised; the Other can affect me."[49] Doug was affected by his relationship with Jeanine; affected by his care for her, but also by the concomitant effects of doubt, guilt, and worry. And yet, like so many of our participants that engaged in these deeply affective relations with the most precarious children, Doug did not know what had ultimately happened to Jeanine.

The Risks of the Ethical Relation

Remaining open to the Other is a risk in that one cannot know in advance what the Other will do or say, what the Other needs or wants. Openness, thus, requires vulnerability and receptiveness to the unforeseeable and unpredictable needs of the Other.[50] While the Otherness remains constantly beyond one's grasp, the purpose of being open to the Other is not to come to understand the Other, but rather to "sustain a mode of relation where the love comes into being through response to the Other."[51] As we see with Stacey when she declared her decision to simply love Chris, even though she did not even have him as a student yet, she did so as a way of respecting the alterity of the Other. Although her colleagues "warned" her about him, she saw a boy who "no one else seemed to want to spend any time with." Stacey actively rejected her colleagues' stance of presuming to know him as "difficult" and instead, attentive to his precarity and respecting his alterity, Stacey "decided to make it [her] mission to engage, nurture, and love him."

Stacey did not and could not know what would come from her efforts nor did she seem to want anything in return. Her commitment reflected her own vulnerability in the loving relation: her willingness to be uncertain, to be altered, and to risk her own self-assurance.[52] Stacey, like Doug, demonstrated a willingness to be open to the unknown and to bear the consequences of the unforeseen effects. According to Todd, it is this continual receptiveness that "ground[s] love's ethical potential."[53] Todd writes:

> This meaning of love therefore suggests that it is not what I know about the Other that is important for establishing connection,

but that I simply am for the Other in my feeling for her; I learn from and respond to her difference.[54]

These teachers—Stacey, Doug, Faye, and Michelle—simply *are* for the Other: playing on the floor without an ulterior motive, being curious and attentive, and waiting patiently for a child's story to be revealed. Their engagements with the Other are "not instrumental, not *for* something else";[55] rather, they are about sustaining an openness to the Other and to the difference of the Other, resolved to cultivate an ethical relationality.

Yet relationships that honour the alterity of Other risk the teachers' own recognizability. In resisting an epistemological imperative to know children, they suspend judgment, and maintain their own vulnerability. The teachers' attention to the precarious ones requires their non-compliance with the expert discourses of teaching. As Stacey describes, there was "a lot of pushback from the other teachers, particularly this one staff member. He would not accept that anything positive could happen with Chris." This illustrates how students who are not recognizable with the frames are "cast as threats,"[56] considered deviant, a danger to the social order of schooling and to society at large. In attempting to engage with the precarious children with openness, Stacey encountered "pushback" and thus risked her own recognizability; that is, she was contesting the power at work, enacting teacher differently from the norms by rejecting definitive knowledge of the Other. George's, Doug's, and Stacey's actions illustrate their obligations to the precarious Others, where "something about [their] suffering stops us in our tracks."[57] Their obligations to the Other requires them to act, yet in doing so, they do not enact the teaching subject as prescribed by the discursive norms of knowing.

Jeanine and Chris are precarious youth to whom these teachers have exposed their vulnerabilities, to whom they have listened without judgment, and to whom they have responded without certainty of outcome and without expectation of reciprocity. The teachers demonstrate their willingness to *learn from* children, an openness to their own vulnerabilities, without an end goal or redemptive tale in mind. Stacey says, in her attempts to "love" Chris, that she "doesn't even know if it made a difference." Yet, Todd reminds us that "the point is we can never figure out completely; we cannot calculate, in some algorythmic fashion, the end result in order to keep our actions safe and ourselves intact."[58] In these relationships with the schools' most precarious children, the teachers expose their own vulnerability; they risk themselves; they doubt their decisions, they are uncertain about the outcomes, and they fear judgement from others. This, I believe, demonstrates the qualities of teachers' obligations to children: an unremitting commitment to an ethical response to the precarious Other while enduring the risks involved.

Teachers' Obligations to Precarious Others

Within the epistemological narratives of mastery, students are "framed" through discursive norms that operate "to produce certain subjects as 'recognizable' persons [making] others decidedly more difficult to recognize."[59] In these stories, Destiny, Chris, and Jeanine were indeed precarious—the ones who did not meet the norms. They were presumed to be known and knowable; dehumanized, objectified, and described as "slow," "lazy," "dull," "difficult," "likely end up in jail," "worth good money," or simply "bad." They were unrecognizable as "students" and were at risk of being—and often were—conceived as lives unworthy of response. The educational system's frames are technologies of power that amplify the precarity of these already precarious children and are politically informed mechanisms to maintain the social order of things.[60]

In the education system's epistemological endeavour that privileges knowledge, teachers are expected to be experts, to *know* and to propagate *knowing about* a child, enlisting hyperactive means of surveillance and assessment, identifying deficit and deviance, foreclosing differences and ignoring the mysteries of the Other. It is this disposition of expert—the perseveration on *knowing* the Other rather than being in an ethical relation with the Other—that can disturb the teacher. As we saw with Michelle and Faye, they were frustrated by the system that privileged rational knowledge (which manifested in testing and surveillance) over their understandings of teaching as being relationally oriented. However, these stories also illustrate teachers' strong sense of educational purpose and demonstrate "the very humility necessary for assuming responsibility"[61] within technocratic education systems.

George's, Doug's, and Stacey's stories also illustrated the nuances of teachers' attempts to be in ethical relation with children, suspending judgments, maintaining an openness to their mysteries, waiting patiently, listening, and loving them. These teachers help us to see the qualities of teachers' obligations to children; centering unknowability and cultivating openness toward the Other—particularly with education's most precarious children. Although tasked with caring for so many children, these teachers engaged with those most precarious—those cast out by the system as unrecognizable. Their commitment to *learn from* the Other demonstrates their resistance to education's epistemological demands that arrive in advance, and their willingness to being changed by the encounter. Because "the precarity of life imposes an obligation on us,"[62] we see in these teachers their attempts to apprehend the precarious Others beyond the frames of recognition. Thus, in cultivating ethical relationships—particularly with our most precarious children—teachers exhibit a tolerance for uncertainty, an openness to the differences of the Other, and a willingness to expose their own vulnerabilities. The ethical response is an unrelenting commitment—but also always a risk.

Acknowledgement: This research was supported by the Social Sciences and Humanities Research Council of Canada [grant number 430-2015-00814].

Notes

1. Janzen and Phelan, "'Tugging at Our Sleeves.'" Quotations from teachers cited in this chapter are drawn from the larger research study, which explores the emotional toll of teachers' obligations to children and teachers' disengagement from the profession.
2. Caputo, *Against Ethics*.
3. Caputo, 5.
4. Janzen and Phelan, "'Tugging at Our Sleeves,'" 12.
5. Butler, *Frames of War*.
6. Todd, *Learning from the Other*.
7. Butler, *Precarious Life*, 29.
8. Janzen and Phelan, "'Tugging at Our Sleeves.'"
9. Todd, *Learning from the Other*, 8.
10. Butler, *Psychic Life of Power*; Davies, "Subjectification."
11. Butler, *Psychic Life of Power*, 2.
12. Butler.
13. Butler, *Giving an Account*, 22.
14. Butler, 22.
15. Ball, "Teacher's Soul," 216.
16. Ball, 221.
17. Todd, *Learning from the Other*.
18. Todd.
19. Todd.
20. Todd, 15.
21. Todd, 15.
22. Cannella, "Scientific Discourse," 36.
23. Butler, *Frames of War*, 141.
24. Butler, *Frames of War*, 14.
25. Janzen and Schwartz, "Behaving Badly."
26. "Middle years" refers to schooling provided for youth aged between ten and fourteen years, that is, Grades 5, 6, 7, and 8.
27. Butler, *Frames of War*, 163.
28. Thomas and Loxley, *Deconstructing*, 55.
29. Butler, *Precarious Life*, 32.
30. Butler, *Frames of War*.
31. Butler, 6.
32. Butler, *Precarious Life*.
33. Butler, *Frames of War*, 6.
34. Butler.
35. Butler, 33.
36. Butler.

37 Butler.
38 Todd, *Learning from the Other*, 50.
39 Todd, 50.
40 Todd, 51.
41 Todd, 51.
42 Todd.
43 Todd.
44 Todd.
45 Todd.
46 Schinkel, "Deep Wonder," 539.
47 Todd, "Teaching with Ignorance," 347.
48 Todd, *Learning from the Other*.
49 Todd, 15.
50 Todd.
51 Todd, 89.
52 Todd.
53 Todd, 88–89.
54 Todd, 73.
55 Schinkel, "Deep Wonder," 549.
56 Butler, *Frames of War*, 31.
57 Caputo, *Against Ethics*, 32.
58 Todd, *Learning from the Other*, 88–89.
59 Butler *Frames*, 6.
60 Butler, *Precarious Life*.
61 Todd, *Learning from the Other*, 16.
62 Butler, *Frames of War*, 2.

Bibliography

Ball, Stephen J. "The Teacher's Soul and the Terrors of Performativity." *Journal of Education Policy* 18, no. 2 (2003): 215–228.

Butler, Judith. *Frames of War: When Is Life Grievable?* London, UK: Verso Books, 2010.

———. *Giving an Account of Oneself*. New York, NY: Fordham University Press, 2005.

———. *Precarious Life: The Powers of Mourning and Violence*. New York, NY: Verso, 2004.

———. *The Psychic Life of Power: Theories in Subjection*. Stanford: Stanford University Press, 1997.

Cannella, Gaile S. "The Scientific Discourse of Education: Predetermining the Lives of Others—Foucault, Education, and Children." *Contemporary Issues in Early Childhood* 1, no. 1 (2000): 36–44.

Caputo, John D. *Against Ethics: Contributions to a Poetics of Obligation with Constant Reference to Deconstruction.* Bloomington, IN: Indiana University Press, 1993.

Davies, Bronwyn. "Subjectification: The Relevance of Butler's Analysis for Education." *British Journal of Sociology of Education* 27, no. 4 (2006): 425–438.

Janzen, Melanie D. "The Aporia of Undecideability and the Responsibility of Teacher." *Teaching Education* 24, no. 4 (2013): 381–394. doi.org/10.1080/10476210.2012.716035.

Janzen, Melanie D., and Anne M. Phelan. "The Emotional Toll of Obligation and Teachers' Disengagement from the Profession." *Alberta Journal of Educational Research* 61, no. 3 (2015): 347–350.

———. "'Tugging at Our Sleeves': Understanding Experiences of Obligation in Teaching." *Teaching Education* (2018): 1–15. doi.org/10.1080/10476210.2017.1420157.

Janzen, Melanie D., and Karen Schwartz. "Behaving Badly: Critiquing the Discourses of 'Children' and their 'Mis'behaviours." *McGill Journal of Education*, in press.

Schinkel, Anders. "The Educational Importance of Deep Wonder." *Journal of Philosophy of Education* 51, no. 2 (2017): 538–553.

Thomas, Gary, and Andrew Loxley. *Deconstructing Special Education and Constructing Inclusion* (2nd ed). New York, NY: McGraw Hill, 2007.

Todd, Sharon. *Learning from the Other: Levinas, Psychoanalysis, and Ethical Possibilities in Education.* New York, NY: SUNY Press, 2003.

———. "Teaching with Ignorance: Questions of Social Justice, Empathy, and Responsible Community." *Interchange* 35, no. 3 (2004): 337–352.

CHAPTER 8

Teaching as a Learned Profession: The Evolution of Inquiry in a Teacher Education Program[1]

Anthony Clarke

Drawing from the theme of academic erudition, if teaching is a *learned profession* then the ability to be curious about, to study, and to inquire into one's practice is a defining feature of that practice. Within the context of teacher preparation, an emphasis on inquiry has long been a mainstay of many North American Bachelor of Education (BEd) programs.[2] For example, inquiry can range from encouraging teacher candidates to be curious about their practice, to educating and supporting them as practitioner researchers.[3] Making sense of these programs within their particular contexts is important for understanding the evolution of inquiry within teacher education as we know it today. This chapter charts this evolution within the context of one North American teacher education program: the University of British Columbia's BEd program. To do so, the analysis draws on Alan Tom's three-part frame for understanding inquiry in teacher education.[4] Central to Tom's frame are three dimensions, posed here as questions:

1. What is the arena of the problematic that is espoused?
2. What is the mode of inquiry that is adopted?
3. What is the ontological status of the phenomena that is assumed?

Each of these dimensions can be considered as a continuum (see Figure 1).

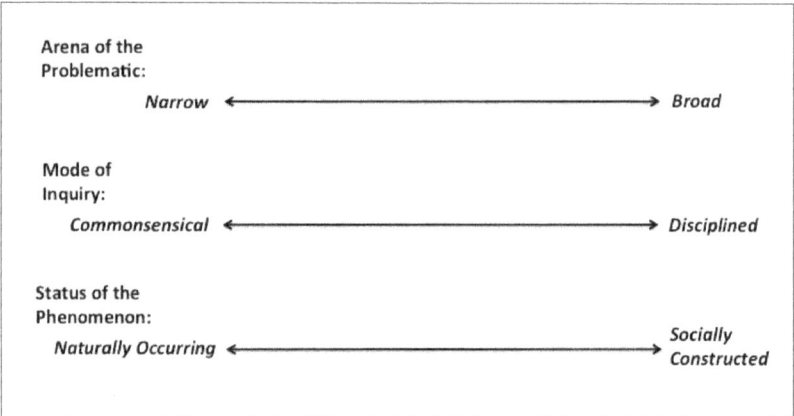

Figure 1: Alan Tom's (1985) three-part analytic frame for examining inquiry-oriented teacher education.

Tom describes the first dimension as follows:

> To make teaching problematic is to raise doubts about what, under ordinary circumstances, appear to be effective or wise practice... While there is consensus that the making of some aspect of teaching problematic is to question that which is taken for granted, no consensus exists concerning which aspect of teaching ought to be the object of problematic thinking... At one end of the dimension is the "teaching-learning process" while at the other end is "society," including educational institutions.[5]

In short, Tom suggests that as we move from one end of the "arena of the problematic" continuum to the other end we go from a relatively narrow to a much broader inquiry focus. For example, we might go from a very limited focus on the behavior of a single child to a more encompassing focus on the child in our midst[6] where the latter asks us to think about the child in the wider context in which schools and societies are situated (See Figure 2).

This shift in focus indicates a richer and more informed understanding of practice, an essential element of any claim to academic erudition within the teaching profession.[7]

The second dimension, the mode of inquiry, directs our attention to the methods and practices endorsed and suggested for undertaking inquiry in a program. These range from very simple methods

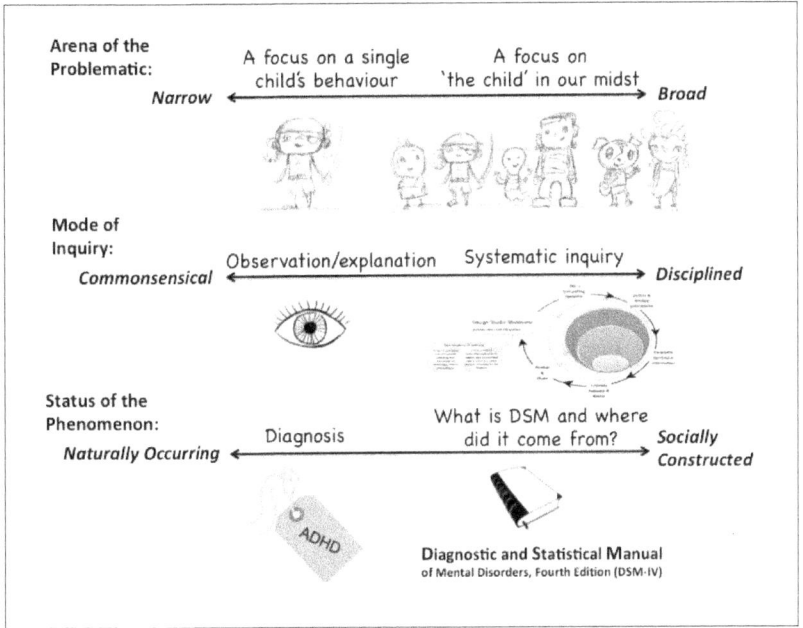

Figure 2: Examples illustrating Tom's (1985) three dimensions of inquiry.

that may be viewed as relatively unproblematic and commonsensical, to more disciplined and nuanced ways of exploring a particular problem or set of problems:

> At one end of the continuum are those inquiry models which stress common sense approaches to deriving knowledge about teaching; at the other end are inquiry models which unite the disciplined study of teaching with a concern for the quality of teacher actions.[8]

Common sense approaches often require less formal preparation and are relatively easy to enact (for example, observation). Disciplined inquiry, on the other hand, requires a greater degree of preparation for and knowledge about inquiry methods appropriate to the phenomenon under study. The latter demands a higher level of academic erudition by individuals, commensurate with their accumulated experience within the profession. It is important to note that higher levels would not be expected of teacher candidates, but the foundations should be laid during their BEd program. A failure to do this jeopardizes its development as lifelong professional pursuit.

Finally, Tom suggests that the ontological status of the educational phenomenon is an important determinant for the sorts of questions one asks and the claims that one hopes to make as a result of the inquiry undertaken:

> In recent years, considerable disenchantment has developed with the assumption that educational phenomenon are natural... These and related concerns have led to a number of inquiry-oriented teacher educators to see educational phenomena not so much as naturally occurring events in need of analysis and understanding but as social constructions in need of thoughtful and wise design efforts.[9]

In Figure 2, the example used to demonstrate this dimension has at one end of the continuum the simple matching of the observations of a child's behaviour with one of the disorders (Attention Deficit Hyperactivity Disorder) listed in the APA's Diagnostic and Statistical Manual (DSM).[10] At the other end of the continuum, inquiry is framed in terms of examining the construction of the DSM itself,[11] for example, asking: "Who created it?"; "Who makes judgments about what is included in it?"; and "Whose interests are being served by it?" As we move along Tom's third continuum, the analytic demands increase, and the expectations for erudition heighten. Both go hand in hand as the practitioner increasingly appreciates education as complex endeavour.[12]

These examples illustrate and help to contextualize Tom's rendering of the three dimensions of his analytic frame for examining inquiry-oriented teacher education. As such they highlight the underlying expectations for academic erudition. These expectations increase as we move from the left to the right of the continua. In this paper, they will be used to analyze the evolution of inquiry in UBC's BEd program over the past sixty years. To facilitate this analysis, a brief rendering of the history of the program follows.

University of British Columbia's BEd Degree Program

The University of British Columbia's BEd program has been in existence for over sixty years. Its history reveals five distinct iterations (or reform efforts) occurring at approximately twelve-year intervals (Table I).

Table I: Five Iterations of UBC's BEd Degree Program.

Year	Program Iteration
1956–1971	The Beginning Years
1972–1986	The Kaleidoscope Years
1987–1999	The New Program Years
2000–2012	The Experimental Years
2012–present	The CREATE Years

Each of these iterations is significant in its own right and has been influenced by a number of factors such as the leadership of the day, ongoing debates in teacher education, and resource availability. One constant through the years has been the relatively stable level of student enrolment in the program (between 700 to 900 students), a factor that is significant in the life of any faculty of education in North America, where competition between various teacher education providers has serious ramifications for the viability of the program offered.

The Beginning Years (1956–1971)

In 1956, pre-service teacher education in British Columbia officially moved from Normal Schools to the newly established Faculty of Education at the University of British Columbia under the leadership of Dean Neville Scarfe. Normal Schools were post-secondary institutions established for the preparation of elementary and secondary school teachers and existed in various places throughout the world from the late-1800s through to the 1950s.[13] The shift of teacher education to the university saw the number of professors and instructors employed in teacher education almost double to forty-two. The initial enrolment figure for pre-service teacher education students was 905 (537 elementary and 332 secondary teacher candidates).

The program developed two routes for teacher certification. First, students could attend the faculty full-time and complete all their coursework (content and pedagogy) over a three-year period. Second, students could transfer into the program after completing a degree in another faculty and then undertake a twelve-month BEd degree. The program was largely prescribed for the students with little or no option for individual choice, experimentation, or inquiry on the part of the students; in short, the university had the knowledge, and they gave it to the students, and the students were expected to apply that knowledge unproblematically in school settings.

The Kaleidoscope Years (1972–1986)

The late 1960s and early 1970s heralded a number of new and innovative ideas in education. For example, educational theorist Jerome Bruner had a marked influence on alternative practices in education (such as the discovery learning model for classroom practice). These practices were embraced at UBC. In 1972, under the leadership of a new dean, Professor John Andrews, the Faculty established a number of alternative field-based teacher education options within the program. The options were based on the individual interest of faculty members. The names given to the various options are indicative of their uniqueness and diversity: Task Oriented Teacher Education (TOTE); Community of Values Education Teachers (COVET); In School Involvement for Teachers of English (INSITE); Low Income Student Teacher Education Network (LISTEN); and the Native Indian Teacher Education Program (NITEP). Involvement in field settings for the different program options also varied greatly, with some options locating their entire program in schools (where, for example, professors and teachers co-taught the program). A sense of inquiry, rooted in the themes taken up by each option, emerged. However, these inquiries were not highly formalized and, at best, were loosely coupled to the students' overall learning experience.[14] The Kaleidoscope years occurred at a time of great prosperity within the province and around the world. Faculty numbers swelled to 276 (distributed across twenty-two departments). Ninety-five percent of tenure-stream faculty were involved in the BEd program. Unfortunately, the excitement was relatively short-lived as key factors that allowed the emergence of the various program options (such as high levels of resourcing) changed shortly thereafter, and their demise was complete by the early 1980s despite the seeming success of the program. Few people know of this colourful past today.

The New Program Years (1987-1999)

As the 1980s approached, two critical factors converged which substantively impacted pre-service teacher education at UBC. First, the tenure and promotion system, which had previously emphasized teaching and service (as evident in the faculty's high level of involvement in pre-service teacher education at that time), shifted to rewarding those who were involved in research and graduate education.[15] Second, there was a global economic recession that had a marked effect on budgets and staffing. As a result of these two factors, human and financial resources were drained from pre-service teacher education. However, enrolment levels remained high, which necessitated a complete transformation of the program.

A teacher education review committee proposed a new two-year post-degree program for the preparation of elementary and secondary school teachers. Unfortunately the University Senate (who oversee all major program revisions) balked at the proposal, noting that they did not believe that secondary school teachers required two years of professional preparation to become teachers. This challenge to the Faculty's autonomy further diminished the BEd program in the eyes of faculty members, and flight from teacher education (to research and graduate education) continued at a heightened pace. As a result, a highly centralized, lock-step curriculum was adopted, called the New Program, which was staffed largely by sessional or contract instructors (85% of the program). The end result was that the New Program reversed most of the modest gains related to inquiry witnessed in the Kaleidoscope Years. The New Program was first offered in 1987 and coincided with the appointment of a new dean, Nancy Sheehan, who as a new arrival to the University, held little sway over the introduction or direction of the reform efforts.

The Experimental Years (2000-2011)

New paradigms of thought and practice arose within education and began displacing the technical rational[16] emphasis evident in in UBC's New Program Years with new and emergent emphases such as teaching as a moral practice appearing.[17] As a result, some faculty members, particularly recent appointees, began to lament the highly structured and fragmented nature of teacher education at UBC (for example, the separation of theory from practice, and the siloed nature of the courses within the program). Fundamentally, the program in its current form was unacceptable to faculty who had a deep interest and willingness to invest their time in teacher education. As a result, from late 1990s onwards a small group of tenure-track faculty sought permission to experiment with a cohort concept (calving off cohort groups of 36 students from the mainstream group of 900 teacher candidates) where they could have some degree of professional autonomy over what and how teacher education was enacted. Further, these early cohorts were built around the research interests of the faculty members involved. These cohorts were reminiscent of the program options witnessed during the Kaleidoscope Years but were more substantive in terms of their theoretical underpinnings. Cohorts created at this time included Problem Based Learning (PBL), Fine Arts and Media Education (FAME), and Community of Inquiry in Teacher Education (CITE). In contrast to the heavy experiential emphasis of the Kaleidoscope Years, the new cohorts sought better integration between on-campus courses and off-campus fieldwork such that theory and practice were intertwined throughout the students' learning experience.[18]

Due to the success reported by these programs after a couple of years, a teacher education review committee was struck to develop a set of principles based on the emerging cohort model and a proposal to change the entire program based on these principles was formally submitted to the British Columbia College of Teachers (BCCT), the provincial teacher registration body established in 1987 that oversaw and approved teacher education programs in the province at that time. As these negotiations unfolded, the issue of a semi-autonomous government body (the BCCT) having oversight over the content of a university program became increasingly contentious (although few, including the BCCT reviewers, disagreed with the main features of the proposed program). A new dean, Robert Tierney, was appointed at this time and sought legal action to resolve the issue. The courts eventually ruled that the BCCT had the right to determine if the program's graduates met the requirements for certification but did not have the right to direct the university as to how they would prepare students for that certification within the program. The legal arguments and associated court case took three years to conclude.[19] At the end, everyone involved in teacher education at UBC was exhausted by the ordeal, and the proposal to reform the New Program was shelved.

In 2006, after a few years of respite following the protracted legal wrangling described above, a re-visioning process called the Community to Re-imagine Educational Alternatives for Teacher Education (CREATE) was established in the Faculty. Following extensive faculty-wide consultation, CREATE developed a new set of principles based on the cohort model. Unlike the preceding committee, discussion about individual courses per se within the program was held in abeyance so that the process of developing educationally sound principles for a teacher education program would not get bogged down in territorial warfare between departments. While this was an admirable aim, the implementation of the principles and associated learning experiences intended for the revised program still had to run the gauntlet of departmental approval and many of the admirable intentions of CREATE were significantly curtailed by the end of the process; concessions such as one-credit courses (in what had previously been a three-credit course economy for teacher education) were used to satisfy department demands, but in reality these concessions only exacerbated program fragmentation that the Experimental Years sought to overcome. Nonetheless, a new direction for UBC's teacher education program was forged with some program-wide emphases surviving and new emphases such as Indigenous education, inquiry, and community field experiences introduced.[20]

The CREATE Years (2012–Present)

After five long years of deliberation, the fifth program iteration, based on the CREATE revisioning, was adopted by the Faculty. It is currently in its sixth year, and although a number of the goals have been achieved—most notably the inclusion of inquiry seminars in each of the three terms of the program—there are still considerable challenges stemming from the frustrations experienced during the five years that it took to develop the CREATE program. For example, the program is more fragmented than the previous one (for example, there are more individual courses than in the previous iteration). This fragmentation has made it impossible for the cohort coordinators to gather the eighteen or so individual course instructors for the cohort so that they can communicate and make decisions together (something that was a key feature of the cohorts in the Experimental Years cohorts). Further, other successes of the Experimental Years were watered down. For example, what was previously a three-week short practicum in the first term was reduced to two-week practicum so that it could be scheduled and managed across the whole program. While this might seem like a small change, it largely undercut years of work by some existing cohorts with schools and school districts in establishing the three-week practicum to take full advantage of the students' early immersion in schools. Further, the first school term was broken into two five-week blocks to accommodate the increased number of one-credit and two-credit courses (in what was previously only a three-credit course economy). As a result, reflectivity seemed to be replaced by intensivity as students struggled to deal with multiple courses with multiple instructors over shortened time periods. Fortunately the Faculty sees the BEd program as a dynamic (not static) and has attempted to respond these challenges. Nonetheless, structural barriers still exist that limit these efforts.

The above five iterations of UBC's BEd program provide an overview of its evolution since its inception. During that time the program has moved from the view of teaching as largely a technical endeavour (born out of the process-product movement) through to an increasing appreciation for the complexity of teaching as a political, moral, and social act (for example, teaching for social justice[21]). The following section of this chapter analyzes these iterations in terms of Tom's three dimensions of inquiry-oriented teacher education.

Inquiry-Oriented Teacher Education: A Historical Analysis of UBC's BEd Program

The following analysis of the five iterations of UBC's BEd program shows that, with one exception, it has been slowly inching its way from left to right along Tom's three continua (Figure 3).[22]

Not surprisingly, the Early Years (1956–1971) were positioned at the far left end of the three continua. This positioning represents the prevalence of a particular view of knowledge held by the academy at that time, specifically, the seductive simplicity of readily codified behaviours that emanated from the positivist paradigm (for example, teacher effectiveness, process-product, and teacher competency research).[23] As Van Manen notes, the enthusiastic application of such theory to teacher education was not unexpected:

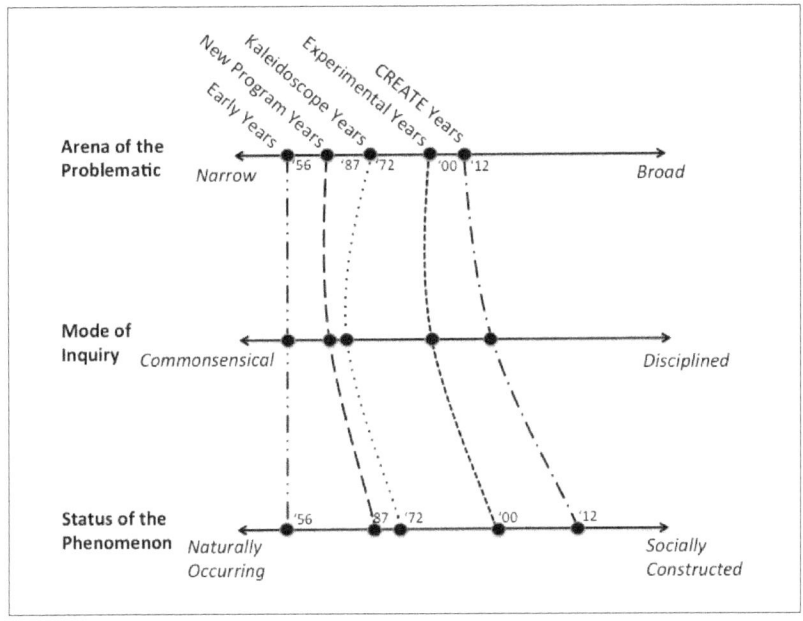

Figure 3: The five iterations of UBC's teacher education program mapped against Tom's (1985) three continua for inquiry-oriented teacher education.

> In a culture where the knowledge industry is strongly dominated by an attitude of accountability and human engineering, it is not surprising that the predominant concern of educational practice [had] become an instrumental pre-occupation with *techniques*, *control*, and means-ends criteria of *efficiency* and *effectiveness*. [original emphasis][24]

Thus, the preparation of beginning teachers was greatly simplified when teaching was viewed as instrumental problem solving.[25] In short, teacher candidates were viewed as technicians who faithfully implemented the results of academic research.[26] As a consequence, the BEd program at UBC became imbued with a technical, almost scientific language that was supposedly an accurate representation of the world. The notion of the teacher as technician was further underscored by the positivist assumption that the problems of practice were generalizable across multiple contexts and, as such, did not require curiosity or inquiry to determine if any adjustments might be required in these contexts.[27] In sum, an instrumental-heavy and inquiry-light focus characterized the program.

The second iteration of the UBC BEd program, the Kaleidoscope Years (1972–1986), was a particularly generative period during which there was a shift in emphasis to experiential learning, influenced by Bruner's "discovery learning."[28] As noted earlier, some program options spent their entire time in school contexts. The program coordinators for the various options were very progressive in terms of encouraging students to broaden the scope of their inquiries to include a wide range of educational phenomena. Limited, however, was the mode of inquiry used to explore the various phenomena that the students were encountering. Recall that action research[29] as a mode of inquiry was only beginning to take root in the 1980s and had yet to have an impact on teacher education in North America; the pre-test/post-test mindset still held considerable sway. Nonetheless this period did see some remarkable changes to the ways in which teacher education was conceived (faculty interests drove their involvement in teacher education) and the changing nature of the way in which phenomena were viewed (as being inextricably linked to practice). The various program options offered during this iteration were among the most ambitious and exciting that the Faculty had ever seen. However, the highly experiential nature of these programs meant that inquiry was mostly based on a trial-and-error model—a process which may or may not have the desired outcome(s)—rather than being guided by more systematic and rigorous inquiry. Britzman's questioning of the old maxim that practice makes perfect speaks to one of the key problems here.[30]

In stark contrast to the freedom given to the different program options during the Kaleidoscope Years, the New Program Years (1987–1999) returned to a centralized structure with an emphasis on codified knowledge. Indeed, this reversal was driven by the reduced number of faculty members (who were ostensibly the experts in teacher education) and the university's insistence on a twelve-month rather than a two-year BEd program, which placed an enforced time-press on teacher candidate learning that continues today. For example, the scheduling of classes into large group lectures and the lock-step nature of the curriculum resulted in a largely balkanized and disjointed program.[31] Further, the flight of faculty from the program and their replacement with contract and sessional instructors reduced the capacity for creating and sustaining a culture of inquiry in the program. In British Columbia, researchers such as Grimmett and McKinnon reacted to this shift in teacher education by advocating for the importance of craft knowledge in learning to teach.[32] This situation was not confined to UBC. In the United States, Goodlad[33] decried the use of what he called shadow faculty and argued that delegating the work of teacher education to less experienced and less knowledgeable instructors diminished the possibilities for a truly vigorous, vibrant, and erudite teacher education program. The upshot was regression on all three of Tom's[34] inquiry-oriented teacher education dimensions during this period.

The Experimental Years (2000–2012) saw a more sustained and deeper investment in inquiry than previously witnessed at UBC. A key factor was the increased degree of autonomy and flexibility that was permitted for faculty members who piloted theme-based cohorts (for example, organizing clusters of thirty-six students with a small group of instructors based on a particular theme such as Problem-Based Learning or Fine Arts and Media Education). The shift away from the lock-step, system-wide oversight of the BEd curriculum allowed for a range of possibilities for inquiry both on and off campus. This shift followed the larger and more inquiry-encompassing Professional Development School (PDS) movement in the United States[35] but without the same level of funding. A deliberate shift from fragmentation to integration of the program elements took place. For example, the arena of the problematic now made sense because the program allowed for contextualized inquiry.[36] Indeed, inquiry was woven into the fabric of the cohorts by virtue of the fact that faculty members were engaged in teacher education research within their own cohorts. As a result, not only were faculty members supporting the students' inquiries but they were modelling the practice of inquiry at the same time. The powerful combination of teacher education and teacher education research was one of the most distinguishing features of the cohorts in the Experimental Years.

As a result of the very positive feedback from students and faculty during the Experimental Years, the CREATE Years (2012–present) formally included inquiry as one of five thematic strands within the B.Ed. curriculum:

> UBC teacher educators consider Inquiry to be a hallmark of teacher education and development.... The CREATE Teacher Education Program revision draws attention to our own research

orientation and encourages teacher candidates to inquire systematically into their own practices.[37]

Furthermore, inquiry was allocated one-fifth of the total number of credits in the program and was embedded in the curriculum through the inclusion of three consecutive inquiry seminars:

> EDUC 450 Inquiry Seminar I is designed to engender: an understanding of teaching as a moral and intellectual activity requiring inquiry, judgment and engagement with multiple others—students, parents, colleagues, scholarly community; an appreciation of the importance of research in understanding curriculum, teaching, and learning; and a desire to engage in one's own educational inquiries—to become students of teaching.
>
> ***
>
> EDUC 451 Inquiry Seminar II is designed to provide opportunities to: engage in teacher inquiry around a theme, a particular curriculum emphasis or an educational issue of one's choosing; demonstrate understandings acquired during course work and develop deeper understandings of a particular area of educational study; and begin to make links between one's inquiry topic and one's practice as a beginning teacher.
>
> ***
>
> EDUC 452 Inquiry Seminar III is designed to provide opportunities to reconsider, reflect upon, and represent their own learning experiences (in the teacher education program) in light of a critical engagement with what it means to be a professional and to be engaged in a profession [through the] creation and presentation of a portfolio or similar document.[38]

These seminars have changed somewhat in the years that followed, but the overall intent is still present. Thus, not only the tenor and tone but also time and credit for inquiry in this iteration represented a significant shift in how inquiry was pursued by both instructors and teacher candidates. For the first time at UBC, all three elements of Tom's continua were collectively addressed as part of the BEd curriculum. This combined effort to bring together the what, the how, and the why of inquiry into one conversation underscores the heightened level of erudition that currently exists around inquiry in the UBC program. However, this enthusiasm must be tempered by the reality that not all instructors within the program fully understand or subscribe to the tenets of an inquiry-oriented teacher education program. There is a constant a need for professional development for instructors to ensure that inquiry moves beyond simplistic conceptualizations to more complex, contested, and uncertain understandings of inquiry.[39] This last point was vividly brought home during a recent department discussion when one professor voiced the following opinion: "What is the purpose of inquiry? What is supposed to be the outcome of inquiry? I think that students would be better off if they spent more time on lesson and unit planning." And another suggested that the time spent in the inquiry seminars should be given back to the curriculum courses because the students need more time to focus on teaching methods.

Lessons Learned

Understanding one's history is important for understanding oneself;[40] therefore, analyses that take into account the history of programs are important for making sense of and suggesting revisions to such programs. The above historical analysis suggests that there are a number of lessons that can be learned, four of which are detailed below.

1. A Need to Balance the System of Schooling with the Educative Agenda

First, the above analysis reminds us of Fenstermacher's[41] caution about two powerful forces at play in all educational institutions: the system of schooling versus the educative agenda. The system of schooling refers to the structural aspects that are necessary for institutions to fulfil their mandate (for example, instructor appointments, class scheduling, recording and reporting practices). The educative agenda is entirely different in its emphasis. The educative agenda is about

> the formation of habits of judgment and the development of character; the facilitation of understanding; the development of taste and discrimination; the stimulation of curiosity and wonder; the fostering of style and a sense of duty; the growth of a thirst for new ideas and visions of the yet unknown.[42]

These elements are central to the notion of inquiry writ large.[43] The inherent tension between the system of schooling and the educative agenda is very clear in the analysis of UBC's BEd program over the past sixty years. For example, at times there has been the freedom to explore and experiment. There is also evidence of a more technical-rational, one-size-fits-all approach to student learning. Many factors can be attributed to impacting the balance between these two forces: the level of faculty involvement in teacher education, resource allocation, university mandates, conceptions of teaching and learning, and so on. The important lesson to be learned is that the tension between the two can never be fully resolved but rather needs to be managed such that both can mutually co-exist without one imposing itself unduly to the detriment of the other. The generative outcomes evident in the Experimental Years are perhaps the best example of the benefits that a harmonious relationship between the two can offer. This is best captured by the term enabling constraints, that is, acknowledging the conditions that define a system but not allowing them to limit the possibilities within that system.[44]

2. A Need for Greater Appreciation and Understanding of School Contexts

Another lesson learned is that even in the most progressive institutional environments (for example, the context of the CREATE years), teacher candidate inquiry is conditional on the knowledge and experience that those leading inquiry have of the contexts in which the teacher candidate's inquiries are typically situated: schools. The Kaleidoscope and Experimental years are instances where there was a strong alignment in this regard. While this is not a necessary condition, it clearly has an impact on how and in what ways teacher candidate inquiry is taken up and guided. The more distant the inquiry instructors are from schools and the more distant their research is from schools, the more challenging it is for programs to support teacher candidate inquiry. Faculties of education need to hire those who not only understand the notion of inquiry in rich and informed ways but who also have both the knowledge of and experience in the contexts in which those inquiries are embedded. This level of erudition is essential for ensuring movement from left to right along Tom's three continua for any teacher preparation program that hopes to substantively support and sustain inquiry.

3. The Benefits of Modelling Inquiry within the Program

The third lesson is that when instructors inquire into teacher education as they simultaneously work to support teacher candidate inquiries, there are synergies that promote and support inquiry in ways that are otherwise hard to sustain. This was certainly the case during the Experimental years when the faculty members of cohorts such as PBL, FAME, and CITE were actively involved in teacher education research within the context of the cohorts themselves. Papers, presentations, and books were generated during this period that spoke to issues in teacher education in ways that is not often seen in university settings. This issue also speaks to the importance of encouraging and attracting research faculty into teacher education, as their expertise and knowledge of inquiry practice can be extremely valuable in supporting teaching as learned practice. In short, faculty members were modelling the very practice they hoped their teacher candidates would take up. This stands in stark contrast to circumstances where instructors either do not engage in research and inquiry or their activity is divorced from the settings in which the teacher candidates' inquiries are embedded. If teaching is a learned activity, and inquiry is a defining feature of that practice, instructor inquiry and teacher candidate inquiry ideally ought go hand in hand in this regard.[45]

4. The Danger of Scaling Up and Dumbing Down: Better to Smarten Up and Scale Down

Another key lesson to emerge from the historical analysis of the BEd program is the danger of attempting to scale up individual successes found in pervious versions of the program. While the notion of scaling up has merit, the problem arises if there is a failure to distinguish what is unique and particular about those successes and whether or not the move from the particular to the general can be reasonably achieved. Can you duplicate something that is unique? Unfortunately, sometimes scaling up a unique success results in a dumbing down of the character and intent of that success. For example, during the Experimental Years some individual cohorts explored unique alternatives to regular practice. One cohort explored the idea of a short-term practicum in the first term. After several years of experimentation and in consultation with the schools, they settled on a three-week short practicum, the timing of which was always negotiated with the cluster of schools that provided placements for the students in the cohort. However, when scaling this idea up (to the whole program), the early practicum experience was cut to two weeks and the timing was set at a time that suited the university rather than being something that was negotiated with the schools. The cohort that had initiated the three-week short practicum was forced to abandon the practice and was required to conform with a program-wide mandate for a two-week short practice at the university-decreed time. As a result, much of the success of the three-week short practicum for that particular cohort was lost as the early field practice idea went mainstream.

Attempting to distinguish between how much to scale up and how much to scale down (that is, how to allow for uniqueness) will always be a challenge. However, acknowledging difference and allowing for that possibility within a program may result in richer and more generative learning for all involved.

Final Word

The above historical analysis of the BEd program provides both insight into and lessons learned over sixty years. The outcome constitutes a form of institutional memory without which important knowledge is lost.[46] The importance of teacher candidates developing a disposition for inquiry has often been a goal of teacher preparation both at UBC and beyond. This goal lies at the heart of teaching as a learned profession, a profession with responsibility for the intellectual growth of the young and continuing study by the more experienced members of the profession. This is defined in the introductory pages of this text as "academic erudition." Alan Tom's analytic frame serves as a useful guide to evaluate inquiry as it has been taken up in UBC's BEd program. There is evidence that there has been significant movement from left to right along all three dimensions of Tom's[47] dimensions over the past sixty years. More than ever before, inquiry is seen as complex, contested, and uncertain. It is not simple and fixed. This is the reality of teaching, learning, and learning how to teach. The arena of the problematic, the mode of inquiry, and status of the phenomenon have provided important signposts for charting this movement, and that movement indicates a higher level of erudition than ever before. There are undoubtedly other important waypoints and signposts. However, from Tom's perspective, inquiry-based teacher education is alive and well at UBC.

Notes

1. An earlier version of this paper was published in a Chinese-language journal: Anthony Clarke, 研究型教师教育: 教育学本科培养计划 的历史分析及启示 (Researching Teacher Education: Lessons Learned from an Undergraduate Education Program). *Southwest University Journal of Teacher Education* 1, no. 5 (2014), 5–14.
2. Tabachnick and Zeichner, *Issues and Practices*; Sleeter et al., "Scaffolding Conscientization"; Cochran-Smith and Lytle, "Beyond Certainty"; Britner and Finson, "Preservice Teachers' Reflections."
3. Clarke and Erickson, *Living the Research*; Donnell and Harper, "Competing Agendas"; Ortlieb and Lu, "Improving Teacher Education"; Zeichner, "Alternative Paradigms."
4. Tom, "Inquiring into Inquiry-oriented Teacher Education."
5. Tom, 37.
6. Arendt, *Between Past and Future*.
7. Hardy, "In Support of Teachers' Learning."
8. Tom, "Inquiry," 38.
9. Tom, 41.
10. American Psychiatric Association, "Diagnostic and Statistical Manual."
11. Zur and Nordmarken, "Status and Money."
12. Davis et al., *Engaging Minds*.
13. Labaree, "An Uneasy Relationship."
14. Worthen et al., "Evaluation of Alternative Teacher Education."
15. Sheehan and Wilson. "From Normal School."
16. Schön, *The Reflective Practitioner*.
17. Paley, "Heart and Soul."
18. Clarke and Echols, "Brief History."
19. Young et al., "Challenges to University Autonomy."
20. Irwin, *CREATE Program Planning Document*.
21. Kumashiro, *Against Common Sense*.
22. Tom, "Inquiry," 38.
23. Boydell, "Issues in Teaching Practice Supervision Research"; Shulman, "Paradigms and Research Programs."
24. Van Manen, "Linking Ways of Knowing," 209.
25. Boydell, "Issues"; May and Zimpher, "An Examination of Three Theoretical Perspectives"; Schön, *Reflective Practitioner*.
26. Krogh, S. L., "Reflecting on Reflective Thinking"; Simmons et al., "A-ha Moments"; Zeichner and Liston, "Teaching Student Teachers."
27. Erickson, "Qualitative Methods"; Nolan and Huber, "Nurturing the Reflective Practitioner"; Selman, "Schön's Gate."

28   Bruner, *Toward a Theory of Instruction.*
29   Carr and Kemmis. *Becoming Critical."*
30   Britzman, *Practice Makes Practice.*
31   Hargreaves and Macmillan, "Balkanization."
32   Grimmett and MacKinnon, "Craft Knowledge."
33   Goodlad, *Our Nation's Schools.*
34   Tom, "Inquiry."
35   Wilson and Berne, "Acquisition of Professional Knowledge."
36   Mishler, "Meaning in Context."
37   CREATE, Frequently Asked Questions, 1.
38   CREATE, "Inquiry."
39   Fenwick, "Responsibility."
40   Duchan, "What Do You Know."
41   Fenstermacher, "Policy Development."
42   Scheffler, "Basic Mathematical Skills."
43   Darling et al., *Collective Improvisation.*
44   Davis et al., *Engaging Minds.*
45   Clarke and Erickson, *Living the Research.*
46   Linde, *Working the Past.*
47   Tom, "Inquiry."

Bibliography

American Psychiatric Association. *Diagnostic and Statistical Manual of Mental Disorder, Text Revision.* Washington, DC: American Psychiatric Association, 2000.

Arendt, Hannah. *Between Past and Future: Six Exercises in Political Thought.* London, UK: Faber & Faber, 1961.

Boydell, Deanne. "Issues in Teaching Practice Supervision Research: A Review of the Literature." *Teaching and Teacher Education* 2, no. 2 (1986): 115–125.

Britner, Shari L., and Kevin D. Finson. "Preservice Teachers' Reflections on Their Growth in an Inquiry-Oriented Science Pedagogy Course." *Journal of Elementary Science Education* (2005): 39–54.

Britzman, Deborah P. *Practice Makes Practice: A Critical Study of Learning to Teach.* Albany, NY: SUNY Press, 1991.

Bruner, Jerome. *Toward a Theory of Instruction.* Cambridge, MA: Belkapp Press, 1966.

Carr, Wilfred, and Stephen Kemmis. *Becoming Critical: Knowing through Action Research.* Geelong, VIC: Deakin University, 1983.

Clarke, Anthony, and Frank Echols. "A Brief History of Teacher Education at the University of British Columbia." *50th Anniversary Yearbook*. Vancouver, BC: UBC Faculty of Education, 2007.

Clarke, Anthony, and Gaalen L. Erickson, eds. *Teacher Inquiry: Living the Research in Everyday Practice*. London, UK: Psychology Press, 2003.

Cochran-Smith, Marilyn, and Susan L. Lytle. "Beyond Certainty: Taking an Inquiry Stance on Practice." In *Teachers Caught in the Action: Professional Development that Matters*, edited by Ann Lieberman and Lynne Miller, 45–58. New York, NY: Teachers College Press, 2002.

CREATE. "Inquiry EDUC 450, EDUC 451, EDUC 452." Retrieved October 31, 2019 from https://teach.educ.ubc.ca/inquiry/.

CREATE. "Frequently Asked Questions about the CREATE Program and Process." Retrieved October 31, 2019 from teach.educ.ubc.ca › files › 2013/07 › CREATE-FAQ.

Darling, Linda F., Gaalen L. Erickson, and Anthony Clarke, eds. *Collective Improvisation in a Teacher Education Community*. Berlin/Heidelberg, DE: Springer Science & Business Media, 2007.

Davis, Brent, Dennis Sumara, and R. Luce-Kapler. *Engaging Minds: Changing Teaching in Complex Times*, 2nd ed. Mahwah, NJ: Lawrence Erlbaum, 2008.

Donnell, Kelly, and Kelly Harper. "Inquiry in Teacher Education: Competing Agendas." *Teacher Education Quarterly* 32, no. 3 (2005): 153–165.

Duchan, Judith F. "What Do You Know About Your Profession's History? And Why Is It Important?" 2002 *The ASHA Leader* 7, no. 23 (December 2002): 4–29. Retrieved from https://leader.pubs.asha.org/article.aspx?articleid=2292435.

Erickson, Frederick. "Qualitative Methods in Research on Teaching." In *Handbook of Research on Teaching: A Project of the American Educational Research Association*, 3rd ed., edited by Merlin C. Wittrock, 119–161. New York, NY: Macmillan, 1986.

Fenstermacher, Gary. "Policy Development and Teacher Education: An Educative Agenda vs. a System of Schooling." Invited presentation at the University of British Columbia, Vancouver, BC, May 1992.

Fenwick, Tara. "Responsibility, Complexity Science and Education: Dilemmas and Uncertain Responses." *Studies in Philosophy and Education* 28, no. 2 (2009): 101–118.

Goodlad, John I. *Teachers for Our Nation's Schools*. San Francisco, CA: Jossey-Bass, 1990.

Grimmett, Peter P., and Allan M. MacKinnon. "Craft Knowledge and the Education of Teachers." *Review of Research in Education* 18 (1992): 385–456.

Hardy, Ian. "In Support of Teachers' Learning: Specifying and Contextualising Teacher Inquiry as Professional Practice." *Asia-Pacific Journal of Teacher Education* 44, no. 1 (2016): 4–19.

Hargreaves, Andy, and Robert Macmillan. "The Balkanization of Secondary School Teaching." In *Subjects in Question: Departmental Organization and the High School*, edited by L. S. Siskin and J. W. Little, 141–171. New York, NY: Teachers College Press, 1995.

Irwin, Rita. *CREATE Program Planning Document*. Vancouver, BC: UBC Faculty of Education, 2011.

Krogh, S. L. "Reflecting on Reflective Thinking in Methods Classes: Where the Buck Finally Stops." Presentation, Annual Meeting from American Educational Research Association, Washington, DC, April 1987.

Kumashiro, Kevin K. *Against Common Sense: Teaching and Learning Toward Social Justice*. 3rd ed. New York, NY: Routledge, 2015.

Labaree, David F. "An Uneasy Relationship: The History of Teacher Education in the University." In *Handbook of Research on Teacher Education*, 3rd ed., edited by M. Cochran-Smith, S. Feiman-Nemser, and D. J. McIntyre, 290–306. New York, NY: Erlbaum/Routledge, 2008.

Linde, Charlotte. *Working the Past: Narrative and Institutional Memory*. Oxford, UK/New York, NY: Oxford University Press, 2008.

May, Wanda T., and Nancy Zimpher. "An Examination of Three Theoretical Perspectives on Supervision: Perceptions of Preservice Field Supervision." *Journal of Curriculum and Supervision* 1, no. 2 (1986): 83–99.

Mishler, Elliot G. "Meaning in Context: Is There Any Other Kind?" *Harvard Educational Review* 49, no. 1 (1979): 1–19.

Nolan, James E., and Tonya Huber. "Nurturing the Reflective Practitioner through Instructional Supervision: A Review of the Literature." *Journal of Curriculum and Supervision* 4, no. 2 (Winter 1989): 126–145.

Ortlieb, Evan T., and Lucia Lu. "Improving Teacher Education through Inquiry-Based Learning." *International Education Studies* 4, no. 3 (August 2011): 41–46.

Paley, Vivian Gussin. "The Heart and Soul of the Matter: Teaching as a Moral Act." In *The Educational Forum* 55, no. 2 (Winter 1991): 155–166.

Scheffler, Israel. "Basic Mathematical Skills: Some Philosophical and Practical Remarks." *Teachers College Record* 78, no. 2 (1976): 205–212.

Schön, Donald A. *The Reflective Practitioner: How Professionals Think in Action*. New York, NY: Basic Books, 1984.

Selman, Mark. "Schön's Gate is Square, But Is It Art?" In *Reflection in Teacher Education*, edited by Peter P. Grimmett and Gaalen L. Erickson, 177–192. New York, NY: Teachers College Press, 1988.

Sheehan, Nancy M., and J. Donald Wilson. "From Normal School to the University to the College of Teachers: Teacher Education in British Columbia in the 20th century." *Journal of Education for Teaching* 20, no. 1 (1994): 23–37.

Shulman, Lee. "The Paradigms and Research Programs in the Study of Teaching." In *Handbook of Research on Teaching: A Project of the American Educational Research Association*, 3rd ed., edited by Merlin C. Wittrock, 3–36. New York, NY: Macmillan, 1986.

Simmons, J. M., G. M. Sparks, and A. B. Colton. "A-ha Moments while Grappling with the Question: 'What Do We Mean by Teacher Reflective Thinking?'" Presentation at Reflective Inquiry Conference, Orlando, Florida, October 1988.

Sleeter, Christine, Myriam N. Torres, and Peggy Laughlin. "Scaffolding Conscientization through Inquiry in Teacher Education." *Teacher Education Quarterly* 31, no. 1 (2004): 81–96.

Tabachnick, B. Robert, and Kenneth M. Zeichner, eds. *Issues and Practices in Inquiry-oriented Teacher Education*, vol. 3. London: Falmer Press, 1991.

Tom, Alan R. "Inquiring into Inquiry-oriented Teacher Education." *Journal of Teacher Education* 36, no. 5 (1985): 35–44.

Van Manen, Max. "Linking Ways of Knowing with Ways of Being Practical." *Curriculum Inquiry* 6, no. 3 (1977): 209.

Wilson, Suzanne M., and Jennifer Berne. "Teacher Learning and the Acquisition of Professional Knowledge: An Examination of Research on Contemporary Professional Development." *Review of Research in Education* 24, no. 1 (1999): 173–209.

Worthen, Blaine R., Thomas O. Owens, and Beverly Anderson. *Evaluation of the Alternative Teacher Education Programs of the University of British Columbia Faculty of Education (A Report to the Policy Council of the University of British Columbia Faculty of Education)*. Portland, OR: Northwest Regional Educational Laboratory, 1975.

Young, J., C. Hall, and A. Clarke. "Challenges to University Autonomy in Initial Teacher Education Programmes: The Cases of England, Manitoba and British Columbia." *Teaching and Teacher Education* 23, no. 1 (2007): 81–93.

Zeichner, Kenneth M. "Alternative Paradigms of Teacher Education." *Journal of Teacher Education* 34, no. 3 (1983): 3–9.

Zeichner, Kenneth, and Daniel Liston. "Teaching Student Teachers to Reflect." *Harvard Educational Review* 57, no. 1 (1987): 23–49.

Zur, O., and N. Nordmarken. "DSM-5: Diagnosing for Status and Money—Summary Critique of the DSM-5." Retrieved October 18, 2012 from http://www.zurinstitute.com/dsmcritique.html.

CHAPTER 9

A Renewed Understanding of Learning to Teach: Aristotle, Confucius, and My Mother's Stories

Ying Ma

With the overwhelming pressure to implement policies of standardization, assessment, and accountability, teacher success is often largely determined by test results in countries such as China and Canada and many other countries around the world (for example, the international PISA test, SATS in England, NAPLAN in Australia, provincial examinations in Canada, Gaokao in China). In an era of performativity, the languages of competencies, skills, and scores rule supreme in educational institutions. Teaching and teacher education are now, as Clarke and Phelan make clear, "subject to the same managerial norms as those that dominate in the business sector."[1] Any renewal of teaching and teacher education will require different languages to guide educational thinking and practices; such languages must enable educators to engage in moral conversations about what is good for students.

In this chapter, I address the concept of ethical engagement[2] in teaching, which is largely missing from the overwhelming managerial concerns about "what works"[3] rather than what is "educationally desirable."[4] To do so, I return to ancient Aristotelian and Confucian moral languages[5] to conceptualize and situate ethical engagement. I draw upon my mother's stories of learning to teach and teaching during the Cultural Revolution in China,[6] the excess of which points to what the existing dominant managerial schemes neglect. I then bring her stories into conversation with Aristotelian and Confucian ethics by first outlining the major virtues of both wisdom traditions—*phronesis* (practical wisdom), *philia* (friendship), and *ren* (humaneness)—and then by excavating their insights in relation to my mother's stories. Specifically, I repeatedly return to my mother's stories, especially to her interaction with her university teacher Mr. Zhao, from different interpretative angles in Aristotelian and Confucian languages. In so doing, I argue that engaging ethically in teaching involves teachers'

a. negotiation between the particulars of everyday life in the classroom and their more general schemes of understanding;
b. judgments being informed by both reason and emotion; and
c. willingness and capacity to build educational relationships with their students.

In the concluding section of the chapter, I return us to the contemporary context, where I suggest a possible extension of *phronesis* as a framework for teaching and teacher education.

A Brief Overview of Aristotelian *Phronesis* and *Philia* and Confucian *Ren*

Understanding Aristotelian *phronesis* and *philia* and Confucian *ren* can help us, I suggest, interpret my mother's stories of acting ethically among conflicting and even demoralizing government agendas. They jointly provide conceptual resources to understand ethical engagement with self and others, which ask us to reconsider the particular circumstances of teaching and learning.

Aristotle divides virtues into moral virtues and intellectual virtues. Moral virtues are concerned with excellences of character (such as courage, moderation, justice); intellectual virtues include *episteme* (systematic knowledge, scientific knowledge), *techne* (craft, art, skill), *phronesis* (wisdom, prudence, practical wisdom), *sophia* (wisdom, theoretical wisdom, intellectual accomplishment), and *nous* (intelligence, intuitive reason). The intellectual virtues are interrelated and are connected by *phronesis* to the moral virtues. *Phronesis* is considered an executive or "architectonic"[7] virtue, marshalling the requisite intellectual and moral virtues to support and enable right action in a particular context, which, as I understand, contributes to engaging ethically with self and others.

Aristotle elaborates in Books VIII and IX on the importance of *philia*, which is often translated as friendship. Here Hughes suggests that "*philia* applies to a rather broader spectrum of relationships than 'friendship' does in English."[8] Aristotle distinguishes this desirable *philia* from two other insufficient kinds of *philia*, which are, respectively, in virtue of utility—some good which they get from each other; and because of pleasure—they find them pleasant. Relationships based on mutual admiration of one another's character are the best kind of *philia*. Aristotle suggests "perfect *philia* is the *philia* of men who are good and alike in virtue; for these wish well alike to each other qua good, and they are good in themselves."[9] Aristotle's conception of *philia* provides normative guidance for the kinds of relationships that are desirable if one is to engage ethically.

In the Confucian tradition, the deepest caring and concern for humanity constitutes the core of *ren*. Etymologically the word consists of two parts: The left part of the word "亻" means human, and the right part means two. The Chinese character itself suggests its close relation with humans and its emphasis on communication among people. Confucius does not provide us with a fixed definition of *ren*; rather, it is the fluidity and indefiniteness in the practice of *ren* that distinguishes it. Confucius refers to *ren* as a general virtue that encompasses all other moral characters. He also uses *ren* as a particular virtue that contrasts with virtues of *zhi* (wisdom), *yong* (courage), and *yi* (propriety), with emphasis on love towards others. The seemingly contradictory definitions reveal that *ren* is not anchored in the binary conceptualization of the universal and the particular. *Ren*, in both similar and different ways from *phronesis* and *philia*, is conceptually helpful when considering what ethical engagement could involve.

My Mother's Stories: Three Considerations

My mother became a teacher when China was undergoing a devastating ten-year Cultural Revolution. In 1971, without having the experience of being enrolled in any teacher education programs (all universities were shut down at that time), with students just three years younger than her, my mother became a teacher "for the first time." The first years of her teaching were intimidating. She didn't exactly know what to teach or how to teach. "It was like wading across the stream by feeling the pebbles," she says. In the year

1979, after she had taught in the middle school for eight years, the Cultural Revolution drew to an end and universities were reopened. She was finally admitted to a teacher education program at a normal university[10] in Beijing, from 1979 to 1983. She became a teacher "for the second time" upon her graduation. She then taught for another thirty years before her retirement.

She once shared with me a story about one of her university teachers, Mr. Zhao. When the Cultural Revolution had just drawn to an end, books that challenged communist ideologies were still labeled as "forbidden books." As an undergraduate student, my mother secretly read and copied the "forbidden books." She shared those handwritten copies with her classmates in university. However, one day, her teacher Mr. Zhao discovered her secret. She was very nervous and scared of the severe consequences associated with reading and sharing forbidden books. Mr. Zhao asked her to go to his office. He pulled a chair and let her sit next to the desk. He nodded approvingly when he held some pieces of my mother's hand-copied poems. He didn't talk much but listened tentatively to my mother when she mustered her courage to share her passion for those books. Then his mouth broke into a gentle smile, he handed her a wrapper to conceal the books, and he let her go. For my mother, this is a long-kept memory.

The Negotiation between the Particular and the General

To engage ethically, for both Aristotle and Confucius, does not include applying given general rules or theories rigidly to particular practices. Rather, it involves constantly attuning oneself to the particular and negotiating with the general. Consider, for example, Mr. Zhao's refusal to conform to regulation in the face of his student's transgression. Consider, also, my mother's initial experience of teaching without any formal preparation wherein she navigated the stream of the classroom by "feeling the pebbles" of her particular context.

Scholarly works have explored the intertwined and mutually embedded relationship between theory and practice in *phronesis*. *Phronesis* is characterized as a form of ethical knowing "in an acting situation and ... about the exigencies of this concrete situation."[11] *Phronesis*, as Aristotle explains, "is not only concerned with universals; ... it has to do with action, and the sphere of action is constituted by particulars."[12] *Phronesis* brings theory and practice into mutually informative dialogue. Dunne suggests "no divorce (of theory and practice) is admissible,"[13] whereas Kristjansson describes the relationship as "a theory: one which duly informs and is informed by practice."[14] It seems to me that theory and practice are not binary concepts. Rather, their interaction with each other is where ethical engagement is located.

Mr. Zhao was informed by the particular encounter with his student, and managed to negotiate and expand the general framework available to him. If Mr. Zhao had only sat in his office reading about school regulations, a student who read and distributed the forbidden books—thereby breaking the school rules—would have been categorized as a disobedient pupil in need of disciplining. If Mr. Zhao had only studied the theory about teaching, he would have merely cared about how effective his teaching was to promote the prescribed goals and would have found those forbidden books useless or disrupting. However, seeing a student whose eyes shone when reading the forbidden books, who touched and was touched by those books, and who copied the books in a delicate style of calligraphy, Mr. Zhao attuned himself to the particular encounter; he allowed himself to be addressed by the educational passions of his student. He listened attentively to her and responded to the particulars of her situation rather than following preset rules. As Kristjansson points out, such a capacity for response "can be acquired only by an individual who has been initiated into a particular practice and has learned to direct his activities."[15] Mr. Zhao tried to act according to his best judgment in light of what was good and desirable for a particular student but also, perhaps, in relation to his own commitments and values.

Embedded in the rough ground, *phronesis* is "not a type of rootless situational perception that rejects all guidance from ongoing commitments and values."[16] Here Dunne tells us:

> I take Aristotle to be indicating in this dense passage that experience is not a matter of exposure to "one damned thing after another" but rather of particulars giving rise to, and then being perceived in the light of, universals; and of universals neither cancelling the particularity of the percepts from which they have arisen nor becoming invulnerable to modification by new percepts.[17]

In that most devastating political era, my mother, like her teacher Mr. Zhao, initiated dialogue between the general and the particular—theory and practice—in a peculiar way. When my mother was finally accepted to university after teaching for eight years, she had to interact and negotiate her prior teaching experience with the theoretical knowledge offered in university. As such, she was more interested in initiating conversations about her previous teaching than learning theories to apply in the future. She pondered, questioned, negotiated, challenged, and reflected about her previous experiences of teaching in the space and time provided by university. My mother did not follow a hierarchical application mode, nor could she get stuck in the repetitive and self-containing undergoing. She started from the particular and brought it into conversation with the universal. Teachers with *phronesis* use rules only as "summaries and guides; it [*phronesis*] must itself be flexible, ready for surprise, prepared to see, resourceful at improvisation"[18] and "avoid settling into mere routine."[19] *Phronesis* is anchored in a to-and-fro, creative process between the particular and the general, which, I believe, is a foundation for ethical engagement in teaching.

Confucius, like Aristotle, also pays close attention to the particular and its dialogic relationship with the general. *Ren*, not unlike *phronesis*, unifies the concepts of universal and particular. Here Sim notes that "the *phronimos* act as a kind of concrete universal, exemplifying how the right ends are pursued in particular instances by using the right means."[20] Mou also suggests that *ren* is a form of "concrete universal."[21] *Ren* is flexible and concrete, while it is universal and provides guidance. The inherent tension in *ren* allows for *ren*'s creative manifestations rather than being absolute and rigid. In its concreteness, *ren* could be *xiao* (filial love) of a child towards his parents. And Confucius offers more particular understandings with regards to *xiao*.[22] Confucius responds to his disciple Fan Chi and suggests *xiao* means "serving parents in accordance with the rituals,"[23] while the master says to Ziyou, "*xiao* means more than serving parents and must have reverence."[24] As Mou observes, "the manifestations of *xiao* are endless, it is always in its concreteness. Yet it shows a universal truth (*ren*) in its concreteness."[25] I am reminded of the ancient Chinese tale about Shennong, who is the legendary originator of Chinese herbal medicine and author of the book *Shennong Herbals*. Shennong always begins with particulars: He tastes each herb and experiences its unique taste, forms, smell, and effects, and therefore becomes better able to discern and discover its properties—to really understand at a deep level. This process is comparable to learning about *ren* and practicing *ren* by attending to its endless particular expressions. I believe that Mr. Zhao embodied *ren* in his concrete displays of "respect, forgiveness, trust, sensitivity, and generosity."[26] Pulling up a chair and letting my mother sit at the table showed his respect; nodding appreciatively for my mother's hand-copied books revealed his generosity; letting my mother go without questioning her displayed his trust. He also manifested his sensitivity to the particular circumstances and offered my mother his support through the subtlety of a book wrapper. These could all be understood as the concrete practices and manifestations of *ren*.

My mother's attendance at university *after* eight years of teaching represents a prioritization of the particular in teaching. Her teacher Mr. Zhao was also a keen observer, an attentive listener, responding to the particular encounter rather than trying to be a master of teaching. They both understood that "messy, confusing problems defy technical solution"[27] and responded to the best of their understanding in the swampy lowland of teaching.

The Integration of Reason and Emotion

The book wrapper story continues to linger with and in me. When I was a high school teacher, I was very familiar with the zero-tolerance policy toward the students who broke school rules. As a result, I now wonder what could explain Mr. Zhao's actions? Why did he refuse to punish the student who failed to follow the rules? Why would he risk himself at such a tense moment in China's history? What were the resources Mr. Zhao drew upon in that encounter with my mother? In concealing the forbidden books, what did the book wrapper reveal? I understand, to engage ethically—to attend to others at the right time, in the right place and in the right manner—involves, as Aristotle and Confucius tell us, the activation of mutually informing reason and emotion.

I find emotions underlie my mother's stories—particularly her feelings of admiration and appreciation for Mr. Zhao and his feelings of empathy for her. Indeed, *phronesis* never excludes the emotional dimension. Aristotle suggests emotion, as the non-rational part of the soul, can also participate in reason in order to enable morally responsive relationships. He says: "In the moderate and courageous person it is presumably still readier to listen, for in him it always chimes with reason";[28] and "the appetitive and general desiring part does participate in reason."[29] Emotion and reason are by nature inseparable, "like the convex and concave in the case of a curved surface."[30] Emotion makes a strong presence in one's moral life and is always weaved into reason to inform one's judgment and action. To this pedagogical end,

Nussbaum indicates the significance of emotion for Aristotle. The "Aristotelian position accepts," she stresses, "emotional attachment as an intrinsically valuable source of richness and goodness in human life."[31] Dunne also examines the importance of emotion's participation in reason: "He (Aristotle) does not believe that beings such as ourselves can hold a rational stance outside a certain kind of patterning of emotion."[32]

In my mother's interaction with Mr. Zhao, emotion was brought into dialogue with reason to generate ethical action. On the one hand, Mr. Zhao's reasoning capacity could inform him that the rule of forbidding books was a tool of political hegemony; that it suppressed thought and was oppressive of the young. He might also reason that if he publicly supported my mother, he might be expelled from school. On the other hand, Mr. Zhao probably felt extreme disgust toward the rule and great sympathy for my mother. The choice of either supporting my mother publicly or punishing her according to the school rule represented the push and pull of emotion and reason. A more imaginative and ethical space then emerged in the tension. In the end, Mr. Zhao used a book wrapper to convey his feelings of sympathy toward my mother in a discreet way and, at the same time, protected himself and my mother from becoming victims of the political regime. To engage ethically, for Mr. Zhao, involves a dynamic relationship "between reason and the emotions/desires."[33] Mr. Zhao's emotional response to political hegemony and the pains of his students, together with his capacity to reason, jointly informed his ethical engagement.

In the indivisible relationship between emotion and reason, what needs to be noted is that emotion has an important cognitive role to play and can complement and enhance reason. Emotions, for Aristotle, are "not simply blind surges of affect … rather they are discriminating responses closely connected with beliefs about how things are and what is important."[34] Mr. Zhao's emotion informed him about what he valued and deemed important, which "could easily be lost from sight during sophisticated intellectual reasoning."[35] Being emotionally empathetic, Mr. Zhao learned that he valued the good life of his students; from his emotions of anger and contempt about the rule, Mr. Zhao learned about his own longing for freedom and his desire to defy the political hegemony. His sympathy towards his student and anger towards the political authority were inextricably associated with what he valued and helped him better perceive the situation. Emotions are "not only not more unreliable than intellectual calculations, but frequently are more reliable, and less deceptively seductive."[36] Bearing its cognitive nature, emotion enables discernment and judgment about a situation. Indeed, the unification of emotion and reason calls the prevalent view of rationality— "rationality without the interference of unreliable, animal, seductive emotions"[37]—into question. To put it briefly, reason and emotion need to be brought together. Reason unaccompanied by emotion is not sufficient for *phronesis*. Reason helps cultivates appropriate emotion, while emotion participates in reason and may make it more reliable. Mr. Zhao's book wrapper revealed a necessary tension and a mutually interactive relation between emotion and reason, characteristic of ethical engagement.

Confucius recognizes the significance of human emotion. In *Li Ji*, we read that "emotion is the land for sages to plow ... *ren* nourishes the land and sustains the process."[38] And Mencius[39] also affirms the moral subject's unification of reason and emotion. Aristotle emphasizes the mutually informative relation between emotion and reason in *phronesis*, while for Confucius and Mencius there is no separation between emotion and reason in *ren*. For Mencius, every human being possesses emotion and reason, expressing itself as "the four buddings":[40] the dispositions of compassion, of shame and dislike, of yielding and deference, and of discriminating between right and wrong. For Confucius, *ren* means to love people, and it is important to love people with differentiations. In *Analects*, when Confucius responds to Fan Chi's question about what is *ren*, Confucius suggests: "... being *ren* is to love people";[41] and the master also says: "... the person with *ren* could like people and dislike people."[42] *Ren* is emotionally charged yet does not embrace blind love or universal love. Mencius fiercely criticizes Mozi's universal love: "Mozi's universal love does not recognize fathers ... universal love is a kind of beast love."[43] One should know who or what is worthy of being loved and who or what should be blamed and criticized. Loving others lies in one's discernment and judgment in each particular context. Pang interprets, in a person of *ren*, "... to dislike people could be complementary to loving people."[44] Loving people does not mean treating all people in identical ways. Fan argues, "Confucian *ren* requires differentiated love, not equal love. It is love with distinction, and care with gradation."[45] Loving people requires specific knowledge of that particular person and developing a trusting relationship with him or her in order to express your love in the right way and at the right moment, something that varies from person to person, from one circumstance to another. Confucian *ren*'s love is differentiated love based on the knowledge of what is good for the other party.[46] I believe Mr. Zhao, in his attentiveness to his students, tried to understand the uniqueness of his student and responded accordingly. He appreciated my mother's particular passion towards literature—as a student majoring in mathematics—protected her from becoming a victim of the political authority, encouraged her to pursue her passions cautiously, and brought about the best for her.

Having discussed the interplay and integration of emotion and reason through Aristotle and Confucius, I continue to wonder what kinds of emotions are desirable to bring about ethical engagement. Aristotle and Confucius both seem to emphasize the importance of the mean or the intermediate state of emotions. Aristotle shows that some emotions are named in such a way that they are combined with "badness from the start"[47] and raises the examples of malice and shamelessness. Nevertheless, the goodness or badness of emotions could not be solely decided upon in terms of the types of emotions. Rather, it largely depends on the appropriate extent of emotions. Aristotle elaborates on the intermediate state of emotion in relation to excellence of characters:

> … excellence of character is an intermediate state … between two bad states, one relating to excess and the other to deficiency (in a particular context); and that it is such because it is effective at hitting upon the intermediate in emotions and in actions.[48]

The degree of emotions is intricately related to the types of the emotions (for example, the over- and under-indulgence of courage could correspond to rashness and cowardliness) and helps to determine its goodness or badness. In a similar way, Confucian *ren* takes the mean of emotion to its core: "*junzi* (the person with *ren*) embodies the mean, while *xiaoren* (the small person) acts contrary to the mean."[49] Hitting the mean is like "hitting the target in archery,"[50] and emotions need to "be stirred … in their due degree according to the mean. The mean is the great root from which grow all the human actions in the world."[51] It has been compared to archery—it is important to hit the target. A person with *ren* always stirs emotion appropriately—capable of hitting Aristotle's golden mean of moral behaviour. In the book wrapper story, I observe the intermediate emotions in Mr. Zhao. His courage was manifested in his refraining from acting rashly, that is, supporting my mother's reading choices regardless and fighting against official policies. Mr. Zhao's courage was also embedded in his not choosing the safe road of strictly following the school rule. Mr. Zhao did not act impulsively, nor was he cowardly or compliant. Courage for Mr. Zhao, in that particular moment, emerged as the appropriate state between these two extreme states and was manifested in the subtlety of the book wrapper. Also, Mr. Zhao didn't allow either his feelings of sympathy towards my mother or the feeling of defiance towards the rule to go to extremes, thereby enabling him to perceive the situation more accurately. Emotions need to be attended to and attuned to the situation at hand so as to bring about their intermediate states; they must not be suppressed, controlled, or even eliminated. A process of "cultivating, refining, and educating"[52] appropriate emotions, in their intermediacy, can contribute to one's judgments.

Building Ethical Student-Teacher Relationships

Decades have not worn out the connections between my mother and her teacher Mr. Zhao nor between my mother and her own students. My mother's students visit her during spring festivals, which are important days for family gatherings and the reunion of friends. Although my mother has lost contact with Mr. Zhao, she still keeps the book wrapper in a wooden chest as a mark of her gratitude and admiration for her cherished teacher. Phelan reminds us the "intrinsic goods of teaching are relational."[53] What does this mean in the context of my mother's relationship with Mr. Zhao? What constitutes ethical teacher-student relations for Aristotle and Confucius?

Based on Aristotelian understanding of desirable *philia*, I believe his advice upon the ethical relationship between students and teachers is two-fold. First, the mutual respect and mutual admiration are the foundations of *philia*. And second, ethical student-teacher relationships are associated with good characters.

Mutual respect does not merely imply having good manners, or being polite toward each other. It involves the consideration about "what is good for his sake."[54] Loving, for Aristotle, is more of the essence of desirable *philia* than being loved. He praises those who love their friends and help friends become better.[55] Such love is not a coercive love that demands conformity and compliance; however, it is the love that requires mutual respect and admiration of the uniqueness and distinctiveness of a human being. Mr. Zhao showed his utmost respect and care toward my mother, seeing her as a unique person rather than an object to be disciplined and controlled according to school rules. He pulled out a chair for her to sit; nodded approvingly about my mother's hand-copied poems; listened carefully to her; and thought about ways to protect and support her. Mr. Zhao's respect and appreciation of my mother not only earned her respect and admiration back (Mr. Zhao might not expect it), but also helped him grow as a teacher in his attempts to understand and attend to the needs of his students better.

Second, building upon mutual admiration and respect, the best form of *philia* involves cultivating the good characters of each other and "bringing the best out of people."[56] The teacher-student relationship is often an adult-minor relationship, when the equality in virtues between both parties is rare. However, we need to admit that the direction of virtuous exchange in student and teacher relationships could still be mutual—as "the child's possession of certain morally praiseworthy qualities can enlighten the adult."[57] Aristotle claims that good characters are enduring or permanent and can serve as the foundation for the best form of *philia*.[58] It is not compatible with today's teaching and teacher education when the teacher-student realtionship is too often defined by its instrumental benefits or usefulness, based on external "technical and/or disciplinary"[59] criteria. The relationship between my mother and her teacher was fundamentally based on bringing out the goodness of human beings rather than being driven by prescribed external goals. My mother's passion for pursuing something she loved regardless of the potential punishments probably impressed and inspired Mr. Zhao, while his determination of making his own judgment rather than safely following the rule could be contagious and further sustain my mother's courage.

With its emphasis on human relations, Confucius's conception of *ren* contributes further to unpacking what could be involved in ethical relationships. Confucius believes that

> ... participating in relationships (such as those between parents and children, siblings, emperors and ministers, friends, as well as those between teachers and students) is partially constitutive of living well. It is not clear that Aristotle fully does justice to these relationships.[60]

Confucius spends much time and enjoys a very close relationship with his disciples. He often helps relieve the financial burden of his poor student Yuanxian; visits his ill student Ran Boniu; mourns over the deaths of his students Yanyuan and Zilu. Some compare Confucian student-teacher relationship to friendship,[61] while some others believe it is similar to the father-son bond. *Li Ji* observes the parallel ordering of emperors, fathers, and teachers. It records the importance of "serving emperors, fathers, and teachers without any reservations—taking good care of them when they are alive, mourning for their death for three years after they die."[62] This doctrine in *Li Ji* resonates with another saying by Confucius: "Yan Hui treats me as his father."[63] For Confucius, the student-teacher relationship is similar, to some extent, to familial bonds and as close as friendship. I believe, in Confucius' eyes, the relationships between teachers and students, friends, and family members fundamentally share the similar root in the love of *ren*. For Confucius, the filial love could be expanded to the love of *ren* between teachers and students. In spite of the adjacency with familial love, friendships, and teacher-student relationships in Confucius, I notice that the teacher-student relationship anchored in *ren* distinctly creates space for the students to make their appearance and for teachers to welcome the newness students introduce. Below I elaborate on these two aspects of desirable student-teacher relationship: For one, the love of *ren* could serve as the basis for understanding ethical teacher-relationships; for another, the teacher-student relationship is distinguished by its generating space for the newness in the younger generations.

Primarily, Confucius would suggest that good teacher-student relationships emphasize love of *ren*, which derives from a harmonious family and is extended to others and to a harmonious society. Yu captures it as follows: "… the idea of *ren* as love is the expansion of the roots of filial love."[64] When Yan Hui, his favorite disciple, dies, Confucius, like his father, wails wildly: "Heaven is destroying me, Heaven is destroying me."[65] Confucius does not mourn over Yan Hui's death out of obligation as his teacher or to follow some prescriptions. It is apparent that there is as much love of *ren* involved in the relationship between Confucius and his disciples as between familial members. As I have discussed earlier, the loving relationship is not prescribed but characterized by spontaneity and liveliness embedded in the uniqueness and particularity of circumstances. Mr. Zhao managed to create a private public space and rebuilt the respectful and trustful relationship between himself and his students in inhospitable political circumstances. As Pinar suggests, the classroom is simultaneously "a civic square and room of one's own."[66] Mr. Zhao animated the private public space through a loving heart of *ren*: His gentle smile not only eased my mother's anxiety but also resisted the suppression from the public; his book wrapper not only protected my mother from being punished but also conveyed a caring message. *Ren* is embodied in Mr. Zhao's listening, in his smile, in his letting my mother go without much questioning, and in the offer of the book wrapper. *Ren* came to grow and flourish in the animated relational space. Rather than "concentrate on the daily routines, trying to be cool and disengaged, as functional and impersonal as machines,"[67] Mr. Zhao's relationship with my mother embodied a particular form of relation. It went beyond a professional-amateur or trainer-trainee relationship, where teachers often follow their prescribed roles and train their students to achieve those outputs deemed by the institution as appropriate. In contrast, Mr. Zhao built an emotionally charged, caring relationship with a particular student, which Confucian *ren* particularly embraces.

Second, ethical student-teacher relationships are also distinguished for generating the newness and encouraging the younger generation to make their appearance. Admittedly, in Confucian texts, we can find numerous ethical boundaries for different social roles and relationships. When Fan Chi asks about *ren*, the master replies: "In private life, courteous, in public life, diligent, in relationship, loyal."[68] Pang says, "Emperors with humaneness; ministers with loyalty; fathers with love and care; children with filial love; older brothers with friendliness; younger brothers with respect."[69] I realize these moral norms might have their historical, cultural limitations and might risk maintaining and reproducing the existing social norms and structures. However, I also note that good ethical norms for distinct roles and relationships could help people learn how to live well together with others and allow for some ethical spaciousness for people to flourish. Mou reminds us: "Morality is not to constrain people …. Morality is to open and realize human beings."[70] Mr. Zhao earned respect from my mother by respecting her by offering her a chair, in nodding to her approvingly, and in listening to her attentively at the first place. The respectful relationship between Mr. Zhao and my mother goes beyond good manners and etiquette. It generates more genuine and richer conversations between two human beings and opens them to more ethical possibilities and engagement.

The invitation for newness and differences in *ren* relationships is at the heart of ethical possibility. A relationship anchored in *ren* is not to regulate and conform people to absolute rules, but to bring out the goodness by attending to their uniqueness and newness. Confucius suggests: "… the disciples' pursuit of *ren* is not necessarily slower than the teacher's";[71] and Han Yu, in the Tang Dynasty, also writes about how the disciples are not necessarily behind the teachers, while the teachers are not necessarily wiser than that disciples. In a conversation with his disciples about their future inspirations, Confucius does not negate anyone but in a humble way expresses his own of idea of the importance of rituals and music.[72] In my mother's story, Mr. Zhao did not explain to her clearly or predict what good (or bad) could come out of the forbidden books. The lack of explanation, prediction, and certainty in Mr. Zhao's interactions with my mother not only revealed his humility but constituted an invitation to the new and to a future as yet unknown to him and his students.

With and beyond Aristotle and Confucius

To engage ethically in teaching is fundamentally about attuning oneself and responding appropriately to particular others and circumstances, such that one contributes to a good and flourishing life. Indeed, ethical engagement in teaching is not a grand theory for us to master, but a never-ending request for people to reflect upon their own lived lives and their efforts to live well with others. My reading of my mother's stories in all their texture and particularity constitutes my own search for significance and insight into how to live and engage ethically as an educator. Through Aristotelian and Confucian lenses, my mother and her teacher, Mr. Zhao, teach us that it is important to sustain a dialogue between the particular and the general by constantly being open to the particular and revising the general; that reason chiming with emotion can provide resources for ethical engagement; and finally, that the ethical relationships worthy of the name embrace mutual respect, love, and welcome newness. Today's predominant managerial discourses around teaching and teacher education are challenged by these ethical languages, which hold that teachers are not to manage and train their students for better marks but are to encounter them as human others and prepare to be addressed by their particularity; teachers are not advised to contain their emotions and wear cold professional masks but need to bring emotion and reason into mutual illumination, and cultivate appropriate emotions; teachers are not reduced to the roles of regulators and disciplinarians but elevated as human beings devoted to forging truthful relationships with one another.

Of course, listening to Aristotelian and Confucian traditions does not necessarily mean their insights exhaust the stories or provide superior ways to understand. As David Smith suggests, we need to face the truth that "no one tradition can say everything that needs to be said about the full expression of human experience in the world."[73] I transform the lived stories of teaching within the managerial scheme through borrowing Aristotelian and Confucian moral languages. Teleological approaches to ethics advocated by Aristotelians and Confucians presume a level of consensus inconsistent with today's pluralistic, democratic society. It raises further questions about who gets to decide what is true, good, right—and educational. Caputo's notion of "meta-*phronesis*"[74] as the ability to cope with and judge among competing and incommensurable schemata seems to challenge the teleological pursuit and hence offer a messier but more truthful framework for teachers and teacher educators in today's context.

Meta-*phronesis*, a more radically conceived *phronesis*, "undergoes a colder, more merciless exposure to events."[75] Meta-*phronesis* does not suppose a general agreement or consensus about the schemata, and it is constantly shaped and formed by events. The more radical, decentered meta-*phronesis* could push one up close "against the face of ethics,"[76] bearing the potential of transforming the singular notion of goodness in the teleological pursuit. In today's pluralistic and democratic world, teachers and teacher educators often find themselves in the conjunction between cultures and traditions. The goodness of life should be plural and open-ended, and welcome ongoing discussions. The notion of goodness should not be measured against restricted schemes but embedded in particular human experiences. They need to be given space not merely to preserve someone's own cultural heritage and social customs, but to be exposed to, learn about, and appreciate alternatives and other possibilities of understanding life without necessarily agreeing with one another. It is a relentless pursuit and an open-ended inquiry about the meaning and significance of life together with others. As Greene suggests, it is "to look inquiringly and wonderingly on the world in which one lives. It is like returning home from a long stay in some other place."⁷⁷ Teachers and teacher educators are encouraged to respect, include, consider, and negotiate among different schemata and paradigms, to render the familiar unfamiliar, and hence to develop a better ear to hear the resonances of education.

This chapter listens to the ancient voices of Aristotle and Confucius and brings them into conversation with my mother's stories. In my retelling of them I do not aim to yield settled conclusions; rather, I hope to spur and pursue new aspirations and possibilities for understanding teaching and teacher education. Not only are managerial discourses challenged but Aristotelian and Confucian traditions are extended in dialogue with today's context. Again, to cite Greene, I will "keep trying, in order to stay alive and keep alive the sense of possibility, knowing well that there are no guarantees."⁷⁸

Notes

1. Clarke and Phelan, *Teacher Education and The Political*, 2.
2. Ethical engagement refers to teachers exhibiting moral judgment and action, often amidst conflicting and demoralizing political demands.
3. Biesta, "Why 'What Works' Won't Work," 1.
4. Biesta, *Beautiful Risk*, 129.
5. Moral language focuses upon the normative and axiological concerns and claims in life. It helps investigating and making judgments about what is good and worthwhile and how we ought to live together with other people.
6. The Cultural Revolution, also known as the Great Proletarian Cultural Revolution, was a sociopolitical movement that took place in China from 1966 until 1976. Initiated and launched by Mao Zedong, at the time the Chairman of the Communist Party of China, the Cultural Revolution was aimed at advocating pure communist ideology and eradicating capitalist and traditional elements from Chinese society. In contrast to today's neoliberal discourse around privatization, deregulation, free trade, and free market, the Cultural Revolution is characterized by its centralized political power control, regulation, and the imposition of Maoist thought.
7. Reeve, *Practices of Reason*, 76.
8. Hughes, *Aristotle on Ethics*, 168.
9. Aristotle, *Metaphysics*, 1156b7–9.
10. The term "normal school" refers to an institution that aimed to train schoolteachers in the early twentieth century. The terminology is preserved in the official names of such institutions in China even after these schools gained university status.
11. Risser, *Hermeneutics*, 107.
12. Aristotle, *Nicomachean Ethics*, 1141b15–18.
13. Dunne, "Virtue, *Phronesis* and Learning," 52–53.
14. Kristjansson, *Aristotle, Emotions and Education*, 177.
15. Kristjansson, 166.
16. Nussbaum, *Fragility*, 306.
17. Dunne, "Virtue, *Phronesis* and Learning," 61.
18. Nussbaum, *Fragility*, 305.
19. Dunne, *Back to the Rough Ground*, 292.
20. Sim, *Remastering Morals*, 110.
21. Mou, *Nineteen Talks*, 35.
22. Confucius, *Analects*, 2.5; 2.6; 2.7; 2.8.
23. Confucius, 2.5.
24. Confucius, 2.7.

25 Mou, *Nineteen Talks*, 36.
26 Confucius, *Analects*, 17.6.
27 Schön, *The Reflective Practitioner*, 3.
28 Aristotle, *Nicomachean Ethics*, 1102b28–29.
29 Aristotle, 1102b31.
30 Aristotle, 1102a31.
31 Nussbaum, *Love's Knowledge*, 176.
32 Dunne, "Virtue, *Phronesis* and Learning," 62.
33 Yu, *Ethics of Confucius and Aristotle*, 75.
34 Nussbaum, *Love's Knowledge*, 41.
35 Nussbaum, 42.
36 Nussbaum, 36.
37 Nussbaum, 36.
38 Confucius, "Li Ji, Li Yun," 1288–1294.
39 Mencius or Mengzi, living in the Warring States period in China, was regarded as a Chinese philosopher and one of the principal interpreters of Confucianism. He believed in the innate goodness of human nature.
40 Mencius, "Meng Zi, Gong Sun Chou," 238.
41 Confucius, *Analects*, 12.22.
42 Confucius, 4.3.
43 Mencius, "Meng Zi, Teng Wen Gong," 271–274.
44 Pang, *Research on Confucian Dialectical Method*, 18.
45 Fan, *Reconstructionist Confucianism*, 31.
46 Sim, *Remastering Morals*, 28.
47 Aristotle, *Nicomachean Ethics*, 1107a10–11.
48 Aristotle, 1109a20–24.
49 Zi Si, "The Mean," 183.
50 Zi Si, 188.
51 Zi Si, 183.
52 Carr and Harrison, *Educating Character*, 43.
53 Phelan, *Curriculum Theorizing*, 20.
54 Aristotle, *Nicomachean Ethics*, 1156b32.
55 Aristotle, 1159a34–1159b10.
56 Hughes, *Aristotle on Ethics*, 174.
57 Sherman, *Fabric of Character*, 173.
58 Aristotle, *Nicomachean Ethics*, 1156b12–18.
59 Phelan, *Curriculum Theorizing*, 22.
60 Van Norden, "Toward a Synthesis," 64.
61 Ban Gu, *Bai Hu Tong Yi*.
62 Confucius, "Li Ji, Tan Gong Shang," 1181–1187.
63 Confucius, *Analects*, 11.11.
64 Yu, "Virtue: Confucius and Aristotle," 332.

65 Confucius, *Analects*, 11.9, 11.10.
66 Pinar, *What Is Curriculum Theory?*, 38.
67 Greene, *Teacher as Stranger*, 4.
68 Confucius, *Analects*, 11.39.
69 Pang, *Research on Confucian Dialectical Method*, 38.
70 Mou, *Nineteen Talks*, 78.
71 Confucius, *Analects*, 15.36.
72 Confucius, 11.26.
73 Smith, "Farthest West," 26.
74 Caputo, *Against Ethics*, 102.
75 Caputo, 102.
76 Caputo, 103.
77 Greene, *Teacher as Stranger*, 267.
78 Greene, "Autobiographical Remembrance," 11.

Bibliography

Aristotle. *Metaphysics*. In *The Complete Works of Aristotle*, edited by Jonathan Barnes. Princeton, NJ: Princeton University Press, 1984.

———. *Nichomachean Ethics*. In *The Complete Works of Aristotle*, edited by Jonathan Barnes. Princeton, NJ: Princeton University Press, 1984.

Ban, Gu. *Bai Hu Tong Yi* (白虎通义). Retrieved from http://product.dangdang.com/1900017851.html.

Biesta, Gert. *The Beautiful Risk of Education*. Boulder, CO: Paradigm Publishers, 2013.

———. "Why 'What Works' Won't Work. Evidence-Based Practice and the Democratic Deficit of Educational Research." *Educational Theory* 57, no. 1 (2007): 1–22.

Caputo, John. *Against Ethics: Contributions to a Poetics of Obligation with Constant Reference to Deconstruction*. Bloomington and Indianapolis, IN: Indiana University Press, 1993.

Carr, David, and Tom Harrison. *Educating Character through Stories*. Exeter, UK: Imprint Academic, 2015.

Clarke, Matthew, and Anne M. Phelan. *Teacher Education and the Political: The Power of Negative Thinking*. London, UK: Routledge, 2017. Confucius. *Analects*. In *The Complete Collection of Four Books and Five Classics*, edited by Yong Lai, 3–164. Beijing, CN: China's Book Store, 2013.

———. *Li Ji*. In *The Complete Collection of Four Books and Five Classics*, edited by Yong Lai, 1157–1547. Beijing, CN: China's Book Store, 2013.

Dunne, Joseph. *Back to the Rough Ground: Practical Judgment and the Lure of Technique*. Notre Dame, IN: University of Notre Dame Press, 1993.

———. "Virtue, *Phronesis* and Learning." In *Virtue Ethics and Moral Education*, edited by David Carr and Jan Steutel, 49–63. London, UK: Routledge, 1999.

Fan, Ruiping. *Reconstructionist Confucianism: Rethinking Morality after the West*. Dordrecht, NL: Springer, 2010.

Greene, Maxine. "An Autobiographical Remembrance." In *The Passionate Mind of Maxine Greene: 'I am … not yet'*, edited by William F. Pinar, 8–12. London, UK: Falmer Press, 1998.

———. *Teacher as Stranger: Educational Philosophy for the Modern Age*. Belmont, CA: Wadsworth Publishing Company, 1973.

Hughes, Gerald. *Aristotle on Ethics*, New York, NY: Routledge, 2001.

Kristjansson, Kristjan. *Aristotle, Emotions and Education*. Aldershot, UK: Ashgate Publishing Limited, 2007.

Mencius, "Meng Zi." In *The Complete Collection of Four Books and Five Classics*, edited by Yong Lai, 205–361. Beijing, CN: China's Book Store, 2013.

Mou, Zongsan. *Nineteen Talks on Chinese Philosophy (中国哲学十九讲)*. Shanghai, CN: Gu Ji Press, 2005.

Nussbaum, Martha C. *The Fragility of Goodness: Luck and Ethics in Greek Tragedy and Philosophy*, New York, NY: Cambridge University Press, 1986/2001.

———. *Love's Knowledge: Essays on Philosophy and Literature*. Oxford, UK: Oxford University Press, 1990.

Pang, Pu. *Research on Confucian Dialectical Method (儒家辩证法研究)*. Beijing, CN: Zhong Hua Shu Ju Press, 2009.

Phelan, Anne M. *Curriculum Theorizing and Teacher Education: Complicating Conjunctions*. London, UK: Routledge, 2015.

Pinar, William F. *What Is Curriculum Theory?* Mahwah, NJ: Lawrence Erlbaum, 2004.

Reeve, C. D. C. *Practices of Reason: Aristotle's Nicomachean Ethics*. Oxford, UK: Oxford University Press, 1992.

Risser, James. *Hermeneutics and the Voice of the Other: Re-reading Gadamer's Philosophical Hermeneutics*. Albany, NY: State University of New York Press, 1997.

Schön, Donald. *The Reflective Practitioner: How Professionals Think in Action*. London, UK: Temple Smith, 1983.

Sherman, Nancy. *The Fabric of Character: Aristotle's Theory of Virtue*. New York, NY: Oxford University Press, 1989.

Sim, May. *Remastering Morals with Aristotle and Confucius*. Cambridge, UK: Cambridge University Press, 2007.

Smith, David. "The Farthest West Is but the Farthest East." In *Cross-Cultural Studies in Curriculum: Eastern Thought, Educational Insights*, edited by Claudia Eppert and Hongyu Wang, 1–32. New York, NY: Lawrence Erlbaum, 2008.

Van Norden, Bryan. "Toward a Synthesis of Confucianism and Aristotelianism." In *Virtue Ethics and Confucianism*, edited by Stephen Angle and Michael Slote, 56–65. New York, NY: Routledge, 2013.

Yu, Jiyuan. *The Ethics of Confucius and Aristotle: Mirrors of Virtue*. New York, NY: Routledge, 2007.

———. "Virtue: Confucius and Aristotle." *Philosophy East and West* 48, no. 2 (1998): 323–347.

Zi, Si. "The Doctrine of the Mean." In *The Complete Collection of Four Books and Five Classics*, edited by Yong Lai, 181–204. Beijing, CN: China's Book Store, 2013.

CHAPTER 10

Knowing, Thinking, Living: Teacher Education in the Most Enlightened Age

Theodore Christou

Tomorrow is Today

There are moments in history when Tomorrow is Today,
When the mammoth glacier of social trend
taking movement down the Valley of History
can be diverted by men
Into pathways towards Tomorrow.
***
There are moments in history when Today is merely
Today …
inert, unchanging …
When no mustering of energies
Can prod man out of his inertia.
***
Then comes the moment when Tomorrow is Today,
When the flux is at free flow.
Then Man is Captain of his Soul
And the principle of the effective human act
Works in a world at social crisis.
***
I'll say it in this way, then—
***
There is a favored moment … a place …
and a mustering of energies
Which, in unison, will produce an effective
 human act.[1]

This essay articulates a nested framework that may facilitate conversation regarding what it means to know about teacher education, distinguishing between *knowledge of the world*, *thinking about the world*, and *living in the world*. It argues that knowledge of the world is necessary but in itself insufficient. Thinking about the world is broader than, but inclusive of, knowledge, since one is always thinking about facts, figures, and data, which are among the basic elements of knowledge. Living in the world involves the application of knowledge and habits of thought to everyday situations and contexts. This is the enactment of philosophy as a way of life. Within the nested framework of knowledge about teacher education presented here, living in the world encompasses both knowledge and thinking, operationalizing and directing both towards meaningful engagement with contemporary society.

While the framework draws heavily on literature from the teaching and learning of history, it does so because this discipline is in the midst of a paradigm shift that permits a view into the transition from knowing to thinking about the past. Historically, history has focused on memorization of historical content, narratives, and images. It has, more recently, turned away from a focus on content to a concern for historical thinking, requiring scrutiny of perspective-taking, evidence, and the ethical dimensions of history. Yet, historical thinking is not enough. One may think in deep and complex ways about the past without applying any of these habits to lived experience. One may make great inroads with respect to enriching our understanding of the past without taking a single step towards engaging with the present and with the future. Within the present moment, a turn of phrase used by Harold Rugg (one of the most popular and influential educationists of the first half of the twentieth century, who is often forgotten as he stands in the long shadow cast by John Dewey at Teachers College, Columbia), Canadian teacher education is charged with seeking truth and fostering reconciliation. Tomorrow is today, Rugg avers.

In support of this nested framework for knowledge, this essay refers to the work of French philosopher Pierre Hadot, who, appealing to classical traditions that sought to exercise one's abilities to engage with the world meaningfully, argued that philosophy was a way of living. Hadot, an historian of philosophy, who was ordained into the Catholic Church in 1944 and, shortly after, left the priesthood, conceptualized philosophical living as spiritual exercise and discipline in terms akin to those underlying the work of monastics. In living, no matter the context, philosophy set forth a set of exercises one worked on perpetually and persistently. Further, this essay considers some fragments of the poetry composed by Harold Rugg, not normally noted as a poet, who intended to attune educationists to the world around them in order to strive for social change. Lastly, it implicates John Dewey and pragmatic philosophy into the narrative regarding the aims and purposes of teacher education in the present moment.

Knowing the World

Knowledge matters. Whether the context is mythology, fable, one or another dark age, or a space of false news, knowing—right from wrong, fact from fiction, orthodoxy and orthopraxy—is vital to life. Ignorance is only bliss for the faint of spirit, and teacher education ought not to stoop so low. The earth is not flat; at least with respect to the geometrical and physical laws. We are obligated to know about the world so that we are not deluded about the world that we inhabit. A notable caveat is the Socratic adage that knowledge is, substantively, understanding our own ignorance.

Ken Osborne describes *knowing about the world* as "the necessity of knowledge."[2] He does so with respect to historical knowledge, which serves here as a sort of simulacrum. A historian must seek, and be able to seek, factual knowledge about the world. Facts matter. An account that claims, for instance, that a sophisticated alien species descended to earth in order to build the Canadian Parliament buildings would not be historical. The scholarly community—not to mention common sense—would refute the claim on the basis of evidence. Those individuals who took the time to refute the claim about aliens building Parliament would be compelled to seek, and then present, warrants for their contradictory claims. Various combinations of archival data, building records, and personal correspondence might be chosen to refute the spurious claim. Thus, it is as important for historians to have access to evidence as it is for them to have knowledge. The two are inseparable. Osborne offers a pertinent analogy: "If we are confronted with a Holocaust-denier, for example, we can hardly break off the argument while we go off to consult the Internet. We have to rebut the falsehood, then and there, and this requires knowledge."[3]

George Orwell's dystopian novel *Nineteen Eighty-Four* presents a portrayal of a society, Osborne continues, in which people lack both independent knowledge as well as access to such knowledge. Within the discipline of history, the scholarly community serves this purpose of checking and balancing knowledge claims. In principle, historians hunt for new sources and perspectives to examine the past not because it will make their account more original, but because these allow us as a whole to have a richer and more complex understanding of the context under examination. While the inhabitants of Orwell's novel are one extreme of the spectrum, the contestants on trivia shows are the other extreme. The former know nothing about the past except that which has been told them, and the latter—literally, in an etymological sense—are asked to trivialize their knowledge of the past, by recalling facts in isolation of their contexts and meanings. Facts matter, but they do not suffice.

Thinking about the World

The more we know, in a quantitative sense, the more we realize how little we know with respect the infinitude of knowledge. Knowledge breeds modesty. Thus, the old chestnut that proclaims a little bit of knowledge is a dangerous thing, for in pursuit of knowledge we learn that we are ignorant and hold knowledge tentatively. How we think about the world and our place within it matters more than knowledge does. Paradigms and truths change. We cannot trust knowledge. It evolves, trips, falters, and finds new trespasses to explore. To think about the world is to cultivate habits of mind that permit us to question knowledge—whether that is our assumptions, presumptions, or held-for-granted truths—and to hold it up to scrutiny just as scientists may with respect to the material elements of the cosmos.

Because knowledge is often, or always, evolving and transmutable—a matter made evident by historiographical work—the ways that we think about the world bear our attention, particularly in teacher education. The publication of Thomas Kuhn's *The Structure of Scientific Revolutions* demonstrated dramatic changes throughout the history of science in regards to the way we view and interpret our world.[4] Rather than describing a process of increasing, linear progress in scientific knowledge, Kuhn showed complex shifts in the fundamental paradigms operating within communities of researchers and general populations. The latest incarnation of any curriculum document requires careful study, but it cannot be understood without examining the historical moment in which it was created and the context in which it will be interpreted. In history education, for instance, historical thinking matters more than historical knowledge; when one thinks historically, one necessarily thinks about knowledge: facts, figures, dates, and so on. Peter Seixas, retired Canada Research Chair in Historical Thinking at the University of British Columbia, is at the Canadian forefront of this massive endeavour to understand historical thinking and to relate it more intimately to schooling. With Tom Morton, Seixas defines the concept as follows: "Historical thinking is the creative process that historians go through to interpret the evidence of the past and generate the stories of history."[5] They frame the matter in terms of six concepts; each represents a historical "tension, or difficulty, that may be irresolvable in an ultimate way."[6] The "big six" tensions are:

1. Significance: How do we decide what is important to learn about the past?
2. Evidence: How do we know what we know about the past?
3. Continuity and Change: How can we make sense of the complex flaws of history?
4. Cause and Consequence: Why do events happen, and what are their impacts?
5. Historical Perspectives: How can we better understand the people of the past?
6. The Ethical Dimension: How can history help us to live in the present?[7]

Seixas's articulation of historical thinking is framed as the backbone of inquiry learning within Ontario's History and Social Studies curriculum documents, although this framework is pervasive in the contemporary curricular landscape across the country. He is directly cited in those documents:

> Competent historical thinkers understand both the vast differences that separate us from our ancestors and the ties that bind us to them; they can analyze historical artifacts and documents, which can give them some of the best understandings of times gone by; they can assess the validity and relevance of historical accounts, when they are used to support entry into a war, voting for a candidate, or any of the myriad decisions knowledgeable

citizens in a democracy must make. All this requires "knowing the facts," but "knowing the facts" is not enough. Historical thinking does not replace historical knowledge: the two are related and interdependent.[8]

Seixas's framework is reflected in history curricula across the Canadian landscape although Ontario's curricula are most clearly and explicitly grounded linguistically and conceptually with Seixas's historical thinking concepts, articulated here at the University of British Columbia.[9]

Historical thinking is equated with active and inquiry-based learning.[10] Although this equation does not explicitly invoke a social reconstructionist or social justice framework, it does represent history education with active learning, a core progressivist principle in Ontario education.[11] Agency is not explicitly noted as a dimension of historical thinking within Seixas's framework, although history educators could concentrate their studies on this concept without undermining historical thinking. If history demonstrates change, it follows that change is possible and individual actors can be change agents in whatever context they are engaged. In other words, history education as a dimension of citizenship education is both vital and vigorous in relating study of the past with engagement with the present.

The teacher candidates that I work with are compelled to concentrate on historical thinking and inquiry-based instruction rather than on any particular narrative or data sets. Historical thinking is defined as "a way for students to develop the ability to think critically about significant events, developments, and issues, both within the curriculum and in their lives outside the classroom."[12] This aim is frequently alien to these teacher candidates and, what complicates matters, it is alien, also, to the associate teachers that will host them during their practicum placements.

Through what Dan Lortie termed the "apprenticeship of observation," teacher candidates—future history and social studies teachers—have already learned a great deal about history education before their teacher education programs even begin.[13] By virtue of having being students in history and social studies classes for most of their lives, teacher candidates are not blank slates; rather, they have strong beliefs about what history is as a discipline and how it ought to be taught. They are asked to not rely on their instincts or on their memories of how history is taught but, rather, to use historical content as a means of cultivating historical thinking. In other words, knowledge matters but only insofar as it is operationalized through inquiry.

There are four historical thinking concepts identified and laced throughout the curriculum documents: a) historical significance; b) cause and consequence; c) continuity and change; and d) historical perspective.[14] Missing are two of the six concepts iterated in Seixas's framework: a) evidence; and b) ethical dimensions. The explication for these absences must rest with another essay. Thus, we develop a historical fluency gradually, never entirely resolving the past, but always seeking to examine it more critically and with greater sophistication. Facts matter, but what we do with the facts that we recall is a question of greater complexity and, we argue, significance.

Living in the World

We are prompted to think about the world by various media and spaces, in contexts immersed in the business of life and in eremitic silence. When we think about the world and in endeavouring to know about the world, we strive to comprehend our life space and to examine it critically and with a detective's healthy sense of suspicion. What matters more than knowing about the world and thinking about the world is the way that we live in the world. When we examine classical philosophy—its schools as well as its traditions, which will be discussed below—our examinations reveal that it is a way of living in the world. In other words, philosophy is an ongoing struggle to seek knowledge about the world, to think about how knowledge is both constructed and contextual, and to operationalize it meaningfully and increasingly consistently, to shape ourselves and the world we inhabit.

Living in the world means examining our context and our actions even as we shape our time space and act within them. It is the operationalization of our efforts to pursue knowledge of the world and the application of our thinking about the world to our lived existence. In teacher education, it is the aim of enacting a philosophic life. It requires that the teacher candidates move from understanding and contemplating educational questions to working out their solution *in medias res*.

Herein lies the significance of a nested framework of knowledge in teacher education (Figure 1), particularly in the Canadian landscape where citizenship is explicitly invoked within the history and social studies curricula: in the present paradigm, where historical thinking supersedes historical knowledge, we are invited to consider how content knowledge and our habits of thought interact with the phenomenal world. If teacher education concentrates on knowledge of the world—as a category, this may contain disciplinary content knowledge, familiarity with curriculum expectations and assessment criteria, or standards of practice, as beginning points—this is all that candidates will learn (to the extent that retention or recollection of knowledge entails learning).

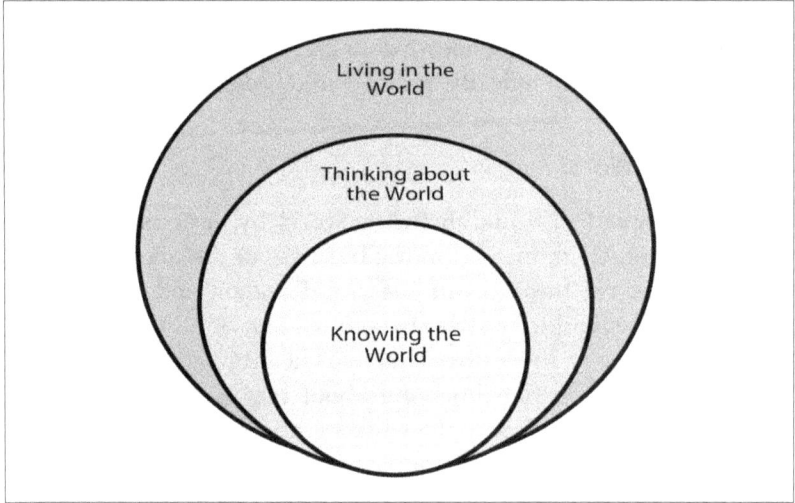

Figure 1: A nested framework of knowledge in teacher education.

This is not to diminish knowledge, which would be akin to neglecting to see that the War of 1812 engaged the United States with Britain's North American colony in the territory that is now Canada, implicating Indigenous communities on both sides of the dispute. If teacher education, rather, concentrates on thinking about the world, it will, by necessity, be thinking about something—that is, knowledge of the world. When considering, in other words, how evidence, continuity and change, cause and consequence, or the ethical dimensions of history help us understand history, we can do so by examining the War of 1812 (or, for that matter, any other historical context and problem).

Further, when we are charged, as we are in 2017, with living in and shaping the world around us as engaged citizens, what we do is put into practice particular ways of thinking while testing knowledge claims by our own understanding. We have thought about the world. In order to do so, we have sought to know the world. And, having practiced both, we seek to live in the world intelligently, ethically, and well.

Tomorrow Is Today

Teacher education, conceptualized as knowing, thinking about, and living in the world, is related to the development of agency and engaged citizenship. We can shape ourselves and the world around us. Both self and society are intertwined in the process of making. We make, are made, even as we hold the potential to sit inertly and reject our potential as change agents and ignore how the spaces that we inhabit determine the conditions of our evolution: moral, physical, intellectual, and social.

Harold Rugg, a protagonist of progressive education as a means of social reconstruction, is part of the canon of curriculum theory courses. He is regarded as a social activist, a perhaps-communist during the Red Scare in the United States following World War II, a researcher and author of a wildly popular textbook series, and colleague of such educational giants as John Dewey, William Heard Kilpatrick, Edward Thorndike, and William C. Bagley at Columbia University's Teachers College.[15] Rugg is rarely, if ever, lauded as a versifier. Yet here he is, composing poetry to foster social mobilization and reform. He is acutely aware of time and, more so, he is prescient with respect to the ability of educational reform to spur social reform.

Here, history, present, and future are not distinct. All are akin to glacial ice sheets, altering the very landscapes that they occupy as they shift, expand, or retreat. This movement is particularly contemporary, associated with a free flow of time. Unlike glaciers, Rugg appears to insist that humans can decisively shape the world around them. Rugg's context was shaped by global warfare, economic instability, political unrest, and ongoing struggle between democratic, fascist, socialist, and radical ideologies. In many respects, Rugg's "today" feels like it is ours.

A forward-looking, hopeful, and robust vision for education and for schooling, which seeks to foster affirmative change in society at large, must work from within a particular social context and consider that setting's complex historical development and relation to other contexts. Progressivism is predicated on faith and hope. Yet, despite all progress we might profess to have made in pedagogy, burning questions remain that cast doubt on our hopeful intimations of what "tomorrow" may resemble. In which direction or to which aims are we progressing? How do we measure or regard such progress? Is all reform necessarily and equally progressive? These questions are not merely posed to suggest that contemporary schools are problematic institutions; this is too commonplace and over-abused a position, anticipating reform manifestos.

These questions presuppose a multiplicity of responses, as there is a gross incommensurability between conceptions of progress in educational discourse. It is dangerous to conflate these conceptions because their orientations are frequently divergent. We must face the understanding that progress in terms of one ideological or ontological framework potentially undermines another. The normalizing effects of many administratively efficient pursuits such as standardized and norm referenced testing potentially restrain, for example, anarchical or liberal thought. Likewise, statistics and ministerial publications, among other indicators of progress or growth, while elucidating administrative criteria of growth, are, in terms of many pedagogical criteria, smokescreens. This is the basic premise of Egan's historical and philosophical study of schooling, *Getting It Wrong from the Beginning*.[16] There is some irony to be derived from Egan's critique; he outlines the parameters of progressive education but is also one of its most prescient critics.[17]

I argue that a particular strand of existential anxiety about the present and a correlative uncertain future are at the root of much of our educational rhetoric and our educational objectives. For the past century, progressivists have implored educationists to (a) focus on the individual child as an emerging being rather than upon a traditional curriculum; (b) make schooling adaptive to the needs of these individuals within a world wrought with flux; and (c) commit to relating school life to the modern, evolving, and rapidly transforming realities of social existence. Schools as conceived and as constructed were seen by progressivist minds as historical appendages that were no longer useful in the modern age.[18]

These three themes read, in sum, as follows: The century to come is qualitatively and quantitatively inimitable to the previous one and the world that we inhabit is in flux. Schools need to be reconceptualized. We must prepare our youth for the world of the future by engaging them actively with technologies available to us in the present. The world that they will inhabit is not the world of the past that we inhabited.

I return to Harold Rugg as a case in point. "It is my thesis," he notes, "that this is our moment. That by taking thought now ... by focusing our total energies on the fulcrum and lifting together ... we can move the social world."[19] Rugg continues: "There's poetry as well as pragmatism / and both are needed."[20] He characterizes poetry as an uplifting force, and pragmatism, which he associates with science and technology, as a directive force. The latter offers structure—technical, administrative, and operative—but it is useless without the former, which is the engine that drives social living.

"We fight two wars in one," Rugg argues.[21] He refers to domestic and international tensions, as this text was largely penned during the Second World War. Yet Rugg also relates this statement to the dual purposes of progressive education. On the one hand, it concerns the central concerns of progressivist thought, which I have already introduced (focus on the individual learner, on active learning, and on the integration of school life with social life). On the other hand, it concerns the functions of progressivism, which, again, as noted, confront the existential realization that the world we inhabit today is qualitatively different from the one that we inhabited as children. Progressive education serves as a means by which we might align schools more meaningfully with contemporary realities and prospective actualities. Progressive education is thus an instrument of change within a world that is perceived to be rapidly changing. Progressivist pedagogical philosophy, in other words, articulates a response to the perceived misalignment between schools and society, even as it increasingly provokes dissonance between those same two institutions or structures.

Within the macrocosm of what is today, it may appear paradoxical to speak of progress in a time that feels particularly regressive. The state of the world today is not particularly happy. In this context, Harold Rugg's poetry is prophetic. Unpacking the verse "the social flux is at free flow," he notes:

> We live at the median of the swiftest social transition in all history. The flux of events and mood is at last at free flow. The adamant of a static society has been shaken apart. Changes in social pattern succeed one another so rapidly that the culture is no longer a matrix into which human life is poured, but seems far more like a kaleidoscope.[22]

Rugg imagined that by the dawn of the twenty-first century, his grandchildren would look back at the twentieth century and see a shift from a world built on industrial foundations to a world grounded in democracy. He aspired to a world that resembled a kaleidoscope. Naively, perhaps, he presupposes the possibility of symmetry and reflexivity within the United States and beyond its borders. Neither is a feature of the world we live in. This is a post-postmodern world, fractured and divided. A post-secular world, in Habermas's characterization.[23] It is a world in which tomorrow is today, where we fight many wars in one:

> You ask me,
>   suppose we win the war,
>   what then?
>   Can we win the peace?
>
> ***
>
> I tell you we are winning the peace now.
> Every victory and every set-back, now,
> Is a campaign in tomorrow's war at home.
>
> ***
>
> So I tell you we must speak of the peace,
> Even while we war.[24]

Rugg was simultaneously responding to a world fraught with change, and he was seeking to change this world, which was fraught with change. The western world was at war in Europe and in the Pacific, and it needed to win this war to engage in another struggle for peace. Both challenges were intertwined. Tomorrow is today.

Rugg, drawing from a personal journal, offers a further analogy that is in equal parts brute and poetic:

> On my desk stands a bronze statue by Alfeo Faggi. The light of my lamp evokes the muscles of a powerful man. "Depression 1934" Faggi called it ... himself momentarily cast down by a sick society. "Reservoirs of Power" would be a better name—for, while the total posture is one of being bowed down ... "depressed"... it is not one of being crushed. Every muscle is taut, coiled to spring up—to carry on, to build anew, to create. I saw a

fine man beaten down like that once in a dreadful bare hand fist fight. And even as he was forced down on his knees I saw his spirit coil his muscles, pour strength into them from hidden reservoirs of power. And springing up at the tenth count, when all seemed lost, he beat his adversary into submission. As I write our world seems beaten down and the moment is at the tenth count. But our world is like that man; muscles are taut, coiled to spring up, to carry on, to build anew, to create.[25]

Here, Rugg's narrative reveals a stoic recognition of human frailty. In this age of extremes, or in any age, we will fall and falter. It is at these moments, "favored" as Rugg defined them, that teacher educators are charged with the task of reconceptualizing their role within their local, provincial, territorial, national, and global contexts.

This reconceptual work, prompted by some moment, is necessarily about today and about tomorrow. It is both grounded in the present and entirely aspirational. Canada's Truth and Reconciliation Commission's ninety-four calls to action represent the most significant moment and challenge that teacher educators face. We are like Faggi's depressed man, wearing the weight of the realization that our history is far from progressive and teeming with instances of what I have elsewhere termed "pedagogical sins."[26] Tomorrow is today. We must create.

The Most Enlightened Age

"What then is education?" asks Søren Kierkegaard; it is, he argues, "the curriculum the individual ran through in order to catch up with himself [sic]; and anyone who does not want to go through this curriculum will be little helped by being born into the most enlightened age."[27] Kierkegaard appeals to an existentialist sentiment. What we learn or, rather, what we may learn, is dependent on the individual. The year 2017 may be an age of enlightenment—there are, sadly, many signs to the alternative—but one is not ever enlightened by virtue of his or her context. One is measured by the way they live. Hence, philosophy, a perpetual search for wisdom, is a way of living.

Thus, Pierre Hadot, conjuring Henry David Thoreau, argues that "there are nowadays professors of philosophy, but not philosophers."[28] Hadot demonstrates that classical philosophy was not a set of doctrines or methods, but a way of life. To be Epicurean or Stoic—to take two examples—was not to ascribe to a club, but to buy into epistemological and ontological frameworks for living. These were the equivalent of exercises one might find to strengthen our body's core, triceps, or hamstrings. In the ancient world, philosophy exercised our minds. It was a means of habituating human life to the pursuit of knowledge, to rigorous habits of mind, and to ways of living ethical and engaged existences.[29] As Robert Wardy has noted, philosophy involved "doing and living."[30] Rather than committing Plato's *Euthyphro* to memory, one ought to be able to read the text, think about it, and use its substantive elements to shape the way one interacted with the world as it was. This means, to quote Hadot, that "we no longer theorize about moral action, we act in a correct and just way."[31]

This is *living in the world*, which, as noted, implicates *thinking about the world* and *knowing the world*. It boils down to teacher education as philosophy. While outlining a philosophy of education, drawing on Rousseau or Vygotsky or any *au courant* philosopher is relatively ubiquitous, being a philosopher, no matter what the age, has connotations of old acetates and boxy briefcases. There are rules that regulate teacher education, and there are rules that we use to regulate ourselves. Both categories are composed of ideas that can be potent and formidable, drawing as they do on authority, creed, and tradition; an amalgam of these and our own experiences shape the way that we think about right and wrong living.

In *The School and Society*, Dewey remarks: "We have a typical idea of the gap existing between the everyday experiences of the child, and the isolated material supplied in such large measure in the school."[32] He continued: "[M]aking the school an organic whole, instead of a composite of isolated parts."[33] We are not speaking of children in teacher education; yet the sense that there is a gap regarding curriculum and learning outside of schools of education is neither new nor novel, but contemporary. Dewey argued further that education and democratic living were intertwined. Schooling ought to be "a form of social life" and a "democratic community."[34] And a democratic society provided "a flexible readjustment of its institutions through interaction of the different forms of associated life."[35]

Conclusions

What this essay identifies as *living in the world* dovetails nicely with what has been termed "historical mindedness"[36]—that is, the application of historical knowledge and historical thinking in the present. Only, living in the world requires more than history. Ken Osborne, for instance, invoked "a way of looking, not so much at history, but at the world at large, that derives from a familiarity with the past and with trying to understand and interpret it."[37] Teacher education in Canada is fundamentally rooted in disciplinary knowledge, however, and not in the foundations of education, which have been associated with educational history, philosophy, and sociology.[38]

As educationists and as teacher educators, our contemporary conceptions of educational research are not always historically minded, but curriculum scholars have long lamented the ahistorical quality of much curriculum work. "Although the curriculum field has witnessed reform after reform in its brief history," Gerald Ponder argued more than four decades ago, "each new generation of curriculum workers has attempted to answer continuing and recurring questions with little regard for their historical antecedents."[39] Herbert Kliebard stated the matter succinctly: "Issues seem to arise *ex nihilo*; each generation is left to discover anew the persistent and perplexing problems that characterize the field."[40]

A historically conscious person examines the past critically and sufficiently. A historically minded individual, on the contrary or as a corollary, looks at the world around them as an engaged citizen and makes sense of it using the tools employed via historical analysis. Historical mindedness is an irrevocable dimension of citizenship; thoughtful action requires historical analysis, which, in turn, demands action in the present that transforms ideas into tangible practices, policies, and practices. According to my understanding, historical consciousness is a personal endeavour that entails finding one's self in a broader historical narrative while being aware of the historical influences on one's own life, while historical mindedness is a way of living in the world that projects an historian's mind-set on every dimension of life as it is. Historical mindedness is, in other words, a way of living in the present that is informed by a particular manner of making sense of the past.

Notes

1. Rugg, *Now Is the Moment*, xiii (ellipses in original text).
2. Osborne, "Teaching of History," 10.
3. Osborne, 10–11.
4. Kuhn, *Scientific Revolutions*.
5. Seixas and Morton, *Big Six*, 2.
6. Seixas and Morton, 3.
7. Seixas and Morton, 10–11.
8. Seixas, *Scaling Up*, 6.
9. The six historical thinking concepts have evolved over time, having been termed "benchmarks of historical thinking" and "elements of historical thinking" in earlier iterations. See Seixas and Peck, "Teaching Historical Thinking," 109–117. Vancouver: Pacific Educational Press, 2004; and Seixas and Morton, *Big Six*.
10. Ontario Ministry of Education, *Social Studies*, 22–23.
11. See Christou, *Progressive Education*. There are two other core elements of progressivist educational rhetoric in Ontario's history: individualized instruction and the relation of learning to contemporary life and society.
12. Ontario Ministry of Education, *Social Studies*, 7.
13. Lortie, *Schoolteacher*, 61.
14. Ontario Ministry of Education, *Social Studies*, 13.
15. See Kliebard, *The Struggle for the American Curriculum*. Even as Rugg was popular, he was also loathed amongst some circles, especially for the political orientation he brought to social studies work, which was painted as leftist and subversive; as part of the Red Scare following World War II, his books were popularly burned and banned. See, for instance, Krane, "Rugg's Books under Fire.".
16. Egan, *Getting It Wrong*.
17. Egan, "Social Studies."
18. Christou. *Progressive Rhetoric and Curriculum*.
19. Rugg, *Now Is the Moment*, 1 (ellipses in original text).
20. Rugg, 4.
21. Rugg, 6.
22. Rugg, 9.
23. Habermas, *Faith and Reason*.
24. Rugg, *Now Is the Moment*, 109.
25. Rugg, 131.
26. Christou, "Stepping Away," 192.
27. Kierkegaard, *Fear and Trembling*, 52.
28. Hadot, "There Are Nowadays," 229. See Thoreau, *Walden*, 14.

29   Hadot, *What Is Ancient Philosophy?* Hadot cites Aristotle's *Politics* 1, 2, 1252a24 in stating: "Our goal, then, is to seize this phenomenon at its origin, remaining quite aware that philosophy is a historical phenomenon which arose at a particular point in time and has evolved up to the present," 2.
30   Wardy, *Doing Greek Philosophy*, 19–20.
31   Hadot, *Philosophy as a Way of Life*, 267.
32   Dewey, *School and Society*, 90.
33   Dewey, 106.
34   Dewey, *Democracy and Education*, 92.
35   Dewey, 105.
36   Bruno-Jofré and Steiner, "Fostering Educative Experiences," 70.
37   Osborne, "Book Reviews," 552.
38   Christou, "Gone but Not Forgotten."
39   Ponder, "Curriculum: Field without a Past?", 461.
40   Kliebard, "Curriculum Field in Retrospect," 69.

Bibliography

Bruno-Jofré, Rosa, and Karen Steiner. "Fostering Educative Experiences in Virtual High School History." *Encounters on Education* 8, no. 1 (2007): 69–82.

Christou, Theodore M. "Gone but Not Forgotten: The Decline of History as an Educational Foundation." *Journal of Curriculum Studies* 41, no. 5 (2009): 569–583.

———. *Progressive Education: Revisioning and Reframing Ontario's Public Schools.* Toronto, ON: University of Toronto Press, 2012.

———. *Progressive Rhetoric and Curriculum: Contested Visions of Public Education in Interwar Ontario.* New York, NY: Routledge, 2018.

Christou, Theodore M. "Stepping Away from the Utopias: Sin and the Myth of Progress in Matters of Pedagogy." *Encounters on Education* 9, no. 1 (2008): 189–194.

Dewey, John. *Democracy and Education.* In *The Middle Works of John Dewey, 1899–1924, Vol. 9: 1916, Democracy and Education,* edited by Jo Ann Boydston, 4–370. Carbondale, IL: Southern Illinois University Press, 1980.

———. *The School and Society.* Chicago. IL: University of Chicago Press, 1907.

Egan, Kieran. *Getting It Wrong from the Beginning: Our Progressivist Inheritance from Herbert Spencer, John Dewey, and Jean Piaget.* New Haven, CT and London, UK: Yale University Press, 2002.

———. "Social Studies and the Erosion of Schooling." *Curriculum Inquiry* 13, no. 2 (1983): 195–213.

Habermas, Jürgen. *An Awareness of What Is Missing: Faith and Reason in a Post-Secular Age*. Cambridge, UK: Polity, 2010.
Hadot, Pierre. *Philosophy as a Way of Life*. Cambridge, UK: Blackwell, 1995.
———. "There Are Nowadays Professors of Philosophy, but Not Philosophers." *Journal of Speculative Philosophy* 19, no. 3 (2005): 229–237.
———. *What Is Ancient Philosophy?* Cambridge, UK: Belknap, 2002.
Kierkegaard, Søren. *Fear and Trembling*. Translated by Alastair Hannay. New York, NY: Penguin, 2005.
Kliebard, Herbert. "The Curriculum Field in Retrospect." In *Technology and the Curriculum*, edited by W. F. Pitt, 69–84. New York, NY: Teachers College Press, 1968.
———. *The Struggle for the American Curriculum, 1893–1958*. New York, NY: RoutledgeFalmer, 2004.
Krane, Jay B. "Rugg's Books under Fire: T.C. Professor's Social Science Texts Banned in Ten States." *Columbia Spectator Archive* Vol. 64, no. 8, 3 October 1940: 1-2. http://spectatorarchive.library.columbia.edu/cgi-bin/columbia?a=d&d=cs19401003-01.2.5&e.
Kuhn, Thomas. *The Structure of Scientific Revolutions*. Chicago, IL: University of Chicago Press, 1970.
Lortie, Dan. *Schoolteacher: A Sociological Study*. Chicago, IL: University of Chicago Press, 1975.
Ontario Ministry of Education. *Social Studies Grades 1 to 6, History and Geography, Grades 7 and 8*. Toronto, ON: Ontario Ministry of Education, 2013.
Osborne, Ken. "Book Reviews: Knowing, Teaching and Learning History and L'histoire à l'école: Matière à penser." *The Canadian Historical Review*, 82, no. 3 (2001): 548–553.
———. "The Teaching of History and Democratic Citizenship." In *The Anthology of Social Studies Volume 2: Issues and Strategies for Secondary Teachers*, edited by Roland Case and Penney Clark, 3–15. Vancouver: Pacific Educational Press, 2008.
Ponder, Gerald. "The Curriculum: A Field without a Past?" *Educational Leadership* 31, no. 5 (1974): 461–464.
Rugg, Harold. *Now Is the Moment*. New York, NY: Duell, Sloan and Pearce, 1943.
Seixas, Peter. *"Scaling Up" the Benchmarks of Historical Thinking: A Report on the Vancouver Meetings*. Vancouver, BC: Centre for the Study of Historical Consciousness, 2008.
Seixas, Peter, and Tom Morton. *The Big Six Historical Thinking Concepts*. Toronto, ON: Nelson, 2013.
Seixas, Peter, and Carla Peck. "Teaching Historical Thinking." In *Challenges and Prospects for Canadian Social Studies*, edited by Alan Sears and Ian Wright, 109–117. Vancouver, BC: Pacific Educational Press, 2004.

Thoreau, Henry David. *Walden: Or, Life in the Woods*. Princeton, NJ: Princeton University Press, 1971.

Wardy, Robert. *Doing Greek Philosophy*. London, UK, and New York, NY: Routledge, 2006.

CHAPTER 11

George Grant's Critique of Education: Civic Particularity, Academic Erudition, Ethical Engagement

William F. Pinar

> *The sadness of English-speaking nationalism in Canada is that so much of it ... wants to be the same as American capitalism, with a maple leaf flag put at the top.*[1]
>
> — George Grant

Celebrating Canada 150+ invited the praise of particularity,[2] if through the critiques remembrance requires. The phrase "peace, order, and good government"[3] is not unique to Canada, of course, appearing in the constitutions of other countries of the Commonwealth. But the terms have a particular history in Canada; they summarize the aspirations of European ancestors who affirmed survival,[4] especially when at war with each other and with the Indigenous peoples whose land they stole.[5] Their struggles required reliance on government, tradition, character, and ingenuity, nefarious as these European ancestors could be, opportunists in already occupied land. At their best good intentions gone awry—as Jan Hare and Jean Barman phrase the work of Christian missionaries Emma and Thomas Crosby[6]—the actions of these European predecessors present educators today with professional responsibilities: remembrance, reparation, reconciliation.[7] We wed ourselves to these elusive, intersecting, and non-negotiable obligations not as social engineers promising to make things right but as ethically implicated professional protectors of that past we are committed to remember and reconstruct.[8] Without academic erudition, we cannot know that past or what we educators can do now to reconstruct it. Teacher education in Canada could be predicated upon its pre-modern pre-colonial past, emphasizing Indigenous knowledge: its spirituality, orality, sustainability, particularity.[9] But not only upon the premodern past, as teachers are obligated to engage their students in the present, structured as it is by colonialism and its effects.[10]

Civic Particularity

> [T]he question of Canada is: Are we going to build an alternative kind of technological society to what they have in the United States? [11]
> — George Grant

The great Canadian educator appreciated that the politics of his era revolved around two questions.[12] The first concerned maintaining "some independence"[13] from an imperialist United States.[14] Regarding that "great Colossus to the south,"[15] Grant conceded that America was "much more advanced" than Canada, but, he added, "I don't use 'advanced' as meaning good," but only as "farther along in the way of what a liberal society becomes," a fact that should compel "Canadians [to] pause": Grant very much hoped that Canada would not follow the same path.[16] The "Great Republic,"[17] he maintained, had become a "monolithic tyranny" characterized by "sophisticated vulgarity."[18] Any society, Grant cautioned, "that puts its trust in affluence and technology results in using any means necessary to force others to conform to its banal will."[19] Despite striking similarities, Canada was no "pale imitation" of America,[20] Grant declared, but "something richer," in part because Canadians appreciate "the dependence of freedom upon law."[21] He continued: "If we in Canada want to be a country, we have to stand on some principle which preserves some communal individuality in the face of the persuasive power of American homogenization."[22] Underline "communal individuality," as Grant affirmed that while Canadians share the American "belief in the individual's inalienable and indestructible rights, which is the chief pride of Western civilization," he qualified: "Free yes—but not so free that by his freedom he endangers the freedom of others and so disrupts the pattern of social order."[23] Grant expressed satisfaction in "new nationalism"[24] of his era, to which he himself had contributed.[25]

The second political question Grant discerned was the negotiation of "workable relations"[26] between French- and English-speaking communities, a "contract with Quebec in which what both parties' needs can be put together."[27] What such a juxtaposition required, Grant emphasized, was "moderation," by which he meant not "weakness" but "clear firmness," the "opposite of intemperance and confrontation."[28] Moderation had not characterized the history between English- and French-speaking peoples, Grant knew, as conscription had been "enforced" in 1917 "against the will of Quebec," thereby sowing "the seeds of an extreme French-Canadian nationalism."[29] In failing to recognize what was at stake for French-speaking peoples in their struggles to preserve language and culture, English-speaking Canadians, Grant concluded, "show that they are not sufficiently alive to the facts of their own destiny."[30] Canada had been intended to be a society more "ordered" and "caring," Grant reminded, decidedly "less violent"[31] than its neighbour to the south. Now everything Canadian was at risk by cultural, economic, and political integration.

Each of these two political questions—Canada's relationship with the United States, and the relationship between English- and French-speaking peoples—is complex in its own right, but each can only be answered, he suggested, together. What could unite Canadians, Neil Robertson suggested (interpreting Grant), "is an attachment to the universality of the pre-modern tradition that is instantiated in differing forms in Quebec ... [and] in English Canada—a shared standpoint deeper than the differences of culture and equally opposed to American modernity."[32] It was America's modernity—its melting pot, in which difference dissolves—that threatened the particularities that constitute Canada.

Given Grant's affirmation of pre-modernity[33] and particularity,[34] had he lived another decade I am sure he would have revised that list to include a third: that of the Aboriginal peoples.[35] To protest the tyranny of modernity—for Grant it was the obliteration of particularity and eternity—he taught "ancient religions and philosophy at university," but Grant recognized that it could also be subverted by "working with the Métis."[36] He told the Canadian Broadcasting Corporation's David Cayley:

> I take for granted that Canada is an entity that will go on; I hope it is able to maintain an indigenous culture; I hope above all French Canada can have a culture that is somehow different from the rest of North America. And I mean by culture quite a

big thing—I don't mean only art galleries and rock concerts, I mean the way in which people live in all sorts of towns and all sorts of situations.[37]

Notice that Grant's answer is expressed on the scale of the nation but also on those differentiated lives that comprise it. About his own life, Grant was clear: Facing the technological dynamo consuming Indigenous cultures all around him, "about all I can do is carry out my private duties and think my private thoughts. There is not much that anybody can do to stop this tyranny from being; one simply has to live through it."[38] Private duties and private thoughts: these two might be brought "together" in the service of survival. As Margaret Atwood[39] famously suggested, survival is the challenge Canadians have always faced. How to survive what seems—given the impending climate catastrophe—a foreclosed future? Where might passage to an alterative future be found? In the past, Grant replied.

Academic Erudition

If one denies the possibility of any returning to the past, and yet one does not believe in the assumptions of the modern experiment, what then is the task of thought?[40]

— George Grant

The past has been likened to a foreign country.[41] Grant journeyed to ancient Greece, inviting us to join him, "to think with" Plato and Aristotle, to discern "their vision of human nature and destiny."[42] In so doing, he imagined that "we come to see our own."[43] With philosophy "dying out," we face nothing "foreign," only the familiar: "our dead-level, conformist society,"[44] he called it. When one has not considered concepts "quite different from [one's] own," Grant cautioned, one tends to coincide with what is, "not even conscious that [one is] living within those limits."[45] Through reactivation of the ancient past, might we peer through the aporia that is the technological sensorium?[46]

Can there be another life than this one, submerged in screens,[47] titillated by images, inundated with information? Can we find passages to life not structured by the corporate triumvirate—calculation-competition-collaboration—not focused on others as means to our ends but as intrinsically important persons, relationships with whom render the present meaningful? Rather than only a conveyance to capital accumulation, can experience become also educational? Can ethics replace economics and politics as the animating forces in private and public life? More a subjective state of mind than a set of behaviors, ethics for Grant led him to position "piety" as prerequisite to the "public good."[48] In educational terms piety denotes a devotion to ongoing study,[49] humbling oneself before the mystery of the world, seeking understanding.[50]

Revelation represents the results of such research, attunement its rule of engagement, contemplation not calculation its *mode d'être*. In contrast to Grant, I shed supernaturalism: less transcendent than immanent, I tend to see what is as containing what can come. I do share Grant's conviction that contemplation can be structured by "charity," by which he meant "giving oneself away."[51] For him charity was no voluntaristic act of generosity that leaves the structure of subjectivity[52] untouched. For example, when, through study, we reactivate the past we are tourists no longer, still lodged within the temporally empty present. Reactivating the past we are, as it were, "going native," not as escapism or an effort to exoticize alterity but in order to dwell within a past world as if our lives in this one depended upon it.[53]

Such openness implies attentiveness but not only the observation that scientific experimentation rightly ritualizes. We are not testing hypotheses to produce outcomes we can operationalize as much as attuning ourselves to what is at stake in the situation that structures us. We are not trying to solve a problem as much as resolve what remains leftover so we *all* can move on. Calculation reproduces the problem, if in different, often novel forms that are sometimes considered "innovation" but on other occasions as collateral damage, variables (not yet) controlled, whose movements cannot be predicted. Productivity is no working through of the injustice of the past; it piles up more and more information, distracting us from the present.

The problem of the present is that calculation substitutes for reason's role in judgment, discernment, attunement.[54] Knowledge, Grant suggested, depends on these: "The close connection between Socrates and Christ lies in the fact that Socrates is the primal philosophic teacher of the dependence of what we know on what we love."[55] Love (I prefer openness) enables attunement to passages from the present, not escape routes but reactivations—or transfigurations—of what has been bequeathed us. "Paul's hymn to love," Grant reminds us, "uses the word *agape* which is best translated as charity; Plato's symposium is concerned with *eros* which is best translated as desire."[56] The reconstruction of private desire into public service is, I suggest, the calling[57] of our profession.

Charity condensed into kindness obscures its educational potential.[58] One learns from others as one engages with the situation that intersubjective presence reveals and invites us to articulate, separately and together.[59] "To be present to one another," Anne M. Phelan writes, "is not a matter of recognition of each other's qualities, qualifications, talents, and shortcomings, which we may display or hide; it is a matter of revelation of a *who* which is implicit in everything one says or does in that moment."[60] Openness to what is revealed—a willingness to allow reality to speak through us, subjectivity as its mediation—becomes one prerequisite of academic erudition. For Plato, Grant reiterates, "the opposite of knowledge is not ignorance but madness, and the nearest he [Plato] can come to an example of complete madness is the tyrant, because in that case otherness has disappeared."[61] It is the apprehension of alterity—its recognition as difference and resonance—not its disappearance in narcissism[62] that justice demands.

Ethical Engagement

It always matters what we do.[63]

— George Grant

If the mistakes of modernity could be rectified through a recovery of the pre-modern past, teacher educators would have a path ahead of (if behind) us. But such a straightforward conclusion is disallowed by Grant's own analysis, Bruce Ward points out, in which "the modern secularization of Christianity was inevitable and justified."[64] Modernity and the sanctification of "progress" are, in this sense, efforts to make good on the ancients' failure to realize justice. "This," A. James Reimer observes (in a different but compatible context), allows Grant "to say very little in the face of the modern oblivion of the eternal."[65] What *did* he say?

Grant spoke to the curriculum, asking (and answering) what knowledge is of most worth over and over again as he studied "what this is that we are."[66] Spurred to study, he worked his way through four academic disciplines—history, law, theology, philosophy—while remaining alert to art, popular culture, and politics.[67] Like Martin Luther, he was determined to see things as they are. Also like Luther,

Grant was determined that things be different than they are.⁶⁸ "How does one then ever move out of the circle of our present destiny?"⁶⁹ Grant asked, answering: "It is by looking at modernity in its greatest power that one is perhaps able even slightly to escape its power."⁷⁰ Submergence in the screen is the stone that Medusa's gaze casts today. Central to the project of education in our time, then, is non-coincidence with what is; the "negative"⁷¹ is Clarke and Phelan's term: not looking the other way, but staring straight into modernity's mesmerizing screens, steadied by academic erudition—in Grant's case, philosophical knowledge:

> As a regenerate Platonist, I would affirm that philosophy stands or falls with its ability to transcend history ... Indeed in speaking about perspectives for philosophy I would say that in homogenized societies of the future, the hope of philosophy will be with those who understand that thought can partake in that which is not dependent on any dynamic context. It will lie with those who can rise above the historicism which has permeated Western thought ... The possibility of standing above "history" must depend on having lived through the awful responsibilities of time.⁷²

Transcendence, then, can occur by the living through of what is: immersion in the moment while being attuned to the eternal. I reach this conclusion by focusing on his use of the verb "partake" in the second sentence of the quoted passage, and his linking of transcendence ("standing above history") with living through the "awful responsibilities of time" (in that last sentence).

Partake means to enter into, and studying Grant affords one the experience of sharing something of the historical moment in which he was embedded, the moment from which he worked to extricate himself through study and teaching. Partake implies sharing with others, communicating what one is undergoing while listening to others, even joining others in taking on together what must be done, to fulfill the awful responsibilities of one's time.⁷³ Partake also means to take part *in* something, implying that one takes on some of the qualities *of* that something. In other definitions of partake, the ingestion of food or drink is mentioned, as if that "something" enters one, altering one's psychic chemistry as it were. In sharing something—entering into it, and being entered—one becomes different.

For Grant that "difference" in which he had partaken may be summarized in the persons of Jesus and Socrates. Studying each—ingesting their words, experiencing something of what each had thought and undergone—enabled academic erudition, ethical engagement, and subjective reconstruction. One is changed by such intellectual, emotional, even mystical immersion; one emerges altered. When not shared with actually present others, study requires quietude, encouraging contemplation of whom and what one is studying *and* of the person studying.[74] However intensely one might re-experience something of ancient Athens or Jerusalem, one returns right here, right now, and that is the second point about Grant's insight I want to underline.

Extricating oneself from the present moment can occur not by planning the future—overcoming the crises technology has created requires more technology—but by reactivating the past. Like the term transcendence, "standing above" history is a spatial yet not necessarily a temporal position. While it implies the detachment that contemplation encourages, "standing above" seems not necessarily split off from the historical moment. Indeed, for Grant, transcendence *depends* "on having lived through the awful responsibilities of time," an adjective suggesting survival through suffering, a noun honoring—fulfilling—the obligations that being embedded in historical time incur. In my terms: transcendence and worldliness are not opposed but reciprocally related, implied in E. Joan O'Donovan's reminder that, for Grant, *"recollecting* the good and *thinking* our deprival are one."[75] As Samuel Rocha appreciates, "To change everything, we must be willing to change nothing and simply recover what we have lost."[76] Simply is not so simple, Samuel Rocha would agree. "What gets repressed is not the lost object," Carla Benedetti suggests, "but the fact that it constitutes a loss."[77] Good riddance, some say to the past; it's the future we embrace: bring it on, come what may.

In our field, "come what may" has been converted to outcomes, in service to which instruction is structured. This interrelation between theory and practice we used to call praxis. Notice that Grant's insight revises the concept considerably, altering both the "thought" and "action" that comprise it, subsuming each in ethical engagement. In the "rediscovery" of the "wisdom" of the past, he hoped, today's "tragic split" between "action" and "contemplation" could be "overcome,"[78] an aspiration Peter Grimmett and Mark Halvorson seem to share when they assert that understanding curriculum and creating it "must co-evolve."⁷⁹ Understanding and co-creation require a certain immersion in the subject, both academic and human. Partaking requires receptivity, even reverence,⁸⁰ but judgment and wisdom too: after all, one doesn't want to partake of (even if one is obligated to know about) the evils of ancient Athens and Jerusalem.⁸¹

Partaking reactivates the past within oneself, not only arming but also disarming one with facts and ideas, no longer strictly structured by the terms of the present as one becomes restructured temporally. By partaking of the past, one can return to this present still partly in the past, "out-of-date," as it were, but in a welcomed way. Subjectively restructured, disarmingly filled with facts and ideas, one declines to coincide with what is. One lives through it, immersed in the moment, attuned to what lies beyond, embodied as that temporal relation can be within one's subjective presence.

Being subjectively present means honoring one's ethical obligations. The present is not only space⁸²—empty, endless opportunity, absolute freedom—it is place.⁸³ And place is not only geographical but also cultural, sometimes spiritual, certainly historical, haunted by what has happened (t)here, endangered by what may come. It is no environment—in the sense of a clean slate—but a situation, already structured, in process, well underway, and within which one has obligations, sometimes unchosen ones. Learning what those are and how one might honour them is surely central to and enabled by academic study and teaching. Obligation requires action. One is free to ignore it all, but Grant is calling us home, another moving image of eternity.

Conclusion

> *What is the most important to be thought is the rethinking of what things are fitted for.*⁸⁴
>
> — George Grant

Grant was no Luddite, Davis emphasizes.⁸⁵ He knew returning to premodernity—to an agrarian economy or one of hunting and gathering—is neither possible nor desirable. Grant did not imagine

> [t]hat we can or should turn back from the technological society. What I am saying is that the great job in Canada now does not lie in further economic expansion and quantitative progress, but in

> trying to bring quality and beauty of existence into that technological world—to try and make it a place where the richness of life may be discovered.[86]

How might such "richness" be discovered?

What Grant is suggesting, Davis writes, is "changing our awareness of who we are and where we stand in relation to what is other than us—nature and other beings—inside the modern world where we are situated."[87] Changing awareness is no simple inner adjustment; it requires an ongoing dialogical encounter with, attunement to, alterity, in service to finding out what one is fitted for. How might the teacher find that out? One clue could be in a recommendation Grant made to prospective teachers. "[T]ry always as much as you can in teaching," he recommended,

> to deal with something where your mind is just moving to. Don't repeat things which your mind has already grasped and put in perfect order. That is, always teach what is really grasping you because otherwise teaching becomes a routine in which one is killed or else one becomes a pompous propagandist. And that is true at any level of teaching from kindergarten to PhD.[88]

Improvisation,[89] Ted Aoki might have termed it, teaching with training but no plan, riffing off what others have said, contributing to an often but not always complicated conversation. Give yourself away to what is "really grasping you," Grant emphasized, express what is without coinciding with it, become attentive to what "grasps" you from beyond it.

Neither is easy and conjoining them even harder, but that is exactly what Grant challenges us to do: "to bring together in the same thought the truth of classical reason and modern technological thinking."[90] No simple synthesis, as Grant knew that it was not possible "to reconcile the metaphysical assumptions underlying premodern philosophy with the ontological assumptions on which modern thought is based."[91] Holding the two together—in what Aoki would call a state of tensionality[92]—can occur in the distance between goodness and necessity, the former refracted (however elusively) within the latter. In loving one's own—family and friends, place and time—one can experience, in Robert C. Sibley's summary, what is beyond calculable reason and will-to-power, and gain some insight into what it means to "not be one's own." In the knowledge of such experience, we are vouchsafed a glimpse beyond the cave ... In other words, only through the everyday realities and particularities of the material world is knowledge of a transcendent good possible.[93]

A cosmopolitan teacher education might move precisely from particularity to universality.[94]

George Grant embodied such an idea, one that invites us teachers to preserve the past through academic erudition, to reconstruct the past through ethical engagement, conducted in the patterns of civic—pedagogical[95]—particularity that are specifically Canadian. In that distinctiveness, imprinted across the curriculum of teacher education in Canada, can be a compelling contestation of the global command restated earlier this month by Jim Yong Kim, President of the World Bank[96]—to convert children into human capital. Against such a soul-crushing conception of education (another instance of good intentions gone awry?) George Grant would have asked the aid of the nation's teacher educators in protecting the precious particularities of this place.

Notes

1. Christian, *George Grant: Selected Letters*, 387–388.
2. Like Ian Angus, I prefer particularity, a concept from Grant's *oeuvre*. For Angus, the term "provides a sounder philosophical basis for the rethinking of the relation between specific identities and human universality than the concept of difference, which tends towards a blindness to, or even outright rejection of, the notion of universality altogether" (Angus, *A Border Within*, 8). The political affirmation of particularity remains aspirational, however, as Angus observes: "Our failure to think through the claims of 'particularity' is evident in the exclusion of indigenous people as founders" (Angus, 76).
3. Robert C. Sibley suggests that the Charter of Rights "is an American document…. It places individual freedom as the central value of political order, effectively displacing the traditional—and more communitarian—ideal of 'peace, order, and good government'" (Sibley, *Northern Spirits*, 230). That English-speaking Canadians have embraced the charter may show the degree to which they have been Americanized.
4. "Arguably," Katherine Fierlbeck writes (commenting on collectivism in Canada), "the tendency to think about the well-being of the group rather than the rights of the individual was an asset in the attempt to survive the hardship of rural homesteading" (Fierlbeck, *Political Thought*, 52).
5. "The very lack of a clear and sustained political voice for First Nations," Fierlbeck notes, "is itself part of the history and political thought in Canada" (Fierlbeck, 9).
6. Hare and Barman, *Good Intentions*.
7. Sibley suggests that "the theme of reconciliation resides at the centre of Canadian political philosophy" (Sibley, *Northern Spirits*, 12). Fierlbeck recounts its contradiction in Canadian history: "The onerous restrictions against Chinese immigrant labourers (including the notorious head tax), the lukewarm response to Jewish refugees, the interment of Japanese-Canada citizens, Quebec's Padlock Act against communists, and various legislation vis-à-vis aboriginal groups are concrete instances of less than tolerant social attitudes" (Fierlbeck, *Political Thought*, 63). I would add to this list the cultural genocide embedded in the very concept of the residential schools.
8. "The process of reconstruction," Anne M. Phelan suggests, "is a cyclical one because it has no beginning and no final end" (Phelan, *Curriculum*, 32). I am reminded of Williams Doll's (Trueit, *Pragmatism*,

122, 139) insistence on "dynamic interplay" within the classroom, animating a "transformatory curriculum."

9   Angus emphasizes: "The incorporation of pre-modern ethnic traditions into a transformed context by multiculturalism and the recovery of the intrinsic worth of nature by the ecology movement are not one-sidedly archaizing tendencies. They incorporate a retrieval of pre-progressive and archaizing tendencies within the gains of modernity, thus rerouting an otherwise one-sided modernity" (Angus, *A Border Within*, 206).

10 "The task," Fierlbeck appreciates, "is how to reconcile the formal equality upon which democracy, in principle, is based with the recognition of difference and diversity required by a modern pluralistic polity." (Fierlbeck, *Political Thought*, 138).

11 Davis and Roper, *Collected Works: Volume 3*, 446.

12 On another occasions—as in the following sentence—economics plays a more prominent role, but I suspect it is the United States, not Canada, he has in mind in this invocation of ancient Rome: "We don't live in a democratic society; we live in a mass, bureaucratized capitalism—the nearest parallel to which is the Roman Empire at its height" (Davis and Roper, 210).

13 Schmidt, *George Grant in Process*, 17.

14 Davis and Roper, *Collected Works: Volume 4: 1970–1988*, 330; Heyking and Cooper, "A Cow Is Just a Cow: George Grant and Eric Voegelin on the United States," 177. America's imperialism, Grant suggested, developed between the conclusion of World War II and onset of the Vietnam War (*Collected Works of George Grant. Volume 4: 1970–1988*, 178), although, during the 1950s, Grant could still write that "for the ordinary person," America "combines openness and kindness as no other" (Davis, *Collected Works: Volume 2: 1951–1959*, 255). John Von Heyking and Barry Cooper suggest that "Grant's critique of the U.S. was fairly consistent throughout his career" although that last line underscores their adjective. Grant himself regarded his antipathy to the United States as "deep" and "ancestral antipathy," given that his ancestors had fled the American Revolution (Davis and Roper, *Collected Works: Volume 4: 1970–1988*, 85).

15 Davis and Roper, *Collected Works: Volume 3*, 436.

16 Davis and Roper, 452. "This rejection of American republicanism, together with the individualist ethos that went with it," Sibley summarizes, "is central to Grant's understanding of the idea that gives Canada its reason for being. So long as that idea holds, particularly among the ruling elites, then Canada is possible. And it is this possibility, this good, that Grant loves as his own" (Sibley, *Northern Spirits*, 119).

17   Schmidt, *George Grant in Process*, 63.
18   Davis and Roper, *Collected Works: Volume 3*, 421. What would Grant say now, in this time of Trump? Vulgarity remains prominent but just the start of what one must say has become of the land of the free and the brave.
19   Davis and Roper, 468. Despite their traditions and present circumstances, Grant allowed that "many Americans have seen with clarity the nature of that which chokes them and seek for ways to live beyond it" (Davis and Roper, 468). Despite our disagreements over abortion, euthanasia, sexuality, and religion—never mind Dewey's pragmatism—Grant might include me in this category.
20   "Anti-Americanism has always been an aspect of Canadian political culture," Fierlbeck reminds, "but it was only in the twentieth century that the expression of anti-Americanism became a clear response to a society built upon the exaltation of individualism, the use of technology, and the force of consumerism. In Canada's geographical and economic vulnerability, Canadians quite quickly became aware of the consequences of this web of modernity" (Fierlbeck, *Political Thought*, 53–54).
21   Davis and Roper, *Collected Works: Volume 4*, 405. For Grant, "the U.S.A. has produced a society where freedom of the individual is a fetish. For instance, during the race riots in Detroit the white Americans, when all too infrequently prevented by the police from beating up their Black fellow citizens, yelled at these police 'Gestapo.' After all, the intervention by the police was the infringement of their right as individuals to beat up the Negroes. At the same time this very individualism has produced in the U.S.A. some wonderful examples of what the free individual can do" (Davis and Emberley, *Collected Works: Volume 1*, 130).
22   Davis and Roper, *Collected Works: Volume 4*, 416. "The pain and insularity caused by scarcity and necessity," Angus suggests, "can be reversed by infusing production with cooperative individuality" (Angus, *George Grant's Platonic Rejoinder*, 88). The two terms—communal individuality and cooperative individuality—intersect and diverge, as the latter can tend toward conformity and the consequent erasure of individuality. Grant's adjective—communal—hints at community and shared experience, perhaps a reflection of his pre-modern preferences.
23   Davis and Emberley, *Collected Works: Volume 1*, 130.
24   "I think it's great that there's new nationalism in Canada; I think it's great that there has been new nationalism of an authentic kind in Quebec" (Cayley, *George Grant in Conversation*, 107). The question of Quebec is Grant's second—after retaining independence from the

United States—political question for Canada. "By the 1990s," Fierlbeck notes, "interest in Canadian nationalism became increasingly eclipsed by the study of nations *within* Canada" (Fierlbeck, *Political Thought*, 37). Grant's analysis suggests the two are inextricably interrelated.

25 I am of course referring to his *Lament for a Nation* (2005 [1965]). Referencing that book, O'Donovan explains that Grant insists that Canada's "persisting political integrity" depends upon the "continuing public articulation of two Christian conservatisms: those of French-Canadian Catholicism and British Loyalist Anglicanism," and specifically the public expression of their "common commitment to an individual and collective 'ethic of self-restraint,' maintained socially by a 'high degree of law,'" where "Grant finds the *raison d'être* of Canada's separate political existence" (O'Donovan, "Law, Love and the Common Good," 135). This "Indigenous tradition of virtue," she continues, one that renders "Canadian nationhood worthy of loyalty, protection, and, indeed, lament. Its recollection renders the attachment of Canadians to their political past an act of patriotism rather than nostalgia, by setting the object of their particular affection in relation to the universal common good." (O'Donovan, 135.) As I suggest soon, had Grant lived another decade he would have emphasized too the history and presence of Aboriginal peoples.

26 Davis and Roper, *Collected Works: Volume 4*, 335.

27 Davis and Roper, 337.

28 Davis and Roper, 337. "Moderation is not only needed from our political leaders," Grant emphasized, "but from the rest of us."

29 Davis, *Collected Works: Volume 2*, 150. Anti-conscription and anti-English riots occurred in Quebec, Grant reminded. (Davis, 151).

30 Davis and Roper, *Collected Works: Volume 4*, 416. In 1979 Grant was awarded an honorary degree from the University of Toronto, and in 1980 another one by the University of Guelph; on both occasions he spoke on the same subject: Canada and Quebec (see Davis and Roper, 415).

31 Emberley, "Foreword," lxxx.

32 Robertson, "Freedom and Tradition," 160. "What Grant recalled," Peter C. Emberley explains, "… was the pre-modern substance of Canadian patriotism. This patriotism, unlike its simulacrum nationalism, evoked not merely an imaginary identity, but a tradition and a place—organizations of time and space constituting our unique British heritage. Being a Canadian had meant being grounded in these historical legacies" (Emberley, "Preface," xiii). The English and French settlers (invaders) were pre- even anti-revolutionary all right, but not entirely pre-modern, although of course exploitation even genocide are not limited to modernity.

33 As "a Platonist within Christianity," Sibley suggests, Grant's "consciousness is pre-modern at its deepest philosophical level." (Sibley, *Northern Spirits*, 114).

34 "As a Christian Platonist," Anthony J. Parel suggests, "Grant's love for Canada has its basis in the love of particularity" (Parel, "Multiculturalism and Nationhood," 142). Parel does not "see any danger here of the Grantian love of the particular degenerating into Canadian xenophobia." (Parel, 147).

35 "When we go into the Rockies we may have the sense that gods are there. But if so, they cannot manifest themselves to us as ours. They are the gods of another race, and we cannot know them because of what we are, and what we did" (Atwood, *Survival*, 82). At first, I decoded these sentences as suggesting pantheism, but Margaret Atwood associates them with Indigenous peoples. If so, here is Grant's acknowledgement of both cultural incommensurability and cultural genocide.

36 Christian and Grant, *The George Grant Reader*, 101. "Although he [Grant] saw no way for the demise of local Indigenous cultures to be avoided," Gary G. Caldwell notes, "he very much admired those who resisted" (Caldwell, "Grant and Quebec," 29). For Grant, Robertson suggests, what "unites" Canadians is an attachment to the universality of the pre-modern tradition" (Robertson, "Freedom and Tradition," 160). While Grant was focused on the cultures Europeans brought, his view acknowledges implicitly, I suggest, members of the First Nations.

37 Cayley, *George Grant in Conversation*, 109.

38 Christian and Grant, *The George Grant Reader*, 101.

39 Certainly that was—is—the case with Aboriginal peoples but also true of their European occupiers, both French and English. Atwood points out: "Quebec authors have been just as addicted to Survivalism as have those in the rest of Canada. But the attitude and its corollaries have been with them longer, and are, if anything, more extreme. In addition to the bare survivalism they share with the rest of Canada—survival in the face of a harsh climate and a recalcitrant land—and the sense that their survival may be the survival of an archaic form of life, which they also share—they emphasize cultural and religious survivalism" (Atwood, *Survival*, 247–248).

40 Grant, *Time as History*, 65.

41 "The nineteenth-century German architect Karl Friedrich Schinkel," John Toews reminds, was among those who imagined the "past as a foreign country," and one "that could function as a model and norm for the present. But for Schinkel the past lived in the present through all of the historical forms in which its principles had been

transfigured and passed on through time. To think historically was not to make an imaginative leap into a past world, but to view oneself within the flow of time in which historical forms were in a constant process of making and remaking" (Toews, *Becoming Historical*, 175). For Schinkel those forms were architectural; they can also be curricular, evident in this present effort to reconstruct the present of teacher education through "reactivating" the thought of George Grant.

42 Grant, *Philosophy in the Mass Age*, 26.
43 Grant, 26.
44 Grant, 26. Thanks to the Bill and Melinda Gates Foundation, United States public schools are now enlisted in the cause of "dead-level" conformity. Long committed to destroying public education in the US, the Foundation granted $900,000 to develop 80 videos, five to fifteen minutes in length, featuring "high-performing" teachers in the Washington, D.C., district, as they teach decimal numbers and the Marshall Plan. Motoko Rich reports that the videos function as a complement to Washington's teacher evaluation scheme, known as Impact, in which teachers are judged on student test scores and classroom observations. (Versions of these are used across the United States.) Because observers assign numerical ratings, many teachers called for demonstrations of "excellent" teaching. "Teachers were saying to us, 'Just be very clear about what good teaching looks like'," said Kaya Henderson, Washington's school chancellor (quoted in Rich, "Show and Tell for Teachers," A14). If we can turn teachers into robots, perhaps students will follow? Of course teachers will fail—if they remain human and imperfect—rationalizing the use of actual robots, boosting profits of those companies that manufacture them and cutting the costs of public education by eliminating health insurance (repair insurance instead) and pensions.
45 Grant, *Philosophy in the Mass Age*, 26.
46 For Grant, Harris Athanasiadis points out, "all cultures and traditions are progressively being swept aside before technological culture. It is becoming increasingly universal and homogenizes all ways of thinking and living" (Athanasiadis, *George Grant and Theology*, 125). James Doull, a close colleague of Grant's at Dalhousie, also decried the "devastating uniformity of technological society" (Doull, "Naturalistic Individualism," 31), reminding us that: "In the older culture from which Canadians received their institutions it was not assumed that the economic realm had this priority but that it was subservient to the state and, in other ways, to the family and the church" (Doull, 30).
47 In Angus's terms: "The encounter with the primal, unhistorical, is an annihilation of temporal relations into the purely spatial extension of

a thick present" (Angus, *A Border Within*, 133). Fusion with the screen is "thick" with simulated sensation, not embodied duration. Samuel D. Rocha says it more simply: "More and more, glowing rectangles tell us what to think, feel, and believe. I am staring at one right now. Under this dictatorial regime, it is hard to be still or silent, much less to exercise the imagination" (Rocha, *Tell Them Something Beautiful*, 69).

48 Grant, *Technology and Empire*, 50.

49 Phelan notes that "the time of study is without destination or end" (Phelan, *Curriculum Theorizing*, 31).

50 As Grant came to rely on Simone Weil, Barry Cooper notes, he came to consider the "true purpose of education to be the cultivation of a capacity for attention … which is to say the capacity to do right." (Cooper, "A Imperio usque ad Imperium," 28).

51 Grant, *Technology and Empire*, 35; see also Davis and Roper, *Collected Works: Volume 4*, 943. "The supreme figure of the Western world other than Christ," Grant wrote, "is Saint Francis. He asserts the supremacy of charity" (Davis and Roper, 579–580). In his interview with Cayley (1995, 174), Grant worries the word has become convoluted: "… *charity* has become such a lousy word, I just like to use *love*."

52 "Subjectivity," Phelan reminds, "is an event rather than a project of completion; the teaching subject is always in 'a state of becoming' and never fully realized…. This means that subjectivity is only possible in a world of plurality and difference" (Phelan, *Curriculum Theorizing*, 3). I would add that subjectivity requires actual, not only virtual, experience; Emberley references the "ravages technology wreaks on human subjectivity" (Emberley, "Preface," xvi).

53 Perhaps this is a third space, but it requires a double consciousness, e.g., non-coincidence with the situation-at-hand. "[I]t is necessary on the one hand to avoid a scholarship that by its immersion in the past castrates our thinking about what it is to exist now," Grant understood, "and on the other to avoid an immediacy that trivializes by persuading us that we are understanding the modern when in fact we are being carried along by the waves of its dynamism." (Grant, *Time as History*, 32).

54 "Experience is a key condition for the cultivation of *phronesis* as discernment," Phelan explains, to which I might add lived or actual, not virtual, experience. "Experience," Phelan continues, can contribute to the "deepening of insight and wisdom" (Phelan, *Curriculum Theorizing*, 17).

55 Grant, *Technology and Justice*, 72.

56 Grant, *Technology and Justice*, 73. Desire demands satiation. Love invites devotion. "Because *eros* is aspiration toward something beyond itself to something eternal, unhanging, perfect, and final,"

Grant wrote (Davis and Roper, *Collected Works: Volume 4*, 1008). In modernity, *eros* becomes means to another end: mastery, wealth, power. In the ancient world, Grant suggests, we would be considered fools, as "universal human satisfaction" was considered in principle impossible due to "human dependence" and "weakness" (Grant, *Technology and Empire*, 99).

57   The concept is spiritual, and teaching is not the only profession with its sacred subtext. While the call comes from the world, that world is also inside us, as Sonya Sikka makes clear in her association of Heidegger with the medieval German mystic Johannes Tauler: "Like Tauler's notion of call, then, this voice [of conscience, in Heidegger] provides an 'interior' and thus individual attestation of a higher possibility for the self, and in recalling it to this possibility, it calls the self back in from its everyday lostness and falling, its average absorption in the world. Furthermore, while the actual performance of the call does not, for either Tauler or Heidegger, lie within the self's own power of choice, the failure to hear the call does, at some level, involve a decision for which the self is responsible. Ethical engagement with one's self is a prerequisite to professionalism" (Sikka, *Forms of Transcendence*, 202).

58   This a very different sense of potential that Tyson E. Lewis (Lewis, *On Study*) decries, i.e., monetizing talent. Grant historicizes this development within "English-speaking modernity," with its "exaltation of motion over rest, of potentiality over actuality, of interest as detached from virtue" (Davis and Roper, *Collected Works: Volume 4*, 84). Given these circumstances, Grant reaffirms the integrity of study when he asserts: "Learning—[one] must do it at one's own pace, must do it one's own way. I can point out places to learn, which may be helpful, [or] may not…. The great thing about learning is to keep one's proper independence and yet not stop listening to the other—sometime[s] [a] waste, sometime[s] not" (Davis and Roper, *Collected Works: Volume 3*, 677).

59   What Grant wrote about a superb storyteller seems pertinent here: "He or she must be there as an individual, and yet open to otherness" (Davis and Roper, *Collected Works: Volume 4*, 436). Perhaps the importance of presence derives from Christian culture as it summarized by Grant (referencing Strauss): in Islam and Judaism "revelation comes in the form of law … while in Christianity it comes in the form of a being" (Davis and Roper, 829). Law becomes personified and enacted inter-subjectively, a whiff of eternity within time.

60   Phelan, *Curriculum Theorizing*, 3.

61   Grant, *Technology and Justice*, 73.

62 "[N]o matter what you do," Carla Benedetti writes, "you are prisoner to the already-given. This is the way late-modern learning is: modernity sees itself in the mirror and is paralyzed by its own gaze" (Benedetti, *The Empty Cage*, 210). That mirror is a smartphone screen.
63 Davis and Roper, *Collected Works: Volume 4*, 294.
64 Ward, "George Grant and the Problem of Theodicy," 99.
65 Ward, 114.
66 Davis and Roper, *Collected Works: Volume 4*, 133.
67 One must say of Grant's teaching what Gian Maria Annovi knows about Pier Paolo Pasolini's: "The cinema is therefore an art bound up with the director's *personal* expression; it is precisely his unique personality that gives the work organic unity" (Annovi, *Pier Paolo Pasolini*, 86).
68 Unlike Luther, Grant was not anti-Semitic.
69 Schmidt, *George Grant in Process*, 67.
70 Davis and Roper, *Collected Works: Volume 4*, 492. "Staring" at our situation is not what our times encourage, rather distraction through stimulation, likely in increasing doses. When Grant made this point the "strongest stimulations" were receivable "on pay television," but by making that observation it is as if he knew the smartphone was coming (Davis and Roper, *Collected Works: Volume 4*, 492).
71 Clarke and Phelan, *Power of Negative Thinking: Teacher Education and the Political*.
72 Davis and Roper, *Collected Works: Volume 4*, 679–680, n 69.
73 Grant reminds us that "religion," derived from the original Latin verb, *religere*, means "to find together" (quoted in O'Donovan, *George Grant and the Twilight of Justice*, 62).
74 "While teachers have to act in the moment," Phelan explains, "their actions take the form of an active passivity," what she characterizes as waiting and floating, akin to quietude I should think (Phelan, *Curriculum Theorizing*, 23).
75 O'Donovan, *Twilight of Justice*, 129. "Escaping the technological empire requires, in the first place," Angus appreciates, "understanding how deeply we are each caught up in it." (Angus, *A Border Within*, 96).
76 Rocha, *Tell Them Something Beautiful*, 94.
77 Benedetti, *The Empty Cage*, 202.
78 Davis, *Collected Works: Volume 2*, 14–15.
79 Grimmett and Halvorson, "From Understanding Curriculum," 242. Curriculum scholarship, Madeline R. Grumet suggests, "should contain these three themes: curriculum as autobiography, because we are all implicated in the curriculum that has shaped us, and that we in turn, would shape; curriculum as phenomenon, because there is no neutral knowledge and every discipline is saturated with its cultural

history; and curriculum as event, because curriculum ... is a happening" (Grumet, "Imago, Imago, Imago," 87–88).

80   T. F. Rigelhof associates reverence with remembrance: *"Remembering with reverence is a special kind of thinking. Remembering with reverence seeks out the ways that people lived—not what they did or said as such but as the life that animated their actions an their words. Those of us who can reverentially remember can come to know something of what others knew and feel something of what they desired and be nudged by what they loved"* (Rigelhof, *George Grant*, 122–123).

81   For Grant, Robert Meynell explains, "understanding history is an integral part of our power to overcome evil" (Meynell, *Canadian Idealism*, 120).

82   "We are present overbalanced towards space," Angus notes, "inhabiting a highly developed planetary system that is subject to endemic crises" (Angus, *A Border Within*, 173).

83   Phelan notes the "poverty" of the conception of "place in teacher education" (Phelan, *Curriculum Theorizing*, 75).

84   Davis and Roper, *Collected Works: Volume 3*, 626.

85   Davis, "Did George Grant Change His Politics?", 73. "In Grant's most recent work," Angus points out, "he still claims that one cannot simply reject modern technology since it has brought forth essential new human possibilities. Nevertheless, neither can technology simply be accepted because of the threat it poses to justice as individuality and equality" (Angus, *A Border Within*, 95).

86   Davis, *Collected Works: Volume 2*, 163–164.

87   Davis, 163–164.

88   Davis and Roper, *Collected Works: Volume 4*, 968.

89   "Could improvisation," Ted. T. Aoki asked, "be a way to create spaces to allow differences to show through" (Aoki, *"Sonare* and *Videre,"* 368)?

90   Sibley, *Northern Spirits*, 114. Sibley suggests that Grant's "philosophical career reflects this attempt."

91   Sibley, *Northern Spirits*, 114.

92   Aoki, "Teaching as Indwelling," 159.

93   Sibley, *Northern Spirits*, 116.

94   "Particularity need no longer be defined as against universality," Angus points out, "but as the *very condition* for whatever universality the human being may be able to apprehend" (Angus, *A Border Within*, 159).

95   "Today's school," Rocha worries, "is indifferent and even allergic to the civic model; in scope and purpose, schooling is becoming less and less political and more and more economic," adding: "This new economic school is a threat to all" (Rocha, *Tell Them Something Beautiful*, 81).

96   Kim, "Human Capital."

Bibliography

Adams, Michael. *Fire & Ice: The United States, Canada and the Myth of Converging Values*. Toronto, ON: Penguin Canada, 2009.

Angus, Ian. *A Border Within: National Identity, Cultural Plurality, and Wilderness*. Montreal, QC, and Kingston, ON: McGill-Queen's University Press, 1997.

———. *George Grant's Platonic Rejoinder to Heidegger: Contemporary Political Philosophy and the Question of Technology*. Lewiston, NY: Edwin Mellen Press. 1987.

Annovi, Gian Maria. *Pier Paolo Pasolini: Performing Authorship*. New York, NY: Columbia University Press, 2017.

Aoki, Ted T. "*Sonare* and *Videre*: A Story, Three Echoes and a Lingering Note." In *Curriculum in a New Key: The Collected Works of Ted T. Aoki*, edited by William F. Pinar and Rita L. Irwin, 367–376. Mahwah, NJ: Lawrence Erlbaum, 2005.

———. "Teaching as Indwelling between Two Curriculum Worlds." In *Curriculum in a New Key: The Collected Works of Ted T. Aoki*, edited by William F. Pinar and Rita L. Irwin, 159–165. Mahwah, NJ: Lawrence Erlbaum, 2005.

Athanasiadis, Harris. *George Grant and Theology of the Cross: The Christian Foundations of His Thought*. Toronto, ON: University of Toronto Press: 2001.

Atwood, Margaret. *Survival: A Thematic Guide to Canadian Literature*. Toronto, ON: House of Anansi, 2012 (1972).

Benedetti, Carla. *The Empty Cage: Inquiry into the Mysterious Disappearance of the Author*. Translated by William J. Hartley. Ithaca, NY, and London, UK: Cornell University Press, 2005.

Caldwell, Gary G. "Grant and Quebec." In *Athens and Jerusalem: George Grant's Theology, Philosophy, and Politics*, edited by Ian Angus, Ron Dart, and Randy Peg Peters, 29–38. Toronto, ON: University of Toronto Press, 2006.

Cayley, David. *George Grant in Conversation*. Toronto: House of Anansi Press Limited, 1995.

Christian, William, ed. *George Grant: Selected Letters*. Toronto, ON: University of Toronto Press, 1996.

Christian, William, and Sheila Grant, eds. *The George Grant Reader*. Toronto, ON: University of Toronto Press, 1998.

Clarke, Matthew, and Anne M. Phelan. *Teacher Education and the Political: The Power of Negative Thinking*. London, UK: Routledge, 2017.

Cooper, Barry. "*A Imperio usque ad Imperium*: The Political Thought of George Grant." In *George Grant in Process*, edited by Larry Schmidt, 22–39. Toronto, ON: House of Anansi, 1978.

Davis, Arthur, ed. *Collected Works of George Grant. Volume 2: 1951–1959*. Toronto, ON: University of Toronto Press, 2002.

———. "Did George Grant Change His Politics?" In *Athens and Jerusalem: George Grant's Theology, Philosophy, and Politics*, edited by Ian Angus, Ron Dart, and Randy Peg Peters, 62–79. Toronto, ON: University of Toronto Press, 2006.

Davis, Arthur, and Peter C. Emberley, eds. *Collected Works of George Grant. Volume 1: 1933–1950*. Toronto, ON: University of Toronto Press, 2000.

Davis, Arthur, and Henry Roper, eds. *Collected Works of George Grant. Volume 3: 1960–1969*. Toronto, ON: University of Toronto Press, 2005.

———. *Collected Works of George Grant. Volume 4: 1970–1988*. Toronto, ON: University of Toronto Press, 2009.

Doull, James. "Naturalistic Individualism: Quebec Independence and an Independent Canada." In *Modernity and Responsibility. Essays for George Grant*, edited by Eugene Combs, 29–50. Toronto, ON: University of Toronto Press, 1983.

Emberley, Peter C. "Foreword." In *Lament for a Nation*, Carleton Library Edition, by George Grant, XX–XX. Montreal, QC, and Kingston, ON: McGill-Queen's University Press, 2005.

———. "Preface." In *By Loving Our Own: George Grant and the Legacy of Lament for a Nation*, edited by Peter C. Emberley, xi–xxvi. Ottawa, ON: Carleton University Press, 1990.

Fierlbeck, Katherine. *Political Thought in Canada: An Intellectual History*. Peterborough, ON: Broadview Press, 2006.

Grant, George. *Lament for a Nation: The Defeat of Canadian Nationalism*. 40th anniversary edition, edited by Andrew Potter. Carleton Library Series. Montreal, QC: McGill-Queen's Press, 2005 (1965).

———. *Philosophy in the Mass Age*. Toronto, ON: Copp Clark Publishing, 1966 (original work published 1959).

———. *Technology and Empire*. Toronto, ON: House of Anansi, 1969.

———. *Technology and Justice*. Toronto, ON: House of Anansi, 1986.

———. *Time as History*. Toronto, ON: University of Toronto Press, 2001 (original work published 1969).

Grimmett, Peter P., and Mark Halvorson. "From Understanding Curriculum to Creating Curriculum: The Case for the Co-Evolution of Re-Conceptualized Design with Re-Conceptualized Curriculum." *Curriculum Inquiry* 40, no. 2 (2010): 241–262.

Grumet, Madeleine R. "Imago, Imago, Imago." *Journal of the Canadian Association for Curriculum Studies* 12, no. 1 (2014): 82–89.

Hare, Jan, and Jean Barman. *Good Intentions Gone Awry: Emma Crosby and the Methodist Mission on the Northwest Coast.* Vancouver, BC: University of British Columbia Press, 2006.

Heyking, John Von, and Barry Cooper. "'A Cow Is Just a Cow': George Grant and Eric Voegelin on the United States." In *Athens and Jerusalem: George Grant's Theology, Philosophy, and Politics,* edited by Ian Angus, Ron Dart, and Randy Peg Peters, 166–189. Toronto, ON: University of Toronto Press, 2006.

Kim, Jim Yong. "Human Capital in the 21st Century." Speeches and Transcripts. Who We Are. The World Bank. November 4, 2014. Accessed October 20, 2017 at http://www.worldbank.org/en/news/speech/2014/11/04/human-capital-in-the-21st-century. Accessed October 20, 2017.

Lewis, Tyson E. *On Study: Giorgio Agamben and Educational Potentiality.* New York, NY: Routledge, 2013.

Meynell, Robert. *Canadian Idealism and the Philosophy of Freedom: C.B. Macpherson, George Grant, and Charles Taylor.* Montreal, QC, and Kingston, ON: McGill-Queen's University Press, 2011.

O'Donovan, Joan E. *George Grant and the Twilight of Justice.* Toronto, ON: University of Toronto Press, 1984.

———. "Law, Love and the Common Good." In *By Loving Our Own: George Grant and the Legacy of* Lament for a Nation, edited by Peter C. Emberley, 135–151. Ottawa, ON: Carleton University Press, 1990.

Parel, Anthony J. "Multiculturalism and Nationhood." In *George Grant and the Future of Canada,* edited by Yusuf K. Umar and Barry Cooper, 139–150. Calgary, AB: University of Calgary Press, 1992.

Phelan, Anne M. *Curriculum Theorizing and Teacher Education: Complicating Conjunctions.* New York, NY: Routledge, 2015.

Reimer, A. James. "Do George Grant and Martin Heidegger Share a Common Conservatism?" In *'Two Theological Languages' by George Grant and Other Essays in Honour of His Work,* edited by Wayne Whillier, 49–57. Queenston, ON: Edwin Mellen Press, 1990.

Rich, Motoko. "Show and Tell for Teachers, Inspired by Reality TV." *The New York Times,* August 16, 2012.

Rigelhof, T. F. *George Grant: Redefining Canada.* Montreal, QC: XYZ Publishing, 2001.

Robertson, Neil. "Freedom and Tradition: George Grant, James Doull, and the Character of Modernity." In *Athens and Jerusalem: George Grant's Theology, Philosophy, and Politics,* edited by Ian Angus, Ron Dart, and Randy Peg Peters, 136–165. Toronto, ON: University of Toronto Press, 2006.

Rocha, Samuel D. *Tell Them Something Beautiful: Essays and Ephemera.* Eugene, OR: Cascade Books, 2017.

Schmidt, Larry, ed. *George Grant in Process: Essays and Conversations*. Toronto, ON: House of Anansi. 1978.

Sibley, Robert C. *Northern Spirits: John Watson, George Grant, and Charles Taylor—Appropriations of Hegelian Political Thought*. Montreal, QC, and Kingston, ON: McGill-Queen's University Press, 2008.

Sikka, Sonya. *Forms of Transcendence: Heidegger and Medieval Mystical Theology*. Albany, NY: State University of New York Press, 1997.

Toews, John. *Becoming Historical: Cultural Reformation and Public Memory in Early Nineteenth-Century Berlin*. New York, NY: Cambridge University Press, 2008.

Trueit, Donna, ed. *Pragmatism, Postmodernism, Complexity Theory: The Fascinating Imaginative Realm of William E. Doll, Jr*. New York, NY: Routledge, 2012.

Ward, Bruce. "George Grant and the Problem of Theodicy in Western Christianity." In *'Two Theological Languages' by George Grant and Other Essays in Honour of His Work*, edited by Wayne Whillier, 94–104. Queenston, ON: Edwin Mellen Press, 1990.

Education

Series Editors: Nicholas Ng-A-Fook and Carole Fleuret

Our *Education* series seeks to advance thought-provoking research within the broader field of education. Scholarly works in this series examine educational research from a multidisciplinary perspective and address a variety of issues in the field, including curriculum studies, arts-based education, educational philosophy, life writing, foundations in education, teacher education, evaluation, and counselling.

Recent titles in this series

Michelle Forrest and Linda Wheeldon, *Scripting Feminist Ethics in Teacher Education*, 2019.

William M. Pinar, *Moving Images of Eternity: George Grant's Critique of Time, Teaching, and Technology*, 2019.

Pierre Jean, *Planification de formations en santé : Guide des bonnes pratiques*, 2019.

Thomas R. Klassen and John A. Dwyer, *Décrocher son diplôme (et l'emploi de ses rêves !) : Comment maîtriser les compétences essentielles menant au succès à l'école, au travail et dans la vie*, 2018.

Timothy M. Sibbald and Victoria Handford (eds), *The Academic Gateway: Understanding the Journey to Tenure*, 2017.

Lise Gremion, Serge Ramel, Valérie Angelucci, and Jean-Claude Kalubi (eds), *Vers une école inclusive : regards croisés sur les défis actuels*, 2017.

For a complete list of our titles, see:
press.uOttawa.ca

Printed in December 2019
at Imprimerie Gauvin
Gatineau (Quebec), Canada.

www.ingramcontent.com/pod-product-compliance
Lightning Source LLC
Chambersburg PA
CBHW061345300426
44116CB00011B/2000